Georges Bataille

Modern European Thinkers

Series Editor: Professor Keith Reader,
University of Newcastle upon Tyne

The Modern European Thinkers series offers low-priced introductions for students and other readers to the ideas and work of key cultural and political thinkers of the post-war era.

Edgar Morin
Myron Kofman

Pierre Bourdieu
Jeremy F. Lane

Walter Benjamin
Esther Leslie

André Gorz
Conrad Lodziak and Jeremy Tatman

Gilles Deleuze
John Marks

Guy Hocquenghem
Bill Marshall

Régis Debray
Keith Reader

Julia Kristeva
Anne-Marie Smith

Georges Bataille

A Critical Introduction

Benjamin Noys

Pluto  Press

LONDON • STERLING, VIRGINIA

First published 2000 by Pluto Press
345 Archway Road, London N6 5AA
and 22883 Quicksilver Drive,
Sterling, VA 20166–2012, USA

British Library Cataloguing in Publication Data
A catalogue record for this book is available from the British Library

ISBN 0 7453 1592 5 hbk

Library of Congress Cataloging in Publication Data
Noys, Benjamin, 1969–
    Georges Bataille : a critical introduction / Benjamin Noys.
       p. cm. — (Modern European thinkers)
    Includes bibliographical references.
    ISBN 0–7453–1592–5
       1. Bataille, Georges, 1897–1962—Criticism and interpretation.
    I. Title. II. Series.
PQ2603.A695 Z795 2000
848'.91209—dc21
                                                                    00–024889

Designed and produced for Pluto Press by
Chase Production Services, Chadlington, OX7 3LN
Typeset from disk by Stanford DTP Services, Northampton
Printed in the EC by TJ International, Padstow

Contents

Acknowledgements

I would like to thank Geoffrey Bennington for his patient supervision of the DPhil from which this book has developed and for his continuing encouragement of my work. I would also like to thank the British Academy for the three-year award which made that DPhil possible and the staff of the Graduate Research Centre in the Humanities at the University of Sussex for their help. I want to thank all the staff at Pluto Press for their belief and support for this book, particularly Keith Reader and Anne Beech. I am grateful to James Tink and Ben Rumble for reading drafts of this work and their feedback, to Matt Fletcher for all his help, and to my family, Diane, Charles, Alison and Danny. Above all I would like to thank Jane Gillett, to whom this book is dedicated and without whom it would have been impossible.

Abbreviations

Refer to the major works by Bataille and to *The Critical Reader*.

Accursed Share Vol. 1 (AS1)
Accursed Share Vols 2 and 3 (AS2/3)
The Bataille Reader (BR)
Bataille: A Critical Reader (CR)
The College of Sociology (CS)
Eroticism (E)
Encyclopaedia Acephalica (EA)
Guilty (G)
The Impossible (I)
Inner Experience (IE)
L'Abbé C. (AC)
Literature and Evil (LE)
On Nietzsche (ON)
Story of the Eye (SE)
The Tears of Eros (TE)
Theory of Religion (TR)
The Trial of Gilles de Rais (TG)
Visions of Excess (VE)

Introduction

All profound life is heavy with the *impossible*.
Georges Bataille (IE, 58; BR, 88)

Georges Bataille (1897–1962) is still probably best known as a writer of erotic fiction and as a precursor of poststructuralism, but what do we really know about Bataille? During his lifetime he was a somewhat obscure figure, not widely read but closely supported by a few important friends: Michel Leiris, Maurice Blanchot, Jacques Lacan and Pierre Klossowski, among others. He lived a contradictory life, both the calm life of the professional librarian and the dissolute life of a libertine. After his death he began to gain popularity and the readers that he had so desired, but he still remained obscure. Now Bataille has an ambiguous fame as the writer of excess; disturbing, shocking, perhaps even mad. In an age that so admires excess Bataille has become more and more accepted, even lauded as the prophet of transgression.[1] The literary works that he published under pseudonyms in order to avoid prosecution for obscenity are now 'modern classics' that have been assimilated into the Western canon,[2] and the intensity of his other unclassifiable writings are reduced to interesting footnotes to the intellectual history of poststructuralism.[3]

The problem with this assimilation and appropriation of Bataille is that it is a profound *failure* to read Bataille. As we will see Bataille did not seek admirers and he regarded apologists for his work with suspicion. The promotion of Bataille as a counterculture icon cannot accept that he is still, as his friend Michel Leiris described him, 'the impossible one' (in CR, 167). Bataille recognised early in his intellectual career that he would remain isolated but, 'This isolation, as far as I am concerned, is moreover in part voluntary, since I would agree to come out of it only on certain hard-to-meet conditions' (VE, 91; BR, 147). Although Bataille has become more popular since his death he has not left this state of isolation because most readers of Bataille have not confronted the hard-to-meet conditions that he imposes. To draw him out of it, to introduce Bataille, requires that we try to understand these conditions.

Firstly, it will be a matter of finding out what hard-to-meet conditions Bataille imposes on us, his readers. Once this has been done it will then be possible to approach the relation between Bataille's life and work, after we have seen how Bataille demands to be read. For Bataille the life and work of a writer could not be held apart, and his own writings demonstrate how events in his life constantly impinge on his work and open it to new forces. It is these openings between Bataille's life and work that will lead to the readings of Bataille in the chapters that follow. Finally, in this introduction I want to consider how Bataille leads us into 'the labyrinth of thought' (AS2/3, 370). The labyrinth is Bataille's image of thought, and it is a labyrinth from which we cannot escape. By leading us into the labyrinth Bataille demonstrates why it is impossible to appropriate his work and why he still remains a vital figure in modern European thought.

The hard-to-meet conditions that Bataille imposes on us are made most explicit in 'The Use-Value of D.A.F. de Sade (An Open Letter to My Current Comrades)', which was probably written between 1929 and 1930 but was unpublished at the time. Even here the conditions are not set out directly but through the question of how we should read the scandalous and pornographic writings of the Marquis de Sade. Bataille identified with Sade (1740–1814), the aristocratic libertine who supported the French revolution. Sade was both imprisoned in the Bastille by the *ancien régime* and in a lunatic asylum after the revolution, as his works were disturbing to monarchists and to republicans alike.[4] Bataille is concerned with the nature of the scandal of Sade's works and how they can still remain a scandal for us. Moreover, on many points Bataille's 'physics and metaphysics are not essentially different from those of the Marquis de Sade'.[5] It is not surprising then that Bataille should link his own fate to that of Sade.

So, although Bataille's essay is ostensibly about Sade, and in particular 'the brilliance and suffocation that the Marquis de Sade tried so indecently to provoke' (VE, 93; BR, 149), it is also a reflection on the same effects in Bataille. When Bataille writes about Sade he is never writing only about Sade but also about himself. He is concerned with two dominant reactions to Sade: the violent rejection of Sade's works and the admiration of Sade's works. The first reaction is probably more prevalent and more familiar, so familiar that Simone de Beauvoir could write an article entitled 'Must we Burn Sade?' in 1951.[6] However, Sade has also had his admirers and this was particularly true of when Bataille was writing. The surrealists had rediscovered Sade, along with Lautréamont, as a proto-surrealist. For Bataille it was Sade's 'most open apologists' (VE, 92; BR, 148) which concerned him more because, as he commented in his later work *Eroticism* (1957), 'Those people who used to rate de Sade as a scoundrel responded better to his intentions than his admirers do in our own day: de

Sade provokes indignation and protest, otherwise the paradox of pleasure would be nothing but a poetic fancy' (E, 180).

Those who reject Sade respond *better* to his intentions than his admirers do, because his admirers find, or make, Sade acceptable. They turn the paradox of pleasure, where pleasure for Sade always turns on pain, into a 'poetic fancy'. Rather than Sade having an impact on how we think about the world his admirers make him into part of a 'thoroughly literary enterprise' (VE, 93; BR, 149). There is little doubt that Bataille had the surrealists in mind when he wrote that 'The behaviour of Sade's admirers resembles that of primitive subjects in relation to their king, whom they adore and loathe, and whom they cover with honours and narrowly confine' (VE, 92; BR, 148). When the surrealists transformed Sade into a literary precursor they were not only establishing their avant-garde credentials by appropriating him, they were also making his work available as a work of literature. Sade could eventually become a part of the literary canon, and his scandalous works could be imprisoned within the library and the bookshop.

Bataille has also faced similar gestures of rejection and appropriation, which is no doubt why he considered so much to be at stake in the reading of Sade. During his lifetime Bataille was first rejected by the surrealists, being expelled from the group in 1929, and then later rejected by existentialism, when Jean-Paul Sartre described him as a case needing psychoanalysis.[7] He had alienated himself from the two dominant radical movements of French and European intellectual life at the time, condemning himself to a marginal existence. Even when he was admired this admiration led to an unacknowledged appropriation of his work. Lacan would draw on Bataille's writings which analysed the violence essential to sexuality to develop his concept of *jouissance*, a shattering enjoyment that is 'beyond the pleasure principle'.[8] Despite using Bataille's work Lacan did not make direct reference to it, and Bataille's contribution to Lacan's thought was erased.[9] In Chapter 1 I will try to recover some of Bataille's distinctiveness from this Lacanian appropriation.

It would be after his death that there would be steady increase in the number of Bataille's admirers, and all too often they would treat him as part of a thoroughly literary enterprise. Although these admirers make powerful claims for the importance of Bataille, comparing him to Joyce or seeing him as the heir of Catholic decadence,[10] this power is still limited to a *literary* power. We can resist these gestures of rejection and appropriation of Bataille by examining how he resists them when they are applied to Sade. Bataille was rightly pessimistic about this resistance: 'In fact even the gesture of writing, which alone permits one to envisage slightly less conventional human relations, a little less crafty than those of

so-called intimate friendships – even this gesture of writing does
not leave me with an appreciable hope' (VE, 91; BR, 147).
However, although Bataille was without 'appreciable hope' he
could not surrender Sade to his admirers any more than we can
surrender Bataille.

Firstly, Bataille analysed and tested the limits of the gestures of
rejection and appropriation. He argued that despite the fact that
they *appear* as opposites, in fact whether Sade is rejected or admired
he is actually treated in the *same* way. When Sade is rejected he is
immediately expelled but when he is appropriated he is first
assimilated and *then expelled*, and the result is the same in both cases.
These processes treat Sade as a *'foreign body'* (VE, 92; BR, 148)
which must be expelled to maintain purity. Rejection is more open
about this act and more open about the horror the foreign body
provokes. Appropriation is a more complex gesture which uses the
foreign body, first assimilating it and then gaining pleasure from
expelling it. For those who assimilated Sade he was only 'an object
of transports of exaltation to the extent that these transports facilitate
his excretion (his peremptory expulsion)' (VR, 92; BR, 148).

This process has also happened to Bataille as well as many other
'extreme' or 'transgressive' writers and artists. They are put to use
to produce a controlled pleasure by being appropriated and then
excreted. In this way we can come to terms with the most extreme
works and actually exploit the scandal they provoke. However, this
appropriation can never completely control the foreign body or
make it completely safe for the cultural market place. The foreign
body that cannot be dealt with is the one that still remains despite
being expelled. Both Bataille and Sade play the foreign body that
exists on the limit, that cannot be safely contained within or held
outside. As Bataille explains, these gestures try to excrete Sade but
Sade offers an economy that wallows in excrement. This will open
a thought of the heterogeneous, of *'unassimilable elements'* (VE, 99;
BR, 155), which can neither be rejected nor appropriated.

It also means that Bataille cannot be either rejected or appropriated: to reject Bataille is to fail to read him but to become an
apologist for Bataille, to celebrate him,[11] is also to fail to read him.
What Bataille requires is a reading that respects the heterogeneity
of his thought, a thought that is of and at the limit. In this book I
will explore this reading to argue that any introduction to Bataille
has to try and negotiate with his heterogeneity without simply
excreting it. What we have seen is that we can only arrive at Bataille
through Sade, because it is Sade who poses the problem of the
foreign body. For Bataille there are two tendencies in Sade's
writings: firstly, 'an irruption of excremental forces' (VE, 92; BR,
148) and secondly, 'a corresponding limitation' (VE, 93; BR, 149).
These two tendencies are in conflict, with the excremental forces

challenging the limitations that arise from their eruption. The two tendencies are also reflected in the reception of Sade, which has responded to the eruption of his writings with limitations by either rejecting them or confining them by admiration. Instead Bataille analyses eruption as the essential movement of Sade's writings and as the destruction of *all* limitations. In this way he tries to free Sade from the limitations imposed by his readers.

The 'violent excitation' (VE, 101; BR, 158) of Sade's work shakes those who reject it and those who try to appropriate it. It threatens to overflow the limitations in which they try to confine Sade. Bataille is also an irruptive force of violent excitation, and this accounts for the excitement of reading him. The irruptive forces which are condensed in Bataille's works threaten to destroy any reading that imposes a sense on Bataille or tries to place him within limits. To do so is to destroy the thought of freedom that is central to all of Bataille's work. If we do not read Bataille as a thinker of freedom then we do not read him at all. He has to be read *between* the gestures of rejection and appropriation for the heterogeneity of his writings and the heterogeneity he exposes at work in *all* writings to be uncovered. For Bataille 'the certainty of incoherence in reading, the inevitable crumbling of the soundest constructions, is the deep truth of books' (ON, 184). Bataille's objective is to expose all writing to the violent excitation of the heterogeneous and so to force us to confront the impossibility at the heart of thought.

Lived Experience

Bataille noted that 'Nietzsche wrote "with his blood"; to criticise or, better still, to test him, one must bleed in turn' (BR, 334). To criticise or test Bataille also requires that we bleed in turn and that we experience how Bataille wrote with *his* blood. Bataille's life was a turbulent one, lived out between irruptive forces and their corresponding limitations. I do not intend to provide an exhaustive description or chronology of his life but to select irruptive events from it which overflow into his work.[12] These events give us an essential background to the readings of Bataille that follow and place these in context. However, Bataille's 'life' and 'work' cannot be regarded as separate because he resists the idea that they can be firmly divided when one is a writer. Instead Bataille ruptures this opposition through '*lived experience*' (VE, 113), which is an experience of irruptive forces that flow between the life and work. His own work makes explicit this interweaving of life and work by always being deeply autobiographical, always written 'with his blood', but in a way that never supposes his own secure identity.

It sends out shock waves from the forces of lived experience that flow through it, shock waves that still cause our thought to tremble.

The most important early event in his intellectual development was his reading of Nietzsche in 1923, which he described as 'decisive' (BR, 113). This gave shape to the conclusion, already made in 1914, that his concern would be 'the formulation of a paradoxical philosophy' (BR, 113). If Bataille took from Nietzsche a taste for a paradoxical philosophy, he would first express those paradoxes in the language of surrealism. The style of his earliest writings is notably surrealist in its fascination with extreme and incongruous juxtapositions, so for example, 'An umbrella, a sexagenarian, a seminarian, the smell of rotten eggs, the hollow eyes of judges are the roots that nourish love' (VE, 6). Although Bataille was using surrealist language, and he always retained a sympathy for surrealism,[13] his writings were more violent and disturbed than many surrealist works. For Bataille the dream was not a royal road to a new superior reality but, as he recorded in a dream during his psychoanalysis (in 1927), a terrifying encounter with a castrating father: 'I'm something like three years old my legs naked on my father's knees and my penis bloody like the sun' (VE, 4).

Bataille himself regarded his work from this period as 'disordered' (VE, 74) and he entered psychoanalysis in 1927 because of the 'virulently obsessive character of his writing' (BR, 114). The analysis helped him personally with his obsessions but did not end his 'state of intellectual intensity' (BR, 114). This intensity would eventually prove too extreme for the surrealists and in the second surrealist manifesto André Breton denounced Bataille as an 'excrement-philosopher',[14] a criticism Bataille would probably have considered to be a compliment! Bataille's analysis of Sade was part of his response to his rejection by surrealism, a response that tried to destabilise the identity of surrealism as *the* avant-garde. One of the important consequences of his break with surrealism was that he joined up with other dissident surrealists, including Michel Leiris, and together with some conservative art historians formed the journal *Documents* in 1929. Not surprisingly, considering this highly unlikely and highly unstable alliance, the journal was short-lived.

The importance of *Documents* is that in its pages Bataille would develop his thought of the subversive image that we will discuss in detail in Chapter 1. That thought has to be understood in relation to his violent break with surrealism and to his desire to develop a paradoxical philosophy. Bataille's relationship to surrealism was not simply negative, he had learned a great deal from its exploration of 'images which form or deform real desires'.[15] However, he would also subject it to a series of deliberately provocative readings which would try to expose surrealism to the excremental forces which it was fast transforming into saleable works of art. In contrast with this attempt to make artistic, and eventually financial, capital from the image, Bataille was fascinated with the 'lightning-flash image' (VE, 78) that would subvert and overwhelm the viewer. This would be an image outside of any aesthetic, political or philosophical use, opposed to and subversive of the propaganda images that would define the 1930s. The experiment of *Documents* would eventually collapse in 1931 but Bataille never lost his fascination with the subversive image.

During this period Bataille also had another decisive encounter, this time with the work of Hegel at Alexandre Kojève's lectures on Hegel's *Phenomenology of Spirit* (1934–39). Kojève exposed a whole new generation of French thinkers, including Raymond Aron, Alexandre Koyré, Pierre Klossowski, Jacques Lacan, Maurice Merleau-Ponty and Eric Weil, to the power of Hegelian philosophy. For Bataille it was a traumatic initiation and he wrote that he felt 'suffocated, crushed, shattered, killed ten times over' by Hegel.[16] It may be that all of his writings after this encounter can be read as a sustained and violent dialogue with the overwhelming force of Hegel. We will see again and again how an internal debate with, and resistance to, Hegel marks Bataille's thought. That is why it is essential to sketch here his initial response to Hegel, because this will be the starting point for all his responses. His first response was to turn the violent effects of Hegel's philosophy on his thought back against Hegel. On 6 December 1937 he wrote a letter to Kojève, known as the 'Letter to X', where he stated that 'I imagine that my life – or, better yet, its aborting, the open wound that is my life – constitutes all by itself the refutation of Hegel's closed system' (CS, 90; BR, 296).

Bataille used his life as an expression of irruptive forces against Hegel's desire to control these forces. Hegel's philosophy depended on controlling these forces, and its power lay in the extent to which it admitted these forces into philosophy rather than rejecting them. In particular it was a philosophy that confronted the heterogeneous moment of death, but only to try and subsume this moment *within* philosophy. Bataille admired Hegel's audacity in trying to subsume death and his lucidity in recognising the threat that death posed to any philosophical system. The problem was that although Hegel had faced death he 'did not clearly separate death from the feeling of sadness' (BR, 289). Philosophy could only confront death in a work of mourning, a labour that gave death *meaning*. Bataille saw this as a retreat from death as impossibility and he responded by taking Hegel *further*. He refused to subsume death within a work of mourning and instead turned to the 'practice of joy before death' (VE, 235–9) which he found in customs like the Irish wake or the Mexican Day of the Dead, where death is faced with pleasure rather than sadness. By combining the 'authentic movement' (BR, 293) towards death of Hegel with the 'blind, pernicious joy' (BR, 290) of the festival he hoped to turn philosophy away from mourning and into delirium.

Although I will analyse Bataille's delirious reading of philosophy throughout this book I am not trying to produce a philosophical reading of Bataille, and in each case it will be a question of pursuing Bataille's resistance to philosophy. He always pursued this work in a series of communities and of friendships, despite his isolation. Chapter 2 will trace Bataille's thought of community as it emerges, paradoxically, from inner experience. Here Nietzsche will return as an essential resource for Bataille to resist Hegel. Bataille not only thought community but he also experimented with community as a practice, and these experiments had high political stakes. Throughout the 1930s Bataille was involved with the extra-parliamentary left and its opposition to fascism. He was not a Leninist or a Trotskyite but what the French would later call, after the May '68 events, a *gauchiste*. A *gauchiste* is an extreme leftist who also contests the idea of the revolutionary party in favour of action by the masses. For Bataille if 'insurrections had had to wait for learned disputes between committees and the political offices of parties, then there would never have been an insurrection' (VE, 162). The political communities with which he was involved refused the party form and would be central to his reflections on community.

He was involved with the Democratic Communist Circle in 1931 and then later helped found Counter-Attack in 1934 at the time of the Popular Front. Counter-Attack attempted to use the popular energies that fascism had aroused among the masses *against* fascism. Such an attempt was deeply ambiguous, leading to charges of a *surfascisme* (super-fascism) which tried to transcend fascism. Although Bataille himself recognised a 'paradoxical fascist tendency' (BR, 115) in the group, which was dissolved because of this, the positions that he took at this time continue to be used as evidence that he was in some way a fascist or complicit with fascism. These political attempts to discredit Bataille seem to have more to do with current debates around literary theory (the Paul de Man affair and the Heidegger affair, for example) than any serious consideration of the depth of Bataille's resistance to fascism in the face of an often widespread capitulation to it at the time. However, in Chapter 2 I will explore further how Bataille resists being reduced to fascism, as well as how he resists the reduction of thought that occurs in any political reading through a freedom that is excessive to politics.

What Bataille found in these leftist political experiments was a desire to seize power, and this pseudo-Nietzschean 'will-to-power' compromised their attempts at liberation. Instead a community could exist which desired freedom rather than power, and Bataille and others formed the secret society *Acéphale* (Headless) in 1936 to bring this community into existence. To counter the fascination with power in politics Bataille used the model of the sorcerer's apprentice who releases energies that he cannot control and which rebound on him (VE, 223–34; CS, 12–23). *Acéphale* was an attempt to release these energies beyond the control of any head or leader (especially the *Führer*). It is mostly famous because of the group's plan to carry out a human sacrifice, a plan that foundered because its members were willing to volunteer to be the victim but there were no willing executioners. However, *Acéphale* is of more interest than the myths that have grown around it. As Blanchot wrote, 'It is, I believe, the only group that counted for Georges Bataille and which he kept in mind, over the years, as an extreme possibility.'[17]

The war and the Occupation would extinguish these experiments in community, including the public face of *Acéphale*, the College of Sociology. The reality of power violently imposed itself on a thought and practice that had tried to disperse power. However, the war was also an experience of freedom for Bataille. Hollier writes that, 'For Bataille, the war is accompanied by an impression – conceivably a scandalous impression – of lightness.'[18] It is also at that time, in 1940, that Bataille met Maurice Blanchot with whom he would remain close friends. Bataille wrote that Blanchot encouraged him to 'pursue my inner experience as if I were the *last man*' (IE, 61; BR, 90) with the 'sounds from distant bombs' (ON, 108; BR, 98) around him. This violent lived experience would also be an experience of lightness. The combination of an experience of violence with an experience of lightness would lead to Bataille's post-war writings on the impossible experience of sovereignty.

In Chapter 3 we will see how Bataille tries to consider a thought of violence that is also recognition of the violence of thought. This act of thought is exposed to danger because a fascination with the exterior forms of violence 'can lead to the worst' (BR, 115). Bataille will confront the problem of how to analyse violence, especially because it is through the violent breaking of limitations that we are led to freedom. Violence is also a challenge to the limitations of language because 'Common language will not express violence' (E, 186). While violence cannot be easily expressed, and we will find Bataille struggling with this problem of expression in Chapter 3, it still remains: 'Violence never declares either its own existence or its right to exist; it simply exists' (E, 188). The war had demonstrated to Bataille not only the dominance of violence, but also how violence broke down limits. It offered a violent freedom, but a freedom that threatened death as the war became a total war that systematically erased the distinction between combatant and civilian. Bataille's war diaries reveal this process but also the necessity of thinking violence and how violence is difficult to reduce to the safety of an historical example.

Bataille wants to express a violence that is radically beyond language, and he searches for *examples* of this violence in acts of sacrifice, in auto-mutilation and in violent criminality. The difficulty is that these examples reduce violence back into language and into a particular historical moment or subject. Violence exists somewhere in the play of the example, existing through examples but also ruining the idea of the example through a violent opening. Bataille's thought and his lived experience exist in this violent tension of violence. Here we are pushed to the limit because it will be at the limit that we experience freedom: 'Freedom is nothing if it is not the freedom to live at the edge of limits where all comprehension breaks down' (I, 40). To live at this edge, where all comprehension breaks down, is to live with sovereignty as an impossible experience that combines violence *with* freedom. Sovereignty has to be understood as a reflection of Bataille's war experience, but also as a transformation of that experience. It is not just a limited response but a response that takes thought violently to its limits.

The violent opening of limitations that emerges in sovereignty, and also through lived experience, is developed by Bataille as a thought of transgression. Transgression is the violent breaking of a taboo, often a sexual taboo, and leads to anguish. Chapter 4 is an analysis of how Bataille reveals transgression through sexual experience. This is not only a matter of theoretical reflection, but also of lived experience. Bataille's post-war writings are often more conventional in form than either his pre-war or war writings. They distance themselves from direct contact with lived experience, and Bataille wrote in *Literature and Evil* (1957) that 'Turmoil is fundamental to my entire study; it is the very essence of my book. But the time has come to strive towards a clarity of consciousness' (LE, viiii). This distancing and drive towards clarity leads to contradictory effects: on the one hand, Bataille's writings are less immediate, more formal and constrain lived experience within the limitations of the historical survey or exhaustive study; on the other hand, because Bataille's writings are more detached from his own lived experiences they have more general effects that go beyond his lived experiences.

The anthropological history of *Eroticism* (1957) and the art history of *The Tears of Eros* (1961) are distant from Bataille's explicit fictional writings and his personal experiences. There is little hint in them that Bataille's analysis of the connections between violence, sexuality and death might have any relation to his four-year affair with 'Laure' (Colette Peignot) which began in 1934. The death of Laure in 1938 'had torn him apart' (BR, 116) and the dissolute life Bataille led at that time is fictionalised in *Blue of Noon*. This biographical reticence is balanced by the deepening of Bataille's thought, where transgression can emerge from sexuality but is no longer confined to sexuality. Sollers writes that 'This opening is achieved not abstractly, but through the body' (CR, 85). Although it begins with the body it also *passes* through the body, opening up beyond it and not remaining confined within it. Transgression is not the property of the body of the pervert, whether we celebrate or condemn that transgression. As we will also see in Chapter 4 this passing beyond opens out eroticism into areas of thought which are usually kept safely away from the erotic.

So, while Bataille intimately relates his life to his work his work cannot be completely explained by his life history. Bataille's writings on eroticism cannot be explained as the result of his own 'perversions' or as some attempt at self-justification for his own desires. It is important that we recognise the limits of biographical explanation and its assimilation of an author to the stability of an identity. I want to examine briefly two possible reductions of Bataille to a secure identity which emerge around his writings on transgression. The first is the reduction of Bataille to his sexual identity, the idea that his sexual experiences explain his writings. The second is the reduction of transgression to a religious identity, and the claim that Bataille is a Catholic writer. Both of these attempts to stabilise transgression have to confront Bataille's own heterogeneity, a heterogeneity which cannot be reduced to an identity and which challenges our tendency to make biographical readings.

Bataille parodies the idea of direct causal connections between his early life experiences and his work in the afterword to his novel the *Story of the Eye* (1928) called 'Coincidences' (SE, 69–74). At first this afterword appears to explain the pornographic sexual narrative that precedes it as the result of a series of shocking childhood memories, focused around the repulsive and obscene figure of Bataille's syphilitic father. What complicates this explanation is that instead of the childhood memories acting as the motivation for the book it is the act of writing that provokes the coincidence of memories (SE, 69), and these memories are deformed by that act of writing (SE, 74). The title of this afterword also points towards Bataille's later work on chance, where the 'gossamer-like lacerating idea of chance!' (G, 73; BR, 41) lacerates identity.

Bataille argues that 'Chance is hard to bear' (G, 73; BR, 41), not least because chance disrupts the stability of the body and identity structured through a linear 'life'. Connections between life and work do exist but they are neither linear nor stable. Already Bataille is leading us into a labyrinth of unstable relations *between* life and work, and between rejection and assimilation. This instability shatters the links on which much of contemporary biography and psychobiography depend. The seventeenth-century philosopher Spinoza had already suggested that there could be ruptures in our lives which altered our identities so completely that we changed identities, and that one of these ruptures is between childhood and adulthood.[19] Bataille sees lived experience as a series of chance ruptures rather than the continuity of identity. Although this is a challenge to psychoanalytic models Bataille does not dismiss psychoanalysis totally: he benefited personally from his own psychoanalysis with Dr Adrien Borel in 1927 and he respected Freud's discoveries. However, he transgresses psychoanalysis almost to the point of parody with his hyperbolic descriptions of Oedipal crisis and castration anxiety. Bataille has a traumatic vision of sexuality but it is not a trauma confined by castration, the Oedipus complex or the nuclear family.

Furthermore, transgression, as Bataille realised, has a close relationship with religion and can be subject to a religious interpretation. Deleuze remarks '"Transgression", a concept too good for seminarists under the law of a Pope or a priest, the tricksters. Georges Bataille is a very French author. He made the little secret the essence of literature, with a mother within, a priest beneath, an eye above.'[20] Bataille may, *at times*, be a very French and very Catholic author but his writings remain irreducible to a national or religious identity. The biographical evidence is ambiguous: although he was raised in a secular environment Bataille became very pious and converted to Catholicism in 1914, perhaps as an act of rebellion against that upbringing. He eventually lost his faith in 1920 because 'his Catholicism has caused a woman he loved to shed tears' (BR, 113) but he never lost a sense of the power of religious feelings (particularly guilt and sin).

Bataille respected the force of these feelings but as *irruptions* that could not be contained within a Catholic dialectic of confession and forgiveness, because transgression did not lead to the priest but to an inexpiable anguish. In *Guilty* he wrote, 'My true church is a whorehouse – the only one that gives me true satisfaction' (G, 12). As Julia Kristeva suggests, 'One might be inclined to attribute Bataille's erotic experience to a Catholicism that was taken on to the limit of its sin-laden logic and would lead to its internal reversal.'[21] Transgression is not a religious concept but the interruption and 'internal reversal' of the sin-laden logic of Catholicism. Once again Bataille exists at the limits, as a foreign body to Catholicism.

By turning away from the directly biographical Bataille's post-war works can better confront the assimilations that impose an identity on him. These more 'systematic' writings are more systematic considerations of the limits of all systems – the impossible. In these works the lived experiences of Bataille no longer belong *only* to him but have *general* effects on all thought. These general effects are taken furthest by Bataille's writings on general economy, which is the focus of Chapter 5. Lived experience is now the experience of an excess which no system can control and which 'must necessarily be lost without profit; it must be spent, willingly or not, gloriously or catastrophically' (AS1, 21; BR, 184). Here is an excess that is not simply individual but traverses every system from the individual to the world and to the cosmos. The opening of the limit which we will trace throughout Bataille's writings, through his subversion of the image, through his reopening of the thought of community, through his violent opening of freedom and through his transgression of the body, is given its most general form in general economy.

In *The Accursed Share* Bataille destroys the framework of political economy in which he is writing. Political economy is led by Bataille into moments of excess which cannot be reduced to political economy: 'I had a point of view from which a human sacrifice, the construction of a church or the gift of a jewel were no less interesting than the sale of wheat' (AS1, 9). The last great critique of political economy had been Marx's *Capital*, but what had been intended as a critique was often transformed by its readers into a manual for a new Marxist political economy.[22] Unlike Marx, Bataille did not operate on the conceptual terrain of political economy and he swept away the residual Marxist desire for 'a good use of economy' (Baudrillard in CR, 192) by destroying the axioms of economy itself.

The Accursed Share is not the final summary of Bataille's writings, but it is an opening where Bataille will trace the contours of lived experience as the convulsive effects of general economy. Bataille's death on 8 July 1962 does nothing either to end this convulsive movement or limit the general effects of his writings. For Bataille 'Death is disappearance' (G, 7) and this disappearance makes it impossible to decide if death is a lived experience, the end of lived experience or is outside of lived experience. Death is an experience at the limit, the limit which not only divides life from death but which also contaminates them by drawing them together. Bataille was fascinated by the possibility that we might experience death through the other, for example, in the spectacle of sacrifice. Sacrifice exposes us to death but also saves us from death: 'Thus, at all costs, man must live at the moment that he really dies, or he must live with the impression of really dying' (BR, 287). However, for Bataille this economy of sacrifice is threatened by a general economy that would expose us to death with no protection. This economy 'threatens with death all who get caught up in its movement' (BR, 290). Bataille's death does not order his thought into the consistency of a career or a life, but it exposes us to the convulsive movement of his thought.

The Labyrinth

After Bataille's death we still remain exposed to the convulsive force of his writings, and he leaves us with a new and perplexing image of thought: the labyrinth. The labyrinth is an image of the path between his rejection and assimilation, and between his life and work. The labyrinth also confronts us with Bataille as the impossible one, because this is not a secure path. I want to suggest the impossible as a guiding thread to lead us into Bataille's work, but this guiding thread cannot lead us safely through the labyrinth. For Bataille 'There are hours when Ariadne's thread is broken …' (IE, 33; BR, 64) and the impossible is a broken thread through which we can become lost in the labyrinth. The reason that we must become lost in the labyrinth is that Bataille's labyrinth is not only a space in which we become disoriented but it is also a *disoriented* space. Therefore, a broken guiding thread is the *only* type of guiding thread that can lead us to an experience of the labyrinth of thought.

The labyrinth is no longer a maze which has a potential or actual solution, but it is a 'space' without an entrance, an exit or a centre. In this disorientation the labyrinth is an image of existence that is determined by what Bataille calls 'a *principle of insufficiency*' (VE, 172). As Bataille explains in his essay 'The Labyrinth' (1935–36) (VE, 171–7) this insufficiency is a principle that dominates all existence. It means that no being is ever complete, ever sufficient, and that because of this insufficiency every being is in an open relation to others. Bataille chooses the image of the labyrinth to describe this state because it captures the effect of disorientation caused by insufficiency, but at the same time the labyrinth is never sufficient and is always in relation to an exterior which cannot be completely specified in advance. The most powerful example of the principle of insufficiency is language, because language imposes itself on us and puts us in relation to others. To be in language is to be in relation to others, a relation that can never be fully mastered or controlled.

Through language the idea that we can exist as self-sufficient is destroyed: 'Being depends on the mediation of words, which cannot merely present it arbitrarily as "autonomous being", but which must present it profoundly as "being in relation"' (VE, 173–4). It is language which discloses the impossibility of an autonomous being, and it is language which places us in an impossible *relation* that we can never master. By placing us in relation language leads us into disorientation: 'One need only follow, for a short time, the traces of the repeated circuits of words to discover, in a disconcerting vision, the labyrinthine structure of the human being' (VE, 174). The labyrinth is not an external structure imposed on existence, which would suppose that we could find in the labyrinth a model that could master this situation. Instead, the labyrinth is the dispersal of this 'being in relation', no longer on the model of a maze that always has a potential solution but now a space of relation that lacks any solution and any sufficient moment that would secure closure.

The labyrinth of 'being in relation' is disclosed by language and it can also account for the reason that we persist in believing in the idea of separate autonomous beings. Although language places us in relation with others these relations are never secure; they destabilise us and they are also unstable themselves. The relation between beings has no more sufficiency than the beings themselves, and it is because of the instability of these relations that we can feel ourselves to be autonomous: 'This extreme instability of connections alone permits one to introduce, as a puerile but convenient illusion, a representation of isolated existence turning in on itself' (VE, 174). It is only because we are so lost in the labyrinth that we can regard ourselves as isolated beings, but this isolation is only ever an effect of the fragility of the relations which form us. The principle of insufficiency leads to the illusion of self-sufficiency, but sufficiency cannot be found.

It cannot be found in the labyrinth itself either as the labyrinth is a 'foggy labyrinth' (VE, 174) and not the clear map of relations between beings. In fact, the guiding thread of impossibility leads us to the centre of the labyrinth where what we find is a 'central insufficiency' (VE, 176). We resist this instability of the labyrinth by creating 'relatively stable wholes' (VE, 175): cities, empires, or a God or gods. These wholes attempt to order the play of the labyrinth and organise the dispersed and fragile relations between beings by organising them around a centre. As the idea of our autonomous being emerged from the instability of the labyrinth and tried to end that instability, so these stable wholes perform a similar function. We impose on the labyrinth a stability which would allows us to map it and so put an end to the principle of insufficiency. The most powerful idea of the centre is that of God, a 'divine sufficiency' (VE, 173) that promises to orient thought. Secular thought has not done away with this idea of a centre, the idea of a relatively stable whole. Science is not as opposed to

religion as may first appear, not least because it too imposes
stability on its object in its 'obsession with the *ideal* form of matter'
(VE, 15). Most of the various 'materialisms' which have attacked
religious explanations of the world have still believed in an ideal
form of matter.

These models of sufficiency suppose a hierarchy where the
principle of sufficiency dominates over insufficiency. Bataille turns
the insufficiency that these models try to confine to the peripheries
of thought against the centre: 'The relative insufficiency of
peripheral existences is absolute insufficiency in total existence'
(VE, 176–7). Rather than the 'weakness' of the peripheral regions
around the centre supporting the sufficiency of the centre the
'weakness' of those regions exposes the centre to the total loss of
sufficiency. The labyrinth is decentred and can no longer be
ordered from the centre outwards or from the top to the bottom.
The whole 'structure' is afflicted with 'absolute insufficiency' and
this changes the whole concept of structure. This decentring of
structure is why Bataille has so often been seen as a precursor of
poststructuralism. Derrida has noted that structure 'has always
been neutralised or reduced, and this by a process of giving it a
centre or of referring it to a point of presence, a fixed origin'.[23]
Bataille destroys this point of presence by exposing it to 'a network
of endless waves that renew themselves in all directions' (VE, 177),
and so prefigures the poststructuralist 'deconstruction' of structure.

These waves overflow and flood the centre, and they will lead us
from the broken thread of the impossible to the broken thread of
difference. The model of the decentred labyrinth, of language that
puts us in relation, and the network of mobile waves can all be
interpreted as a thought of *difference*. Difference here is not a master
concept or a theory but an unstable putting into relation, the
'*nonlogical difference*' (VE, 129: BR, 180) of matter that Bataille
discusses at the end of 'The Notion of Expenditure' (January
1933). I am not arguing that Bataille *is* a poststructuralist, but
rather that Bataille is an anachronism, out of his time, thinking
poststructuralism before it was even named. Instead of giving
Bataille the identity of poststructuralism I see him as the foreign
body that can expose us to a different thinking of his own work
and poststructuralism. This is one reason why Bataille still remains
so central to modern European thought and why the rejection or
appropriation of his work misses the importance of that work by
expelling it as a foreign body. In doing so these gestures refuse to
understand Bataille as central *because* he is a foreign body.

As poststructuralism will change our thinking about Bataille, so
Bataille will also change how we think about poststructuralism.
With Bataille poststructuralism is no longer confined to being a
method of literary study or an academic sub-discipline, but instead

it is a thought of difference. Bataille shares a number of points of reference with poststructuralism and virtually all the major thinkers associated with it have written essays on Bataille.[24] Poststructuralism is most often explained through the linguistic model of difference derived from Saussure, or else the difference at work in Nietzsche, Freud or Heidegger.[25] Bataille, however, is a crucial and often ignored reference, not least because he does not fit easily into pre-existing disciplines. Bataille's difference cannot be so easily reduced to linguistics, psychoanalysis or philosophy and he never offers a theory of difference. The impossibility of deriving a theory from Bataille may be the reason that he is so little read, but when he draws out the impossibility of theory itself he becomes impossible to ignore.

The labyrinth is a model that is at once impossible and unavoidable, a model of thought that cannot be rejected or accepted: for that reason the labyrinth is an image of thought for the way we should read Bataille, between the gestures of rejection and appropriation. It is also an image for the results of that reading, because the dispersed model of relations, of a network that is decentred, is also a model of difference. Through the labyrinth we can begin to respond to Bataille's 'hard-to-meet' conditions of reading. These conditions are important because they suggest *why* we should read Bataille, they are conditions of how we should read the remainder or excess that any reading can neither reject nor assimilate. For Bataille this excess is a lived experience which refuses to establish a safe distance between life and work. It also destroys the distance between the reader and Bataille's writings. His lived experiences not only spill out on to the pages of his writings, they also open his writings to us. Bataille described reading as being 'like a solidified instant, or series of instants detached from the work and the reading of the work' (LE, 188). This book is a series of those instants detached from Bataille to allow us to begin to read Bataille. I want to begin at the beginning, with Bataille's earliest works on the subversive image.

CHAPTER 1

The Subversive Image

In the *Story of the Eye* the narrator, a thinly veiled adolescent Bataille, experiences obscene images that flash through his mind and 'these images were, of course, tied to the contradiction of a prolonged state of exhaustion and an absurd rigidity of my penis' (SE, 30). All of Bataille's subversive images share this contradictory structure of exhaustion and sexual excitement (*jouissance*). They at once exhaust the possible functions of the image and subvert it with a *jouissance* which touches on death and that the image can only indicate but not represent. He pursued these multiple images across various media, including painting, photography and writing to the point where we can find no clear distinction between the pornographic tableaux described in his novel *Story of the Eye* (1928) and the photographic images Bataille commented on in the journal *Documents* (1929–31). I want to trace Bataille's subversion of the image through his analysis of specific images to his subversion of vision itself. *Documents* is the beginning because here Bataille not only writes on images but works with images: *Documents* is a multimedia production. It engages with Bataille's other works at the time and also with his later works, prefiguring his fractured and condensed writings which work by producing images of thought. It also raises the question, why has Bataille had so little impact as a writer on the image?

Perhaps the reason for Bataille's lack of impact is that his subversion of the image can never be assimilated by a theory of the image. It is this impossibility of a *theory* of the subversive image that is first sketched out in *Documents* by Bataille and his companions. At the centre of *Documents* is a series of entries written for a planned critical dictionary, with Bataille and Michel Leiris writing most of the entries until the magazine ceased to exist in 1931. Although this meant that the critical dictionary remained incomplete, from the beginning it was always intended to be incomplete. The incompletion of the critical dictionary was a critique of the tendency of dictionaries to try to define all the significant words in a language by freezing their irruptive energies into stable meanings. For Bataille 'A dictionary begins when it no longer gives the meaning of words but their tasks' (VE, 31).

Instead of being organised by meaning the critical dictionary was organised by the tasks of words, trying to release their irruptive energies. This release often involved a play between the critical dictionary entry for a word and its accompanying image. Moreover, the entries were not originally placed alphabetically (although they have been now in EA) but worked together with their accompanying images in a disjunctive, non-hierarchical 'structure'. The tasks of words would be explored through the selection of words analysed which ranged from the question of materialism (EA, 58) to a discussion of Buster Keaton (EA, 56). Through this selection process links are made between the tasks of words and a strange 'logic' emerges where Keaton's *sang-froid* could be the basis of a materialism of 'raw phenomena'.

After only the first issue of *Documents* one of the co-founders wrote to Bataille that 'The title you have chosen for this journal is hardly justified except in the sense that it gives us "documents" on your state of mind.'[1] However, the journal is far more than a catalogue of Bataille's own state of mind and personal obsessions. Through the critical dictionary he intervenes into the founding classifications that define the meaning of our world. The critical dictionary subverts these classifications by shifting from a word's meaning to its tasks and effects. These effects are also visual, coming through the images that accompany the 'definitions' in the critical dictionary. Bataille and his co-writers are pursuing images that overwhelm the viewer. For Bataille the 'noble parts of a human being (his dignity, the nobility that characterises his face)' (VE, 78) cannot 'set up the least barrier against a sudden, bursting eruption ...' (VE, 78). The critical dictionary registered these bursting eruptions as chance instants in which the image would rear its head and shatter the calm world of the dictionary. The destruction of the classifications of the dictionary would then affect the order of language and of the world itself. Far from being documents of Bataille's state of mind these are documents of sudden bursting eruptions that are impossible to classify.

The critical dictionary is an act of 'sacrificial mutilation' (VE, 61–72) of the classical dictionary. It is 'charged with this element of hate and disgust...' (VE, 71) for the tranquil orderings of a world bound by meaning. In *Documents*, however, there is an anomalous image which appears to remain within this world of meaning. It is a photograph taken in 1905 of a provincial wedding party lined up in two regimented rows in front of a shop (EA, 99) which accompanies an essay by Bataille called 'The Human Face'. The image is anomalous to the critical dictionary because it is so utterly conventional; it is an image out of place. Why is it there when for Bataille 'The mere sight (in photography) of our predecessors in the occupation of this country now produces, for varying reasons, a burst of loud and raucous laughter; that sight, however, is nonetheless hideous' (EA, 100)? What fascinates Bataille is that this conventional image should provoke this reaction, a reaction which combines contradictory experiences of laughter and fear. These supposedly incompatible effects are brought together in this image and make it unforgettable. Although we may laugh at the wedding party it still haunts us with a fear that remains with us even in our most acute moments of pleasure. Bataille comments that it forces a youth to confront 'at every unexpected moment of rapture the images of his predecessors looming up in tiresome absurdity' (EA, 100).

Lodged within the critical dictionary, lodged within its images of base eruption, is this haunting image of propriety. It is an image that has the power to destroy our rapture and to limit the subversive image. The image of the wedding party always threatens to loom up before the subversive image and put an end to the subversion that it promises. What is worse is that these ghosts from the past are not the powerful monsters that once terrified us but banal representations of the provincial bourgeoisie. Once we had to be held in check by horrifying phantoms that possessed a terrible power; now, 'The very fact that one is haunted by ghosts so lacking in savagery trivialises these terrors and this anger' (EA, 100–1). The ghosts of our ancestors destroy the subversive image in two ways: firstly, they block any effect of rapture by appearing before us at our moments of pleasure and secondly, they make the horror they cause us appear trivial. Bataille has to counter this neutralisation of the subversive image or his subversion of the image could always be accounted for as the results of his own personal obsessions.

He subverts this image of propriety by exposing it to the violent irruptive forces that it is trying to hold in check rather than by attacking it from an exterior critical position. The irruptive forces threaten to break apart the image if 'we acknowledge the *presence* of an acute perturbation in, let us say, the state of the human mind represented by the sort of provincial wedding photographed twenty-five years ago, then we place ourselves outside established rules in so far as a real negation of the existence of *human nature* is herein implied' (EA, 101). To read the image in this way is to read the rigidity of the wedding group lined up in rows and organised around the bridal pair not as symbolic of a banal power but as the desperate attempt to control and limit the irruptive forces which circulate around and through the bridal pair. In reading the image to the limit of the frame Bataille detects an 'acute perturbation' that shakes the hold that this image has over us.

This 'acute perturbation' is found through the image and it threatens to negate the image of human nature on which the power of the photograph rests. The wedding photograph presents 'the supposed continuity of *our* nature' (EA, 102), the safe passage from one generation to the next represented by a bridal pair surrounded by their families and friends. The image is a promise of the continuation of the family and also of society. Yet the image is split by the violence which is condensed within it, and this family gathering can be seen both 'as representing the very principle of mental activity at its most civilised and most violent, and the bridal pair as, let us say, the symbolic parents of a wild and apocalyptic rebellion ...' (EA, 101–2). The height of civilisation that the bridal pair incarnates is not the calm transmission of a heritage but a violent repression. Violence is present within what presents itself as civilised non-violence. Bataille agrees with Freud's argument in *Civilisation and its Discontents* (published at almost the same time, 1929–30) that the progress of civilisation demands the increasing violent repression of our violent and sexual drives.[2] Like Freud, Bataille recognises that this control can never be complete and often the stronger the repression the more violent the eruption of our 'civilisation' elsewhere, as both of them witnessed in the slaughter of the First World War.

The image is split by the violence that is required to organise it as a stable image, but this violence also *splits* open the image. In the bridal pair Bataille not only finds the principle of 'civilised' mental activity but also the parents of a 'wild and apocalyptic rebellion'. This counter-violence against civilisation is parasitic on the violence that civilised society imposes on irruptive forces. It opposes the supposed continuity of human nature by exposing the bridal pair as 'monsters breeding incompatibles' (EA, 102). As Bataille shatters the continuity of human nature he releases the subversive forces that the photograph has condensed and attempted to control. In this act of violent rejection the depth of the monstrosity of our ancestors is revealed beneath their trivial appearance. Bataille subverts the most 'normal' of images, the image of a ritual that is supposed to express and secure the continuity and progress of the generations.

The 'normal' image is now exposed as monstrous, by exposing its production of 'normal' human nature as an operation requiring massive surplus violence. Human nature is no longer purely natural, a given fact, but it is a complex arrangement of violent irruptive forces forced into stability. Bataille's work on this image is close to the satirical gestures of the surrealist film-maker Luis Buñuel. Buñuel's vicious parodies of the 'exterminating angel' of bourgeois conformity[3] are mirrored in the frantic violence with which Bataille demolishes the image of the wedding party. However, Buñuel would eventually be seduced by 'The discreet charm of the bourgeoisie', as one of his later films was entitled.[4] Bataille resisted the 'charm' of bourgeois power by not limiting his parody to the bourgeoisie but by taking it to the point where 'the world is purely parodic' (VE, 5).

Bataille resists the danger of parody becoming dependent on what it has parodied by making parody a 'principle' of existence. In doing so he dislodges the concept of human nature, whether bourgeois or otherwise. Bataille is not a humanist, not even a radical humanist who probes the limits of human nature to recover what is 'really' human. His work has been used by Michael Richardson to supply a new social theory of the emergence of the human,[5] but this is a misreading. Bataille is probing the limits of the human to the point where the concept of human nature breaks down: 'Where you would like to grasp your timeless substance, you encounter only a slipping, only the poorly co-ordinated play of your perishable elements' (IE, 94). The concept of human nature is our attempt to grasp a timeless substance theoretically, but all we grasp are perishable elements that slip from our hands. The individual is carried away in a play of perishable elements which cannot be organised by a theory of human nature. Bataille cannot provide a new or 'radical' social theory[6] but subjects social theory to parody that cannot be contained within the confines of theory.

His negation of human nature is not based on belief in 'an order excluding total complicity with all that has gone before' (EA, 101). Bataille is not a writer of radical breaks because these breaks are violent gestures of division and purification. To destroy all complicity with what has gone on before would involve purifying ourselves of the past. The break is dominated by a belief in a new pure state, a new pure human nature (for example, Che Guevara's 'new socialist man'). Bataille's violent class rhetoric of the 1930s does call for the destruction of the bourgeoisie but it is not clear that he means mass *physical* destruction. He is not a writer of purification but a writer of the principle of contagion and contamination (CS, 109). Rather than negating human nature with a break from all that has gone before we negate it by an act of contamination of its purity and propriety. We do not flee the ugliness of our ancestors but we are attracted by it: 'There is absolutely no thought of dispensing with this hateful ugliness, and we will yet catch ourselves some day, eyes suddenly dimmed and brimming with inadmissible tears, running absurdly towards some provincial haunted house, nastier than flies, more vicious, more rank than a hairdresser's shop' (EA, 106).

It is not a matter of destroying the image, of creating a 'pure' subversive image, but of embracing what is hateful and ugly in that image. We are pulled back into the image, running into it out of control. The irruptive forces revealed by Bataille flow out of the image and then flow back into it, disrupting its propriety. However, once Bataille has drawn out these irruptive forces is it not possible that they could be assimilated and put to use by science or philosophy? Could they not be analysed conventionally? These irruptive forces do not settle within the conventional, and the classifications of science or philosophy would be variations on the dictionary classifications which work through imposing meaning. Like the dictionary, science divides up the world into discrete units, trying to impose 'a mathematical frock coat' (VE, 31) on the world. Philosophy, on the other hand, tries to contain these forces within metaphysical wholes. What remains is the leftover, the remainder, which cannot be assimilated. The event of eruption is like 'a fly on an orator's nose' (EA, 102), whose comic effect of 'acute perturbation' mocks the discourses of knowledge.

Philosophy is more audacious because it tries to control the moment of irruption within itself by assimilating it within, but 'It is impossible to reduce the appearance of the fly on the orator's nose to the supposed contradiction between the self and metaphysical whole' (EA, 103). If the fly could be reduced to the position of contradiction then it would simply be a negative moment of the metaphysical whole. It would have escaped the image only to have become part of philosophy. Although Bataille had yet to attend Kojève's lectures on Hegel he was already aware of some rudiments of Hegel's philosophy. He knew, probably from the use of Hegel's dialectic in Marxism, how Hegel would use contradiction as a means of bringing any negative moments within absolute knowledge. The fly refused to remain in the contradictory position, and so the subversive image could not be controlled by a dialectical contradiction. The eruption that explodes out of the wedding party photograph and plunges us back into it also shatters the principle of human nature. At the same time it drags philosophy and science into this turbulent play of forces, subverting them along with the image.

With a rapid movement that is dizzying Bataille moves from the image to science and philosophy, and in doing so he suggests the hidden continuity between science, philosophy and society. What they share is a common repression of the violent irruptive forces on which they depend, but which they cannot fully control. In each case violent forces are repressed and controlled by acts that are themselves violent but which dissimulate this violence. It is this that makes them vulnerable, so when a fly lands on a human face which is trying to present itself as serious and knowledgeable it provokes laughter. There is no fly visible in the photograph Bataille discusses but he can see the fly buzzing around by sliding rapidly through the image. In the flight of the fly in and out of the image the highest of human concerns are dragged into the dirt as the fly is attracted by the odour of the rank and vicious. The fly is a provocation to the image because it cannot be found there. It does not settle within the frame of the photograph but flies out of it, buzzes around it and taunts it like the presence of the acute perturbation that disturbs the calm surface of the image. In this sense it has a *virtual* presence, neither actually appearing in the photograph yet not completely absent from it either. It is the haunting possibility of the subversive image that rests 'in' the photograph but only in so far as it is always spilling out of it.

As the fly escapes from the image of the wedding party it moves on to more explicit images of eruption. The photographs of slaughterhouses at La Villette in Paris by Eli Lotar break a taboo on presenting violence. Bataille notes that 'In our time, nevertheless, the slaughterhouse is cursed and quarantined like a plague-ridden ship' (EA, 73). Eli Lotar has put us back into contact with this work of death through images of animal carcasses, butchers and smears of blood. What these images also reveal is that this violent slaughter, on which many of us non-vegetarians still depend, has become a mechanical and technical activity. In one of the photographs a line of severed animal legs rests against a wall in an ordered arrangement that represses the violence of the slaughter (EA, 74). We are doubly alienated from the slaughterhouse: firstly, we do not wish to see what happens there and secondly, its activities turn death into a productive and neutral event.

This limitation of violence is not a sign of the progress of 'civilisation'. 'The curse (terrifying only to those who utter it) leads them to vegetate as far as possible from the slaughterhouse, to exile themselves, out of propriety, to a flabby world in which nothing fearful remains and in which, subject to the ineradicable obsession of shame, they are reduced to eating cheese' (EA, 73). Our exile from the slaughterhouse does not put an end to the violence but transforms it from something sacred to a technical activity from which we can hide ourselves. This transforming of death into a secret, technical operation has been one of the factors at work in the 'slaughterhouses' of human beings in the twentieth century. Bataille's response is to use these images of the slaughterhouse to break the taboo that protects us from an intimate contact with death. By breaking this taboo he challenges the distance which allows us to transform slaughter into a technical activity, and he puts us into contact with a different experience of death.

Bataille is also nostalgic for a past that is supposed to have achieved a sacred relationship with death, where in the act of sacrifice we found 'a primal continuity linking us with everything that is' (E, 15). He is contrasting the practice of joy before death with the organisation of death into productive meaning. This desire for an intimate experience of death finds its most disturbing form in an image, the photograph of the Chinese torture victim. Although it is contained in his final book *The Tears of Eros* (1961)

Bataille had possessed the image since 1925, when it had been given him by his analyst Dr Adrien Borel (and this might indicate the unconventional nature of Bataille's analysis). It shows a Chinese man undergoing death by cuts: 'The Chinese executioner of my photo haunts me: there he is busily cutting off the victim's leg at the knee. The victim is bound to a stake, eyes turned up, head thrown back, and through a grimacing mouth you see teeth' (G, 38–9). Bataille never commented on it in *Documents* and it is the hidden secret of *Documents*. However, it is no longer secret and has become part of the counterculture appropriation of Bataille circulating on the Internet.

If the wedding party of 'The Human Face' is the most conventional image in Bataille then the Chinese torture victim is, for Bataille, 'to my knowledge, the most anguishing of worlds accessible to us through images captured on film' (TE, 206). He returned to it again and again, in *Inner Experience*, in *Guilty* and in *The Tears of Eros*, as if unable to turn away from it. In his final work Bataille wrote, 'This photograph had a decisive role in my life. I never stopped being obsessed by this image of pain, at once ecstatic (?) and intolerable' (TE, 206). It is decisive because Bataille finds in it an image of an ecstatic death that tears at the limits of the image and provokes his 'last shuddering tears' (TE, 207). Bataille's use of this image makes him vulnerable to the criticism that Adorno made of Heidegger – that he offers 'a regression to the cult of death'.[7] Certainly it is a disturbing, even sickening, image, but it cannot be rejected and should not be celebrated. It reaches us through its violence, and in its violence it demands a response from us.

It firstly provokes complex effects, and this provocative complexity indicates that the image is not unequivocal. Bataille cannot be certain that it is the image of ecstatic death that he desires. The strange beatific grin on the face of the torture victim may not be joy before death but the result of the administration of opium used to prolong or relieve the suffering of the victim (TE, 205). There is an undecidable moment where the grin is indistinguishable from a grimace. This undecidable moment undoes Bataille's claim for a direct access to the 'sacred horror' of eroticism. Rather than having direct access Bataille is forced to interpret the image, and no image, including this one, can offer direct access to the impossible. Instead the impossible emerges in the undecidable oscillation between the grin and the grimace, a decisive moment of reading when any decision lacks a secure foundation.

The image is not only equivocal but it also has tasks for Bataille; it is an opening to a communication with the suffering of the Other. It cannot be passively contemplated because it draws us in by taking us outside of ourselves. It is an experience of ecstasy as *ek-stasis* (standing-outside) that leaves us undone: 'The young and seductive Chinese man of whom I have spoken, left to the work of the executioner – I loved him with a love in which the sadistic instinct played no part: he communicated his pain to me or perhaps the excessive nature of his pain, and it was precisely that which I was seeking, not so as to take pleasure in it, but in order to ruin in me that which is opposed to him' (IE, 120). Bataille is not a sadist, nor is he celebrating death, but for him this image of pain makes a *communication* possible. This image is decisive because it so profoundly overflows its limits, and it catches us up in the movement of death.

By drawing us into the movement of death the Chinese torture victim does not leave us at a safe distance from death. This is in contrast to Christianity which admits the suffering body of Christ but has a tendency to 'wholly and irreversibly obliterate the tortured body'.[8] Bataille thought that 'the success of Christianity must be explained by the value of the theme of the son of God's ignominious crucifixion, which carries human dread to a representation of loss and limitless degradation' (BR, 170; VE, 119). Christianity has exploited this suffering through art, with endless studies of the crucifixion but these representations of 'loss and limitless degradation' have always been contained by the narrative of the crucifixion in which Christ's suffering redeems us. Christianity is a cult of death which denies the power of death through the resurrection and through the imposition of religious meaning on death. The image of the Chinese torture victim restores Christ's suffering body to a degradation without return or benefit.

The Chinese torture victim also challenges the reduction of death to meaning by Hegel, who draws on Christian thought. In particular, Hegel uses the crucifixion and resurrection of Christ as the image of a passage from the infinite to the finite and again back to the infinite. The Chinese torture victim disrupts this circle of spirit by dragging it back down into the suffering body. Bataille resists the dialectical reduction of Christ's pain by an image of suffering that does not lead to meaning. Bataille found the attempt to put the divine to death in the crucifixion of Christ comical (BR, 282). Hegel uses it to add on to the infinite 'a movement towards the finite' (BR, 282) that will eventually return to infinite, but for Bataille to make the divine finite is a cause for more laughter. In laughing at death, which does not mean mocking suffering, we become close to the pain of the Other in the paroxysms of laughter which seamlessly turn into sobbing. This is no 'cult of death' but a demand to experience death as an event that shatters us.

The Chinese torture victim photograph has complex effects: it forces Bataille into reading the image, it opens communication, and it intervenes into the Christian and Hegelian reductions of death. It also complicates Bataille's nostalgia to experience death intimately. As we have seen we can never touch on this fusion with the Other *directly* but only through a mediated contact, a reading. The fantasy of an unmediated direct contact is a result of this necessity of mediation rather than an existing possibility. The image is one of the most powerful ways in which this impossible desire can be sustained because it gives us such a powerful illusion of clarity. Bataille ruptures this illusion by revealing the impossible part of the image that destroys clarity. This involves 'nostalgia' because it opens a different relation to death through the past, a critical relation that passes through the impossible. In doing so Bataille can refuse the idea that we could ever successfully quarantine death and also the idea that we could experience death as such. Instead, the image is an eruption into which we are dragged and where we fall from our position of security, but only through reading.

This falling back is comical as well as critical, for example, in Bataille's critical dictionary entry 'Factory Chimney' (EA, 50–1). The photograph accompanying Bataille's commentary is of a demolished chimney falling like a penis in a state of detumescence. Bataille writes that for him, as a child, the 'most fear-inspiring architectural form was by no means the church, however monstrous, but rather large factory chimneys, true channels of communication between the ominously dull, threatening sky and the muddy, stinking earth surrounding the textile and dye factories' (EA, 51). The collapse of the demolished chimney releases Bataille's childhood anger against it. He attacks the factory chimney because it imposes production on to the world (see Chapter 5 for further discussion of Bataille's displacement of production). In the collapse of the chimney there is 'the revelation of a state of violence for which one bears some responsibility' (EA, 51). We are responsible for the violent imposition of production on the world, but as the chimney falls it reveals the *weakness* of this imposition.

As Bataille remarks in 'The Big Toe' (1929), although we may have 'a head raised to the heavens' (EA, 87, VE, 20) we have a 'foot in the mud' (EA, 87; VE, 20). The fall back is comic and drags us down in the mud. This emphasis on the fall and collapse also explains the violence of his pre-war break with the surrealists. For Bataille the surrealists had a 'completely unhappy desire to turn to upper spiritual regions' (VE, 41). Breton defined surrealism as the search for a superior reality: 'I believe the future resolution of these two states – outwardly so contradictory – which are dream and reality, into a sort of absolute reality, a *surreality*, so to speak.'[9] There is an irreducible difference between Bataille's dragging of the image down into 'base matter' (VE, 45–52) and the surrealists turning upwards away from its sources in the 'basest forms of agitation' (VE, 42). Bataille is certainly close to the surrealists but his assimilation to the surrealists is impossible because of this difference. In fact, through Bataille a different heterogeneous reading of surrealism may be possible.

Bataille argued that the surrealists suffered from an 'Icarian complex' (VE, 37), the impossible desire to soar above base matter like the legendary flight of Icarus. Just like Icarus they would also fall back to earth; their 'higher reality' remained tied to the base agitation from which it emerged. Breton was right in saying that Bataille was an 'excrement philosopher' but Bataille could counter: 'Did Breton think he could exist without excreting?' The most sublime of surrealist flights could never exclude the bowel movements that pulled them down into the dirt. When Bataille wrote about Dali's painting 'The Lugubrious Game', he said, 'My only desire here – even if by pushing this bestial hilarity to its furthest point I must nauseate Dali – is to squeal like a pig before his canvases' (VE, 28). Bataille's squealing like a pig is a Dadaist act of provocation which drags the surrealist image into the dirt. By dragging down the image Bataille also rejected the surrealist model of the avant-garde. The surrealists remained an ultimately hierarchical group with Breton as the 'pope of surrealism' dispensing benedictions and excommunications. By dragging the artist down from his (and it is usually a man) role as visionary or seer of 'higher reality' Bataille also offers a new model of community as egalitarian, non-hierarchical and exposed to base irruptive forces (as we will see in Chapter 2).

Bataille exposed surrealism to the effects that it could not control in its own images. As we have seen he has followed this process of exposure from the most conventional images to the most extreme images. Now, I want to follow the next stage in Bataille's subversion of the image. He is not only concerned with subverting *specific* images but also with a *general* subversion of vision itself. The impossible is widened in its effects to include an impossible moment in every act of vision. To accomplish this further subversion of the image Bataille turns to the eye as the organ of vision which allows us to comprehend any image. This disruption of vision can be found in the entry for 'The Eye' in the critical dictionary (EA, 43–8; VE, 17–19, translations differ slightly). Bataille turns the gaze of the eye back on itself through the photograph of Joan Crawford with bulging eyes which accompanies the article. In an exchange of looks we do not receive the reassuring image of the film star as object of desire or identification but a stare that forces our gaze away in shock, a violent contact between the eye and the eye of another.

This violent displacement of my eye disrupts its usual function: 'It seems impossible, in fact, to describe the eye without employing the word seductive, nothing it seems, being more attractive in the bodies of animals and men. But this extreme seductiveness is probably at the very edge of horror' (EA, 45). The seductive eye is the eye that meets another eye in the look of love, in the amorous look from one eye to another. This joining together of eyes in a look seeks out the truth of love in the eye of another, and in that eye is found either the confirmation of a returned love or the ruin of the refusal of love. The eye is the organ of truth through the clarity of the look, and we discover the truth or falsity of love in the look. What the photograph of Joan Crawford does is to turn our look away in shock and it threatens this model of truth with the eruption of an affect at 'the very edge of horror'.

Bataille connects the seductive look of the eye, where the eye is open to the eye of another, to an extreme vulnerability. Everyday language talks of a piercing gaze and the amorous gaze exists on the edge of a piercing of the eye by the look of another, a metaphoric piercing that slides toward a literal piercing. Bataille recalls Buñuel and Dali's film *Un Chien Andalou* where a razor is drawn across the eye of a young woman (EA, 45; VE, 17) in a scene that remains powerfully shocking. For Bataille the eye can be related to the edge of the razor (EA, 45; VE, 17), because the eye has a violence that threatens the moment of vision. The supposed clarity of the look of love is always a look of violence that is threatened by that violence. Again and again we can find examples in horror films and fiction which exploit our horror of the punctured eyeball, where our organ of clarity and sight is reduced to a flow of matter streaming from a sightless eye socket.

How do we explain our extreme horror of damage to the eye? For Freud this fear of damage to the eyes is the result of castration anxiety, with the eyes and the testicles being equivalent at the level of the unconscious.[10] Bataille is interested in the psychoanalytic exploration of the process of equivalence and substitution around the eye but not in having this chain opened or closed by castration. Roland Barthes has analysed the *Story of the Eye* as a playing along a chain of signifiers by passing 'from *image* to *image*' (in SE, 119). In the novel the eye moves around, between eye (*œil*) and egg (*œuf*) by means of the white roundness they share, and then from the egg to the sun, through the egg's yellow yolk, and on to the testicles (in SE, 121). As Barthes points out, Bataille differs from psycho-analysis because he does not ground this chain of images in castration (in SE, 122). In Bataille we find images circulating in a movement which *blurs* objects, causes them to run into each (both collide and become merged); by this blurring the original image is displaced, it is uprooted into the flows of base matter that flow through the eye.

If in Freud the horror of the punctured eye find its origin in the punctured testicle then Bataille is more literal. The horror of the punctured eye lies in the horror of damage to the eye, because the eye can shift rapidly from being caught in the gaze of love to being plucked out and eaten as a cannibal delicacy (EA, 45; VE, 17). The eye is both powerful and vulnerable at the same time. The very power we attribute to vision, its purity and clarity and its capacity for detecting truth make it vulnerable. This clarity is not only disturbed when we gaze at the unclear or impure, or when the amorous gaze is shaken, but it haunts every act of vision. Vision is possible only through the original violence of the aperture that opens the eye, an aperture which is also a blind spot. The blind spot is the part of the eye which makes vision possible and the part which makes that vision incomplete or impossible. It is the aperture which opens the possibility of vision but which vision cannot comprehend visually, and it is this part of vision which is not part of the vision with which the subversive image communicates.

In his later work *Inner Experience* (1943) Bataille used the blind spot metaphorically to indicate the moment of non-knowledge: 'knowledge which loses itself in it' (IE, 111). He uses it to indicate a point of non-knowledge that ruins Hegel's attempts to assimilate the unknown to the known through action. Hegel cannot resist the effects of 'desire, poetry, laughter' (IE, 111) which take him back from the known to the unknown. As Bataille would put it in 'Hegel, Death, and Sacrifice' (1955): 'On the one hand there is poetry, the destruction that has surged up and diluted itself, a *blood-spattered* head; on the other hand there is action, work, struggle' (BR, 280). Hegel's philosophy is a philosophy of action, work and struggle, but its blind spot is everything that cannot be assimilated to work. Action, work and struggle are disrupted by Bataille's invocation of desire, poetry and laughter. For Bataille the blind spot is useful as a metaphor but 'the blind spot of the eye is inconsequential' (IE, 110). He misses the opportunity to relate the philosophical model of knowledge to vision, and so to relate his own subversion of the image with his subversion of philosophy. We can re-establish this connection by recognising that the blind spot is not only a blind spot of knowledge but also of vision, tracing the same movement of collapse in both domains. Neither philosophy nor the model of vision by which it is supported and which it supports can accept the impossibility of the blind spot.

This impossibility is not a negative fault of vision or of philosophy which could potentially be corrected, because the blind spot is also what makes vision possible. The blind spot is the dilatory opening that makes vision possible and also disrupts vision, making it impossible. In the same way non-knowledge is the opening that makes knowledge possible but knowledge also finds itself 'completely absorbed in it' (IE, 111). The impossible is not a secondary effect that comes to ruin a clear image but the very condition of that image itself. This means that it is impossible to get rid of the impossible, to clear up vision or philosophy. Moreover, the original opening of the blind spot explains why the eye exists on the edge of horror. The event of horror of the pierced eyeball refers back to the fact that the eyeball is originally pierced, and it is this opening that makes vision possible. Our horror is a horror at the violence that makes vision possible and that the eye carries within it, and this does not lessen our horror of violence toward the eye but increases it. It is through recognition of the fragility of the eye as it is, the fact that the eye is already damaged, violated and incomplete, that resistance to violence on the eye can originate.

Bataille subverts not only the image but also the eye itself, thereby subverting the possibility of any theory of the image. How could Bataille's work have been read if it did not conform to theoretical demands? The tasks it sets and its practices of reading the image have disappeared into a silence that has rarely been broken, either in Bataille's lifetime or since his death. Where Bataille's writing on the image has had a subterranean influence is in its appropriation by his friend Lacan. Lacan's theory of the image has had far more influence than Bataille's precisely because it is a *theory*. Lacan has dominated Anglo-American film and art theory while Bataille has been left as the hidden burrowing 'old mole' (VE, 32–44) of the metaphor he borrows from Marx. While Lacan's theory has enjoyed institutional success, in contrast Bataille's resistance to theoretical limitations has left him without an institutional or theoretical home. Lacan has a theoretical master, Freud, and also plays the role of master-thinker himself. Bataille's thought is more modest and subversive; it is a thought without mastery.

The question of the appropriation of Bataille by Lacan is a difficult one because they shared a milieu, common formative intellectual experiences, and Lacan even lived with Bataille's first wife Sylvia after she had separated from Bataille. Furthermore, Lacan's 'success' in Anglo-American academia would need its own history of the misreading and misappropriations he has been subject to, which has yet to be written. It is possible that this history would require consideration of Lacan's own concept of misrecognition (*Méconnaissance*) to explain his misreading. One of the strange elements of that 'misrecognition' is that Lacanian discussions of the image have tended to use the text 'The mirror stage as formative of the function of the I', which analyses the origin of the human subject through the 'mirroring' effect of the mother's look.[11] This ignores Lacan's more detailed discussion of vision and the image in *The Four Fundamental Concepts of Psycho-Analysis*, originally given as seminar XI (1964). Recently this account has begun to receive more attention from Lacanians,[12] and it is striking how close it is to Bataille's subversion of the image.

In the seminar Lacan distinguishes between the eye, which is broadly speaking 'normal' vision, and the gaze which is the object that resists the eye. This distinction becomes necessary because of the effect of desire on vision:

> If one does not stress the dialectic of desire one does not understand why the gaze of others should disorganise the field of perception. It is because the subject in question is not that of reflexive consciousness, but that of desire. One thinks it is a question of the geometrical eye-point, whereas it is a question of a quite different eye – that which flies in the foreground of *The Ambassadors*.[13]

Lacan is referring to Holbein's painting *The Ambassadors*, on which there is a strangely distorted smear which, if viewed from the correct angle, appears as a skull. This is an example of the technique of anamorphosis but Lacan is using it to stress the distortion of vision as an act of desire. The role of desire in vision brings an interruption to vision that eludes reflection, '*the stain*'[14] that marks the image. In *The Ambassadors* this stain is the skull that interrupts the image and almost 'sticks out' from the frame.

On the one hand, Lacan understands the impossible element in vision as an effect of castration. Lacan's impossible is the Real, a concept he introduces to explain the remainder of language and castration that resists symbolisation. The Real only appears in *jouissance*, leftover bits of enjoyment that remain at the edges of the body in what Freud called the 'erotogenic zones':[15] the mouth, the anus and the sexual organs. Lacan adds to these a language that emerges from the lips and a vision from the eye, all that emerges at the edges of the body, from the structure of the rim.[16] On the other hand, Bataille's impossible has no conceptual identity and is not organised by castration or contained by psychoanalysis. Bataille's thought of the impossible cannot be assimilated to a Lacanian reading of the Real, as Fred Botting has attempted to do.[17] Although Lacan argues that the gaze has a 'pulsatile, dazzling and spread out function',[18] it can never be detached from castration or from the body without making it something other than a psychoanalytic concept.

Unlike Lacan, Bataille did not set out to re-found psychoanalysis but instead he used Freud to articulate a reinvigorated and mobile materialism of 'raw phenomena' (VE, 16). The irruptive effects found by psychoanalysis in the unconscious could not be absorbed and organised by psychoanalysis as a discipline or institution. The schisms and splits that afflict the psychoanalytic institution could be understood as the signs of eruptions that psychoanalysis cannot control within itself. In his essay 'The Psychological Structure of Fascism' (1933–34) Bataille explored heterogeneity as a series of resistant phenomena that could not be dominated by the homogeneous organisations of knowledge and society. He drew on the Freudian unconscious but argued that 'it would seem that the *unconscious* must be considered as one of the aspects of the *heterogeneous*' (VE, 141; BR, 126). Psychoanalysis has exploited this heterogeneity to found itself as an institution and practice but it can never completely assimilate it.

Lacan's own violent breaks with the psychoanalytic institution, including those that he founded himself,[19] testify to the heterogeneity of his thought. The difficulty is that Lacan was still attached to psychoanalysis and still attached to castration. This difference might explain why Lacan's theory of the image has had so much more success than Bataille. Despite the difficulty of Lacan's language, far more difficult than Bataille's, it is rooted in a conceptual apparatus familiar to many readers. Bataille argues that this conceptual apparatus cannot dominate heterogeneity. Lacan's discussion was also organised around the philosophical references to Sartre and Merleau-Ponty at a seminar that attracted many important intellectual figures and which will go on to achieve wide translation and distribution. In comparison, Bataille's work on the image was hardly read at the time and is now largely forgotten, although it has recently been rediscovered in the art criticism of Yves-Alain Bois and Rosalind Krauss. In *Formless: A User's Guide* (1997) they use Bataille to argue their position 'that the *formless* has its own legacy to fulfil, its own destiny – which is partly that of liberating our thinking from the semantic, the servitude to thematics, to which abject art seems so thoroughly indentured'.[20] They use Bataille's entry for the critical dictionary, 'Formless' (December 1929) (EA, 51–2; VE, 31) where Bataille takes the 'formless' (*informe*) as 'not only an adjective having a given meaning, but a term that serves to bring things down in the world ...' (VE, 31). Bois and Krauss use the formless to bring down art practice and criticism from its dependence on meaning, especially an abject art that would seem to revel in the obscene and perverse.

Abject art is the art of the remainder, especially the bodily remainder: blood, urine, tears, sperm, excrement, etc. It has often justified itself by reference to Bataille, and especially to Bataille's early writings which we have been discussing. In doing so it assimilates Bataille as part of the new counterculture art market, where modernist eruptions are now re-staged as postmodern commodities for art buyers. The assimilation of this 'counterculture' abject art is evident in the way that it has become absorbed within the marketing of a new 'national culture', despite its ostensibly shocking content. Perhaps the best-known work of contemporary British art is Damien Hirst's 'The Physical Impossibility of Death in the Mind of Someone Living' (1991), which 'is a fourteen foot tiger shark preserved in a tank of formaldehyde, a colourless liquid that resembles water so that, at first glance, the creature appears alive'.[21] It is a work which plays with ideas of the abject: death, impossibility, violence, but at the same time it has become an accepted part of the cultural promotion of Britain. It presents itself as having a *meaning*, '"I want to access people's fears," says Hirst. "I like the idea of a thing to describe a feeling."'[22]

Of course, Hirst is not to blame for the wider cultural exploitation of his work, but this is an example of how abject surrenders to meaning. Bois and Krauss oppose this, and they particularly oppose the theory of abjection proposed by Julia Kristeva in *Powers of Horror*.[23] Kristeva is indebted to Bataille but she provides a more Lacanian reading of abjection where the abject is 'These body fluids, this defilement, this shit …'[24] Although Bataille is concerned with the limits of the body this bodily reading of abjection *ties* it to the body and its waste products. Kristeva has provided a matrix for art criticism and practice which allows it to understand the abject as bodily waste, to confine and limit it within a meaning – no matter how 'shocking' that meaning is. In contrast Bataille's formless is 'like a spider or spit' (VE, 31), mobile or fluid enough to evade classification and meaning, including as the abject. For Bois and Krauss it allows them to intervene against an abject art that has claimed Bataille as its patron saint and to offer an art criticism that is not oriented towards meaning.

The problem that their innovative reading confronts is that if they use formless as a word for what resists form aren't they then giving it a form? Although they recognise that this is a problem they fail to deal with it, they realise that they 'run the risk of transforming the formless into a figure, of stabilising it. That risk is perhaps unavoidable …'[25] The 'perhaps' in this sentence is the sign that the problem of form is more intractable than Bois and Krauss are willing to admit. They have inserted it to hold open the possibility that they can avoid giving the formless form; it is a 'risk' which is only '*perhaps* unavoidable'. However, it is unavoidable, and this strikes at the heart of their use of Bataille. The formless (*informe*) is always in-form, and when they fail to recognise this they turn the formless into a new concept of art criticism and Bataille into the theorist of the formless.

The interpretations of the image by Lacan and Bois and Krauss's interpretation are actually symmetrical and not simply opposed. Lacan anchors the impossible in the event of castration, the leftover

pieces of the body and a 'scientific' concept of the Real giving the
formless *form*. In doing so he becomes part of the philosophical
project of 'giving a frock coat to what is' (VE, 31), as Bataille put
it. On the other hand, the emphasis of Bois and Krauss on the
formless as *completely* formless supplies it paradoxically with a form.
In different ways these are gestures of reduction, either locating
the formless within a frame or locating it as what is always outside
the frame. The impossibility of the subversive image is that is does
not fit into the frame but spills over it. The formless is always *in-
form*, but it is never absorbed by that form. The subversive image
as the impossible is a reading that reads this mobile disruption of
the frame of the image. Matter for Bataille is always '*active*' (VE,
47; BR, 162), never settling within a frame or an image but always
emerging from an image, a word or things.

It is this instability, this flowing out from the image, that makes
Bataille's images reach out to the reader and at the same time resist
appropriation by either the reader or by Bataille's own writings.
These images are never formless *as such*, which would be to
produce and form the formless, but they are formless in the
derangement of form, like the spider or spit. It is the difficulty of
appropriating the subversive image, of producing a theory of the
image from Bataille that is no doubt why he is so little read on the
image. The necessity of reading Bataille lies in this impossibility of
the formation of a theory of the image as well, but it is a difficult
demand to meet. This impossibility is never just a reflection of
Bataille's state of mind; it must be read in images and in the act
of vision. While he wrote about images that communicated
intensely to him, lightning-flash images that obsessed and moved
him, what provoked him was that they produced an affect leading
to *communication*. It was never a matter of personal contemplation
but a sharing with others through the image, the image as the
opening of the Other.

The image was a 'lived experience' of an impossible communication like the disturbing image recounted in 'The Jesuve' (1930):
'It would have been impossible for me to speak explicitly of it, to
express totally what I felt so violently in early 1927 (and it still
happens that I bitterly feel it) in any other way than by speaking
of the nudity of an ape's anal projection, which on a day in July of
the same year, in the Zoological Gardens of London, overwhelmed
me to the point of throwing me into a kind of ecstatic brutishness'
(VE, 78). This image was the 'origin' of what Bataille himself
described as the 'excremental fantasy' (VE, 78) of the pineal eye.
The pineal eye is the fantasy of a blinding moment of vision at
once 'pure' and 'impure'. The pineal gland, which is located in
the skull, is supposed by Bataille to be an atrophied eye which
could explode through 'the summit of the skull like a horrible

erupting volcano' (VE, 74). In the moment of vision this eye at the top of the head is connected both to the sun and the anus in a shattering movement of *jouissance*. Developed before the work of *Documents* the pineal eye fantasy prefigures its concerns with an impossible image and still tries to preserve an ecstatic vision, a 'vision of excess'. Bataille's subversion of the image will never let go of a 'certain disorder' (VE, 78) of lived experience and his desire for 'the celestial eye' (VE, 90) which we lack, but he will displace the fantasy of an unmediated vision of excess.

Bataille had suggested that before 1930, 'I was not insane but I made too much of the necessity of leaving, in one way or another, the limits of our human experience ...' (VE, 74). *Documents* is a continuation of this self-criticism through an active intervention into images. Those who celebrate Georges Bataille often remain within this early fantasy of unmediated access to the impossible. Instead, by his self-criticism, Bataille is not retreating from a delirious thought of the image but deepening the delirium of thought. The pineal eye opens on to his later writings on vision and works with them as a subversion of vision. By giving up on the possibility of the purely impure vision of the pineal eye, Bataille can begin to read the image as subversive in its negotiation with the impossible. No longer confined to certain experiences, this delirium of images spreads its effects across all images and all acts of vision, deranging vision from its position of truth.

As technologies of the image have proliferated and increasingly dominated our lives since Bataille's death, his thought is even more necessary. Guy Debord has argued that we are now living in a 'society of the spectacle'.[26] He worked within Marxist categories of the image as an alienation of human beings from their true desires. Bataille does not regard the image as necessarily inauthentic but as having the potential to form or deform real desires. The subversive image is an image which cannot be controlled by the society of the spectacle and which haunts every spectacle and every act of vision as an intractable *impossible* moment of instability. It is also an image which resists theorisation. Of course, it can be read theoretically, for example, the formless is always in-form, and it is possible to imagine institutes devoted to Georges Bataille (although not without a comic effect). Any reading of the formless has to negotiate with the way the formless takes on form, including an institutional form, or else it would leave the subversive image as a fantasy floating free of any relation to lived experience and so destroy the subversive image.

Bataille's response to theoretical readings is a laughter that destabilises any theory built on his work. Whether Bataille intended the images he chose to be read seriously or not, and whether they are objects for a potential theory, these alternatives are dissolved in sovereign laughter (as we will see in Chapter 3). Sartre wrote about Bataille that 'He tells us that he laughs, he does not make us laugh.'[27] He is right in that Bataille can be very serious about laughter and is not a writer of jokes, but Sartre's own philosophical ambitions mean that he cannot experience the laughter in Bataille. He does not recognise that Bataille can be funny, whether intentionally or otherwise. The subversion of the image is always a practice of joy in the face of death, a sovereign laughter. Sovereign laughter is unsettling and when we read Bataille we experience what Derrida describes when reading Heidegger: 'It's always horribly dangerous and wildly funny, certainly grave and a bit comical.'[28] Bataille also provokes these contradictory tendencies of fear and laughter, a gravity and the lightness of the comical.

This is the difficulty of reading Bataille seriously, as Borch-Jacobsen notes (CR, 165). To read Bataille seriously is also funny, he makes us laugh, not least because we can always slip up on 'all the banana peel-like passages of Bataille' (Borch-Jacobsen, CR, 164). Bataille is constantly tripping us up, tripping up our desire to understand him, to make sense of him and to extract a theory from him. He constantly invites, and even demands, a theoretical reading, while never settling within the limits of the theoretical. In fact it is only in being tripped up by Bataille, falling down, collapsing like the factory chimney, that we could be reading him. Then the pain of the fall and the laughter of others at our tripping over the text stop our reading. When we fall we are liberated from theoretical constraints and the demands of seriousness, but only through the demand to trace the movement of that fall. The lack of seriousness is not an excuse for poor thinking, but rather an opening to the demands Bataille makes on us.

The subversion of the image communicates to us through the blind spot that we can see reflected in the image in an instant of impossibility that stops us short. Stopping short before Bataille is to stop as we are arrested by his formless images. Here we are forced to think and at the same time denied the order that thinking usually demands. When we stop short we also experience laughter: 'Laughing at the universe liberated my life. I escape its weight by laughing. I refuse any intellectual translations of this laughter, since my slavery would commence from that point on' (G, 16). Laughter is freedom and liberation from the imperatives of the universe, the demands of the world as it is. To translate this laughter into intellectual constructions would lead to the enslavement of thought, but that laughter cracks through intellectual constructions. It also leads us to 'crack up', to go mad or to laugh hysterically. We start laughing as the image rises up before us, the image of the ape's anal protuberance, for example. Laughter is the result of the subversion of the image, a laughter that is impossible.

CHAPTER 2

Inner Experience

Bataille's laughter is a laughter he shared with Nietzsche and it is a laughter that shakes us with spasms of joy that bring tears: 'The ambiguity of this human life is really that of mad laughter and of sobbing tears' (TE, 20). Bataille begins laughing when he reads Nietzsche; he begins to laugh at politicians, at philosophers and at all those readers of Nietzsche who presume to have understood him. Reading Nietzsche is a shared experience for Bataille, 'I am the only one who thinks of himself not as a commentator of Nietzsche but as being the same as he' (AS2/3, 367). His identification with Nietzsche alters Bataille's own writing, which will mutate through this shared laughter. This is laughter that laughs at the worst: the rise of fascism and Nazism in the 1930s, their attempts to appropriate Nietzsche as the philosopher of fascism and National Socialism, and then war, defeat and the occupation of France. Reading Nietzsche during this period is not a source of hope for Bataille but an experience of a free and mobile thought, an irruptive laughter that shatters the self. Bataille would inscribe this experience as an inner experience, not an *internal* experience but an inner experience of such intensity that it would make identity flow away. Deleuze noted that 'For Nietzsche, laughter always refers to an exterior movement of irony and humour, a movement of intensities, of intensive qualities ...'[1] Laughter is an inner experience that carries us away, a convulsive movement that can lead to '*the course of a convulsion that involves the whole movement of beings*' (I, 10).

This convulsion sweeps over Bataille and carries him and Nietzsche away from philosophy. While Nietzsche is often defined as a philosopher he is also in an unstable position, neither academically nor institutionally secure within philosophy. His political appropriation by fascism has only increased the idea that Nietzsche held of his thought as dangerous. This thought involved a violent war on the idols of philosophy, religion, politics and science, and Nietzsche intended to 'philosophise with a hammer',[2] to turn philosophy into a 'war machine'.[3] This violent and disordered thought was also an attack on the language of philosophy, an attack that involved the invention of a different style of writing. Nietzsche's style has been described as a literary style, and his writings found their earliest reception among literary writers. The problem of Nietzsche's style is more complex, as Bataille reveals, because his style is heterogeneous to both literature *and* philosophy. The classification of Nietzsche as a philosopher is an attempt to avoid these problems of style and violence, to reduce Nietzsche's attack on philosophy to an episode in the history of philosophy.

Bataille tries to reproduce Nietzsche's violent heterogeneity in his own writings. Together with Nietzsche he evolves his own style of writing, at once indebted and singular. This proximity to Nietzsche also places Bataille in an aberrant position in relation to philosophy. Bataille reads philosophy but it cannot be certain that he ever really became a philosopher, and he certainly never held an institutional or public position as a philosopher. Recently Michael Richardson has argued that Bataille 'is to be considered primarily as a philosopher'[4] but this identity can never successfully impose itself on Bataille. In fact philosophy, and the philosopher, is dissolved in laughter by Bataille, in the laughter he shares with Nietzsche. For Bataille, 'The interest of philosophy resides in the fact that, in opposition to science or common sense, it must positively envisage the waste products of intellectual appropriation' (BR, 152; VE, 96). The philosopher picks through the waste of what remains *after* appropriation, and this is what attracts Bataille to philosophy. However, although philosophy does not leave anything out, including waste products, the problem is that it appropriates that waste as part of a new intellectual system. In Hegel this appropriation of waste products by philosophy was taken the furthest – even death would not escape his system – but for Bataille the result was a farce.

In creating new systems out of intellectual waste products philosophy is always threatened with becoming lost in the heterogeneity it uncovers. The difference with Nietzsche is that he is a philosopher who finds philosophy *impossible* as an act of appropriation and who collapses philosophy into the dispersal of heterogeneity. I want to examine how Bataille sifts through the heterogeneity of philosophy and how he uses this heterogeneity to break up the secure identities of philosophy and of the philosopher. After Nietzsche, Bataille will no longer understand philosophy as a discourse of truth but as a discourse that is unstable and impure. Through the impurity and heterogeneity of Nietzsche's writings Bataille opposes the Nazi and fascist appropriation of Nietzsche to a politics of purity. His essay 'Nietzsche and the Fascists' (January 1937) is written at a time of political urgency, but Bataille does not provide either a purely political or a purely philosophical reading. Both these forms of reading would be re-appropriations of Nietzsche whereas Bataille finds in Nietzsche a thought of freedom that resists *all* appropriations:

'Whether it be anti-Semitism, fascism – or socialism – there is only *use*. Nietzsche addressed *free spirits*, incapable of letting themselves be used' (VE, 184).

There were many different fascist and Nazi appropriations of Nietzsche, but the most intellectually dishonest was the attempt to portray Nietzsche as an anti-Semite. Bataille bitterly rejected these 'anti-Semitic falsifications' (VE, 182) whereby Nietzsche's ironic and critical quotations of anti-Semitic views were presented as his own views. Here 'reading' was a matter of violent de-contextualisation, the excision of surrounding material and the virtual invention of Nietzsche as an anti-Semite. His hatred of anti-Semitism and German nationalism is, quite literally, edited out of his works, particularly by his sister Elisabeth Förster-Nietzsche. Bataille renames her Elisabeth *Judas*-Förster for this act of betrayal (VE, 182), depriving her of any relation to Nietzsche's name in a virulent rewriting opposed to her anti-Semitic violence.

Bataille not only engaged with these obvious falsifications but with the whole range of Nazi and fascist appropriations of Nietzsche. He respected the heterogeneity of these readings as they failed to respect that of Nietzsche's writings. The more pernicious appropriations of Nietzsche were those that were, relatively, 'better' readings of Nietzsche, including what Bataille called 'perhaps the most serious' (VE, 190) Nazi analysis of Nietzsche by Alfred Bäumler. This was a more sophisticated reading of Nietzsche, which imposed meaning on his texts which was not only philosophical but also political. Bäumler 'draws out of the labyrinth of Nietzschean contradictions the doctrine of a people united by a common will to power' (VE, 190). Nietzsche's thought of the will to power is reduced to a philosophical concept and a political principle that is consonant with Nazism. Nazism imposes the image of a unified people upon the dispersion of the labyrinth of Nietzsche's thought, giving that labyrinth a sense. His writings both resist and invite this imposition of unity and sense.

In *Ecce Homo* (1888) Nietzsche had predicted that 'Only after me will there be a *grand politics* on earth.'[5] He made this prediction because his violent attack on philosophy was not limited to philosophy but also to the dominance of philosophical thought over the entirety of our culture. To destroy the basis of Plato's metaphysics was at the same time to declare war on that 'Platonism for "the people"' – Christianity.[6] Not only did Nietzsche's thought challenge Christianity, it also challenged supposedly 'radical' political movements like socialism, which he regarded simply as secularised versions of Christianity. After Nietzsche a grand politics becomes possible because of his destruction of the metaphysics which had dominated and limited both philosophy and the politics derived from that metaphysics. The problem, as Bataille points out, is that since Nietzsche's death fascism 'is the only political movement that has consciously and systematically used Nietzschean criticism' (VE, 185). The fate of Nietzsche's 'grand politics' is to have been transformed into a fascist and Nazi politics. How was it possible that Nietzsche could have been appropriated as a Nazi?

Bataille is not content with rejecting the fascist and Nazi appropriations of Nietzsche's grand politics, he also wants to account for the way that this appropriation is possible. In particular, he is interested in the tendency of fascist and Nazi readings of Nietzsche to isolate the concept of the will to power. What Nietzsche had brought into play in the wake of Platonic and Christian metaphysics was now being put to political *use*: 'The teaching of Nietzsche "mobilises" the will and the aggressive instincts; it was inevitable that existing activities would try and draw into their movement these now mobile and still *unemployed* wills and instincts' (VE, 185). Fascism and Nazism draw on the freedom and energies that Nietzsche releases but only to produce a world where 'life is tied down and stabilised in an endless servitude' (VE, 186). The freedom of Nietzsche's thought is what makes it open to fascist and Nazi appropriation, but at the same time fascism and Nazism fear this freedom.

This is why they are forced to read Nietzsche, not only to appropriate the energies that he releases but also to counter the threat that Nietzsche poses to them. What better way to appropriate a dangerous thought than by transforming it into an ideology that supports the ruling regime? Bataille recognised that 'Official fascism has been able to use invigorating Nietzschean maxims, displaying them on walls; its brutal simplifications must nevertheless be sheltered from the too-free, too-complex, and too-rending Nietzschean world' (VE, 187). Bataille is exposing fascism to what it has tried to shelter from in Nietzsche, a freedom that would expose its own hollow and stunted ideology. His interpretation of Nietzsche is no longer only an academic or philosophical interpretation because in the Nazi and fascist appropriation of Nietzsche freedom is at stake: 'Enslavement tends to spread throughout human existence, and it is the destiny of this free existence that is at stake' (VE, 194). The possibility that the freedom of Nietzsche's writings could be enslaved threatens *all* free existence with enslavement, as Jean-Michel Besnier explains: 'It was necessary to make amends to Nietzsche because the co-optation of his thought for propaganda purposes is, in and of itself, the symbolic destruction of all free existence.'[7]

To expose fascism to the freedom of Nietzsche's writings means exposing them to the heterogeneity in those writings *that they could not read.* To put the will to political use fascism mutilated

Nietzsche's writings by repressing the elements 'that Nietzsche incontestably experienced as an end not as a means' (VE, 191). What fascist and Nazi readings consistently failed to read in Nietzsche, even the most 'sophisticated' readings like that of Bäumler, was the 'pathos-laden experience' (VE, 191) of the eternal recurrence. It was the eternal recurrence that threatened the politico-philosophical concept of the will to power with an experience that was 'too-free, too-complex, too-rending', an experience which literally tore apart the will as a unitary entity. In doing so it also tore apart the dream of 'a unitary community' (VE, 198) based on that will and the exclusion and extermination of heterogeneity.

The eternal recurrence is probably, as Bataille recognised, the 'most inaccessible' (VE, 191) experience in Nietzsche, and its place in his writings is still fiercely contested. For Nietzsche the lesson of the eternal recurrence is 'that all things recur eternally and we ourselves with them, and that we have already existed an infinite number of times before and all things with us'.[8] For Bataille the importance of the eternal recurrence, and of its exclusion by Nazi and fascist readers, is that 'Return unmotivates the moment and frees life of ends – thus first of all destroys it' (ON, xxxiii). The effect of the eternal recurrence is to destroy the idea of an 'end' or a 'use', because the effect of return is to destroy the movement towards an end. Once again (as we saw in Chapter 1) Bataille turns to the return as a movement of falling back and collapse into existence. In this way the return disables the 'ends' of life but this involves a return to life and to existence as such. Rather than life depending for its value or worth on some end or ends, whether chosen or imposed, life has a free existence of its own. Bataille resists the categorisation of life into life that is worthwhile or valuable and life that is worthless, the premise of a politics of life that can lead to the worst.

The eternal recurrence is a very difficult part of Nietzsche's thought: because of its instability, it resists being given a sense. For Bataille's friend, Pierre Klossowski, the eternal recurrence is 'the parody of a doctrine'[9] rather than a philosophical concept. The result of this parodic doctrine is that 'the thought of the Eternal Return in its various extensions already abolishes the identity of the self along with the traditional concept of will'.[10] The eternal recurrence abolishes the concept of will to power as the identity of a community and its leader, on which fascism rests. It is this threat of freedom that fascism must resist by appropriating and enslaving Nietzsche. In response Bataille brings fascism back into contact with the heterogeneity of Nietzsche's writings. Already in his essay 'The Solar Anus' (1927) Bataille had described the world as 'purely parodic' (VE, 5) and shown how the effect of this parody is to destroy all foundations in a 'circular movement' (VE, 5). Now Bataille would again use the parodic circulation of the eternal recurrence to depose the fascist attempts to found a community through Nietzsche.

Bataille's objective in 'Nietzsche and the Fascists' is to explain how it is possible that Nietzsche has been enslaved by fascism and then to shatter that enslavement by the eruption of the eternal recurrence. Fascism and Nazism are taken to their limits and forced to confront the limit of their appropriations of free existence: 'NIETZSCHE'S DOCTRINE CANNOT BE ENSLAVED' (VE, 184). This act has political effects but it is not a counter-politics. Bataille resists any attempt to put Nietzsche to use, whether by the political right or left. Neither does he produce a philosophical reading of Nietzsche that would establish his truth against the Nazi and fascist appropriations. Instead he traces the freedom and heterogeneity of Nietzsche's writings which are irreducible to politics and philosophy. This is an act of resistance, opposing the unitary community of fascism founded on the will to power with what Nancy calls 'the sharing of community'.[11]

Bataille's freeing of Nietzsche from fascist appropriations has had little influence on the discussions of his own relation to fascism. I want to suggest that as a critical reading it is a model which can be used to resist the appropriations which claim that Bataille is fascist. At their most extreme they include the claim by Boris Souvarine, who was a friend of Bataille in the 1930s, that not only was Bataille a fascist but that if he had had the courage of his convictions he would have been a collaborator as well.[12] This claim is complicated by the personal disputes between Bataille and Souvarine while Bataille was still alive. Moreover, Souvarine presents his claims without evidence and Maurice Blanchot has fiercely contested them. In fact, it is relatively easy to reject the charge that Bataille was a fascist (as made by Souvarine): he belonged to the extreme left, he did not collaborate and he always held on to the hope of a libertarian communism. His thought of contagion, communication and heterogeneity could not have been more resistant to a fascist thematics of purity and purification.

At the more 'reasonable' end of the spectrum we find the argument of Nehamas that 'a more serious objection to Bataille concerns his intellectual relationship to fascism. Despite his personal opposition to it, there are elements in his thought that bring him philosophically close to it.'[14] Rather than the outright claim that Bataille was fascist, for which there is little evidence, the claim that Bataille is somehow 'close' to fascism is more difficult to dispute and so more damaging. It has been most persistently argued from within the Frankfurt School, beginning with the comments made by Walter Benjamin that the work of the

College of Sociology displayed a 'prefascist aestheticism' (in CS, 389). Of course, Benjamin's accusation has to be understood in the context of his attendance at the College of Sociology and his participation in debates over its direction. The possibility for further debate would be cut short with the war, and although Bataille preserved Benjamin's notes at the Bibliothèque Nationale in 1940, Benjamin would never return. He committed suicide after being turned back from the border with Spain while fleeing the Nazis. This fleeting moment of contact between Bataille's poststructuralism *avant la lettre* and the Frankfurt School was lost, destroyed by Nazism.

Instead, the dismissive tone of the responses to Bataille (and other French thinkers) by the Frankfurt School has been set by Habermas. Habermas claims that Bataille lacks a principle to distinguish his work from the fascism he is trying to combat (repeating the accusations against Counter-Attack discussed in the Introduction): 'Bataille has difficulty making plausible the distinction that remains so important for him – the distinction between the socialist revolution and the fascist takeover of power, which is merely assimilated to the former' (in CR, 175). He has influenced other Anglo-American commentators on Bataille who work in the tradition of the Frankfurt School Critical Theory, like Richard Wolin and Martin Jay.[14] Perhaps it is, at least in part, the *proximity* of Bataille to the work of the Frankfurt School which has provoked this violent rejection. It may also be that Bataille's thought of heterogeneity is *too* heterogeneous for the political aims of Habermas and the representatives of the contemporary Frankfurt School. Bataille is a threatening foreign body to their thought of communicative reason.

However, the charge of complicity with fascism levelled against Bataille by Nehamas, Habermas and others is a difficult one to answer for several reasons. Firstly, fascism drew on a wide range of intellectual and political currents so it is not difficult to establish some connection between virtually any thinker and an idea or thinker linked to fascism, especially in the 1930s. Benjamin used the work of the jurist Carl Schmitt, who would work with the Nazis as a legal theorist, but that is not enough to 'contaminate' Benjamin with fascism.[15] This leads to the second difficulty in countering these arguments: to attempt to remove a thinker or thought from fascism involves a gesture of purification and resistance to contamination by fascism that follows a fascist 'logic'. As with Nietzsche, Bataille is a heterogeneous thinker who is at once available for appropriation and who also resists that appropriation. This is why it is so important to understand Bataille's reading of Nietzsche, because it is also Bataille's own resistance to appropriation.

Unlike Nietzsche, Bataille has never, to my knowledge, been appropriated by an explicitly Nazi or fascist group either during or after his lifetime. But we cannot purify Bataille of complicity with fascism without destroying the heterogeneity of his writings, so they demand careful consideration. This is not a neutral activity but an activity with political effects, even if those political effects will not be easily reducible to a political programme (whether of left or right). One place to begin with in terms of Bataille's 'relation' to fascism is community because, as Jean-Luc Nancy remarks, Bataille had 'a fascination with fascism inasmuch as it seemed to indicate the direction, if not the reality, of an intense community, devoted to excess'.[16] As Bataille not only tried to think an 'intense community' but also to put it into practice he came into contact with fascism. A great deal is at stake in community, not only for Bataille but also for us still today.

The 'fascination with fascism' among Bataille and his friends is evident in the favourable comments by Roger Callois on the book by Alphonse de Châteaubriant, *La Gerbe des Forces (Nouvelle Allemagne)*, about the formation of 'orders of knights' in Nazi Germany. Callois wrote that 'In a few forsaken fortresses in the heart of the Black Forest and in the Baltics, there is a great endeavour to prepare an elite of young, implacable, and pure leaders for the supreme role of dictators first of the nation then of the world destined for conquest by this nation ... But the undertaking fired more than one imagination' (CS, 381). For Callois these experiments in brotherhood that would lead to the formation of the SS were close to the models which the College of Sociology looked to for a renewal of a 'decaying' society: 'Male societies in primitive populations, initiatory communities, priestly brotherhoods, heretical or orgiastic cults, monastic or military orders, terrorist organisations, secret political associations of the Far East or of troubled periods in the European world' (CS, 381). Bataille was more cynical and more politically astute than Callois about these German brotherhoods, remarking in 'Nietzsche and the Fascists' that 'The account of the role played in Hitler's Germany by a free, anti-Christian enthusiasm, which gives itself a Nietzschean appearance, thus ends on a note of shame' (VE, 190).

Despite this disagreement Callois and Bataille did share a fascination with the conspiratorial secret society, which can be seen in the joint existence of the College of Sociology and *Acéphale*. They were both influenced by French sociology, and in particular the work of Durkheim's nephew, Marcel Mauss. On 28 November 1936 Élie Halévy gave a lecture on 'the age of tyrannies' in which he argued that there was continuity between fascism and Bolshevism. Marcel Mauss wrote a letter to Halévy agreeing with this thesis and also arguing that an air of conspiracy and secrecy characterised these movements:

> I can recognise easily here a phenomenon such as frequently occurred in Greece, which Aristotle described extremely well, but which is especially characteristic of archaic societies, and perhaps everywhere in the world. It is the 'society of men,' with its brotherhoods that are simultaneously public and secret; within such a society the youth society is the one that acts. (CS, 348)

As Denis Hollier points out, 'It is likely that everything that seemed negative to Mauss in this technology of the conspiracy, made it, on the contrary, fascinating to his young disciple, Callois' (CS, 349). To a lesser extent Bataille was also fascinated by the brotherhood of conspirators, but he did not mistake this secret group for the conspirators of political revolution, whether left or right.

Bataille's idea of community, and of the secret society, was borne out of his exhaustion with the political groups he had been involved with in the early 1930s, all of which ended up competing for the possession of power. He looked to 'Brotherhoods, Orders, Secret Societies, Churches' (CS, 145–56), as Callois titled one of his lectures at the College of Sociology, but not as groups which would seize power. Instead Bataille was interested in a transformation of politics, as an epigraph from Kierkegaard that he used for his essay, 'The Sacred Conspiracy', reveals: '*What looks like politics, and imagines itself to be political, will one day unmask itself as a religious movement*' (VE, 178). The unmistakable influence of Nietzsche can be found in Bataille's experiment in community *Acéphale*. This was a secret society that was headless and its symbol was André Masson's drawing of a headless man (VE, 180; on the cover of BR). This headless 'deity' was not a symbol of the condensation of power but a symbol of loss: 'He has lost himself, loses me with him ...' (VE, 181).

In 'Propositions' (January 1937) Bataille developed his model of a society of *freedom*: 'The only society full of life and force, the only free society, *is the bi- or poly- cephalic* society that gives the fundamental antagonisms of life a constant explosive outlet, but one limited to the richest forms' (VE, 199). For Bataille this involved criticising democracy for its failure to form communities which are in contact with our 'fundamental mode of existence' (VE, 198) and criticising fascism for promoting a 'closed and stifling social existence' (VE, 198). Like the 'position' of *Acéphale*, which is the loss of any political position, Bataille risks a great deal by failing to be assigned to one of these competing political ideologies. With the benefit of hindsight Susan Rubin Suleiman has argued that 'it did not occur to Bataille or to other revolutionaries on the revolutionary Left to start defending the bourgeois democracies against the threat of fascism'.[17] What she does not recognise is that for Bataille and many other intellectuals (and workers) democracy could not be defended against fascism because democracy (at least in its bourgeois or capitalist forms) *led* to fascism. Whether this analysis is correct, and I believe it has some merit, it should force us to recognise that Bataille is trying, as Nietzsche did, to elaborate a thought of freedom that does not conform to any political ideology.

Of course, the model of a bi- or polycephalic society, a society with two or many 'heads' or loci of power, is fundamental to democracy. We should not mistake Bataille's exhaustion with democracy for a rejection of any or all democratic forms. Rather it was an attempt to reinvigorate those forms with the energies which fascism was exploiting. The 'stability' of a democracy that levelled differences and neutralised class conflicts only led to a monocephalic democracy which was vulnerable to the violently monocephalic form of fascism. Rather than gather power elsewhere (the working class, etc.) to contest this monocephalic society Bataille looked to the secret society of *Acéphale* to release the energies condensed in the 'head' in a flowing away that would no longer be controlled by the secret society. He dreamed of a society with a plural dispersion of power, a society of fluid exchanges and willing loss rather than a society of accumulation.

Bataille is one of the very few thinkers and activists of the 1930s who did not respond to what Besnier calls the 'generalised disorientation'[18] of the period by seeking a position of security within a political ideology. Through his reading of Nietzsche he responded to this disorientation as a possibility of freedom to be preserved against fascism, Stalinism and bourgeois democracy. It is this difficulty in locating Bataille, in stabilising him, which makes him vulnerable to charges of complicity with fascism. To read Bataille with Nietzsche is to read Bataille *against* fascism by reading this instability as a resistance to fascism. Bataille had firstly detached Nietzsche from his political appropriations, while still tracing the political effects in his work. Now I want to follow Bataille in his turn towards inner experience, as he reflects on the collapse of his dreams of community in the face of war. Where Bataille had previously experimented with a praxis of community now, as Blanchot retrospectively recognises, 'What was in play demanded to be taken up again in the paradoxical form of a book.'[19]

That book was *Inner Experience* (1943) which was the first part of a trilogy, along with *Guilty* (1944) and *On Nietzsche* (1945), which collectively made up what Bataille called *La Somme athéologique*. This was the first of Bataille's organisations of his works within an overarching framework and it parodied the *Summa theologica* of St Thomas Aquinas, the great Catholic theologian. The 'a' added to theology is an attempt to deprive theology of its 'head' (God) and to lead to a new post-Nietzschean 'headless theology'. To write this headless 'atheology' *Inner Experience* was impossible without Nietzsche because it was written after the death of God. It was also an opening of a path to *On Nietzsche* through an experience of meditation and mysticism which is separated from God or divine contemplation: 'being concerned essentially to communicate an inner experience – religious experience, as I see it – outside the pale of specific religions' (IE, 34). This is an inner experience because it has *no* reference outside of itself, either to knowledge or to God.

The experience which Bataille is trying to describe in this series of fragmentary written meditations is also an experience that touches on the impossible. For Bataille the impossible is not an object of experience to be meditated on, like a contemplation of the void, but the possibility of experience as well: 'In this sense, the inner experience is throughout an experience of the *impossible* (the impossible being both that which we experience and that which constitutes the experience)' (IE, 26). The impossibility of this experience and the difficulty of describing it without reducing it to a form of knowledge relate it to Nietzsche's transcriptions of his experiences (in particular of the eternal recurrence). However, the difficulty of transcribing this experience is that it becomes vulnerable to misreading, and in particular to being assimilated within knowledge. Inner experience confronts this problem when it is mistaken for what Susan Rubin Suleiman calls an 'inward turn', [20] all the more so when she goes on to argue that this inward turn is Bataille's inner emigration, a collapse of thought in the face of the occupation. For Suleiman Bataille is practising an ineffectual 'spiritual' resistance against the Nazi occupation which lies ambiguously between resistance and collaboration.[21]

She misconstrues inner experience in two ways: firstly by mistaking it for an experience that is internal to the self, rather than an experience that has no reference to anything outside of itself. Bataille regards inner experience as 'an experience laid bare, free of ties, even of an origin, of any confession whatever' (IE, 3). Suleiman misreads this experience of freedom as a retreat into the self to recover a threatened virility, a transformation of the political conflicts of the 1930s into an internal psychodrama. Nothing, as we will see, could be a worse misunderstanding of inner experience, especially as this experience can always be traced to an experience of community. This first misreading dictates her second misreading of Bataille's inner experience as an internal emigration which is an act of moral cowardice in the face of the demands of the Résistance. Suleiman argues that Bataille's thematics of virility risk sexism but now she argues Bataille should have been man enough to join the Résistance. She fails to recognise that Bataille was ill with tuberculosis and isolated in the country, as well as the stakes involved in joining the Résistance. It is far easier to judge the past than it is to recognise the difficulty of making judgements about situations that we only confront from our own position of relative safety.

Inner Experience can be understood as an act of resistance but one difficult to recognise and it is, as Suleiman thinks, ambiguous. However, it is not ambiguous because it fails to support military resistance to the occupation as Suleiman implies. Rather it is *more* ambiguous than that because it resists the worst through an experience of freedom, which is irreducible to political or military resistance. Bataille's thought may be seen as a luxury but his thought was always a thought of luxury, excess, exuberance, freedom, because for Bataille '*everything is rich*' (AS1, 13). Inner experience is an experience which is rich beyond comprehension, beyond being reduced to being an internal experience and beyond being captured within the concept of experience. Religious experience and meditation can lead us to inner experience but they remain limited by their external aims, with religious experience aiming to be at one with God and meditation aiming to bring calm and lessen pain (IE, 7). Inner experience has no such aim and this is why it passes outside of the 'inner experience' as we usually understand it; as Bataille said, 'I call experience a voyage to the end of the possible of man' (IE, 7).

Inner experience transports us to 'an elusive beyond' (IE, 11) where all forms of external authority, like religion or philosophy, are 'dissolved' (IE, 9). This experience is by no means passive and it cannot be correlated with a lack of action as such, except that it challenges any action that is oriented to external aims. Inner experience is another form of 'action': 'Experience, its authority, its method, do not distinguish themselves from the contestation' (IE, 12). Most of all experience is a contestation of 'the law of language' (IE, 14), the law that remains untouched in calls to political action, which depend on and exploit the power of language. Bataille contests the power of the law of language by what operates within language as its heterogeneous moment, 'the silent, elusive, ungraspable part' (IE, 14) of ourselves. The law of language supposes its dominance over all of language but within language words like silence, which name an experience outside of language, fracture the dominance of language. Inner experience reaches out to these heterogeneous impossible moments that are already 'within' us.

For Roland Barthes 'Language – the performance of a language system – is neither reactionary nor progressive; it is quite simply fascist; for fascism does not prevent speech, it compels speech.'[22]

I am not certain that Bataille would agree completely with this
statement, although he does respect the need for a right of silence
or non-response. Bataille recognises the violent imposition of
language on experience but also that language is fissured by the
violence of experience. Language might be 'fascist' but like fascism
it never achieves the power and completion that it desires. There
is not an opposition between language and experience but a more
disorienting experience of contamination. This also suggests that
we should not oppose eruption to limitation but see them as
mutually implicated processes that cannot be dialectically resolved.
Language is a powerful test case because it imposes itself on us as
a law that we cannot refuse without resorting to language, but for
Bataille this imposition is always incomplete and fractured by inner
experience.

As inner experience disrupts the regulating force of language it
also disrupts the subject of that experience (and this disruption of
the subject by Bataille will be considered further in Chapter 3).
Inner experience is an experience which cannot be gathered, either
within language or within the individual: '*In experience, there is no
longer a limited existence*' (IE, 27). It is always an experience of an
outside, of a community that cannot be held within secure limits.
To make the passage from inner experience as a contestation of
language and the subject to inner experience as community we
must pass through *communication*. Contestation shatters the limits
of the subject and language, and in doing so opens an experience
of communication. As it does so inner experience also contests
being contained within experience. Instead it is an exercise,
modelled on spiritual exercises but irreducible to them, that acts
on experience *itself*.

It can be summarised, before we move on to communication, in
the 'principles' necessary to revise the 'spiritual' life after Nietzsche
that Blanchot suggested to Bataille (IE, 102):

(1) The absence of salvation.
(2) Inner experience is its own authority.
(3) Inner experience is contestation.

Inner experience offers neither salvation nor hope of salvation; it
is a finite experience that promises nothing outside itself. This is
why it is an experience with its own authority, without any external
support or telos. The result of this experience which explores itself
to its limits is a contestation of those limits, of the language, of the
subject, and wherever limits try to limit this experience.

Contestation is the opening of an act of communication, and
this communication opens *against* communication as it is usually
thought. It is no longer an act whereby a message is transmitted
from one subject to another, but what communication (in

Bataille's sense) does is to 'pull the rug out from under' (IE, 54) the subject. Communication does not pull the rug out from under an intact individual or subject, but rather from under the idea of this intact subjectivity. Bataille describes an effect of 'laceration', but laceration is not the violation of an intact subject; instead it is the possibility of communication and the subject. Communication is a flow 'like a streaming of electricity' (IE, 94) and in inner experience there is the possibility of an experience of 'the profound lack of all true stability' (IE, 95) that this flow of communication produces. As we saw in the Introduction it is his instability which allows the idea of an isolated individual subject to emerge but: 'I am and you are, in the vast flow of things, only a stopping-point favouring a resurgence' (IE, 95). The concept of the subject is a dam on the flow of communication which will always be overflowed by communication.

Bataille's notion of communication destroys the concept of inner experience as internal because 'your life is not limited to that ungraspable inner streaming; it streams to the outside as well and opens itself incessantly to what flows out or surges forth towards it' (IE, 94). This streaming outside of communication can involve language but is not limited to language; the flow also breaks apart language through the heterogeneity of words like silence. Communication names an opening that does not belong to the subject or language but which opens them. It is an opening from communication to community, but community also cannot arrest this flow. This uncontrollable flowing to the outside makes *Inner Experience* Bataille's profoundest meditation on the existence of community. It inscribes the existence of community as an opening to the outside even in the most isolated state of 'inner' experience. In fact Bataille experiences it through the isolation of extreme inner experiences: meditations on war, death, pain and violent laceration. In these distressing moments of 'intense communication' (IE, 94) we become aware of the depth of *all* communication. Neither inner experience nor communication is limited to our usual concepts, but Bataille is using them to name something different, something which does not only happen in exceptional events. Already this force of rupture inhabits the most conventional communication or mundane experience.

The effect of communication for Bataille is that the individual 'as subject, [it] is thrown outside of itself, beyond itself; it ruins itself in an undefined throng of possible existences' (IE, 61). In the ruin of the subject in 'an undefined throng of possible existences' inner experience becomes an experience of community. This is a community that Bataille finds through his community with Nietzsche: '*It is from a feeling of community binding me to Nietzsche that the desire to communicate arises in me, not from an isolated originality*' (IE, 26–7). Bataille's communication originates from his feeling of community with Nietzsche, and not as the act of an isolated individual but from being cast into the throng of undefined possibilities that Nietzsche makes possible. Nietzsche runs through *Inner Experience* as a resistance to intellectual appropriation, through a community that is not a unitary community but a community of waste or loss (IE, 134). It will lead Bataille to Nietzsche 'himself', in his study *On Nietzsche* (1945).

Bataille's community with Nietzsche is at the limit of community, unlike the fascist or Nazi appropriations of Nietzsche which use him to found a new community. Instead of putting Nietzsche to use Bataille finds in Nietzsche the unfounding of closed concepts of community through the opening of freedom essential to community. The result is an unconventional reading of Nietzsche that opposes readings that force him into political or philosophical conventions, as Hollier describes:

> But in actual fact this book is no more a book than it is '*on* Nietzsche'. It hardly corresponds to what one expects from the title, to the demands of this form. This inadequacy, one both formal and theoretical as far as the rules of knowledge are concerned, does not, however, constitute an imperfection that Bataille (because he lacked sufficient university training or perhaps was driven by some pathological identification) could not have corrected. On the contrary: down to the most incongruous elements (like the presence in this book on Nietzsche of the most autobiographical of journals occupying three quarters of the volume), it corresponds to the strategy Bataille worked out for a relationship with Nietzsche.[23]

The 'incongruous' elements of this book, such as the autobiographical journals, at once prevent Bataille from imposing himself before Nietzsche and place Bataille in intimate contact with Nietzsche. Bataille comes into contact with Nietzsche in a communication without reserve that puts everything at risk: 'So that it was only *with my life* that I wrote the Nietzsche book that I had planned ...' (ON, xxv).

Political readers of Nietzsche (whether of left or right) are bad readers who depend on 'giving him a cursory reading to exploit him' (ON, xiii). Bataille tries to minimise this exploitation and appropriation of Nietzsche through a communication that exposes us to the freedom of Nietzsche's thought. This is a risky gesture but Bataille also embraces chance, including the chance of misunderstanding Nietzsche or being misunderstood. Bataille is not telling us *how* to read Nietzsche, he is offering an experience of freedom through a community with Nietzsche. He substitutes the instability of inner experience for certainties of the war (for example, as a conflict between 'good' and 'evil'): 'My accomplishment, its sum total, is to have taken risks and to have my sentences fall like the victims of war now lying in the fields' (ON, 7). Bataille's comparison is provocative but it also attests to what is at stake in any experience of chance: the chance of the fatal fall.

We have been drawn by impossible laughter into inner experience and then through inner experience to community. Bataille's 'logic' is a logic of broken threads, unstable reworkings of familiar concepts into something strange. At each point in the chain we have to remember that Bataille is using the old names (inner, experience, communication, community) but subjecting them to eruptions that shatter their security. He is taking up Nietzsche's assault on language as a weapon against the reduction of irruptive forces by supposedly 'stable' concepts. Bataille also draws us into this violent rewriting, observing that 'The communication of two individuals occurs when they lose themselves in sweet, shared slime ...' (ON, 98). In this image Bataille captures something of the claustrophobic and intense experience of reading his work. It is an experience which can break down in perplexity, laughter or boredom in the face of the demands of this 'intense communication'. However, by rewriting our fundamental concepts Bataille forces us into a process which undoes the stability of our thought.

He does not offer us a distanced 'safe' Nietzsche, but offers us a community with Nietzsche which places us in the greatest danger. Bataille's generosity is to make Nietzsche a gift to us outside of the appropriations that marked, and still mark, our understanding of Nietzsche. After Bataille Nietzsche's 'Grand politics' are no longer a Nazi or fascist politics but instead new chances for political thought. Bataille's luck is to have found some of his best readers after his death, readers who can open some of these chances for a thought of 'Grand politics'. He still catches readers today 'in sweet, shared slime' as he failed to catch them during his lifetime. Jean-Luc Nancy is one of these readers, and he has brought out the depth of Bataille's thought of community and the way that his thought responds to the exigency of community. In *The Inoperative Community* (*La communauté désœuvrée*),[24] Nancy has proposed community as a demand that demands to be thought through Bataille.

Nancy has also elicited a response from Bataille's old friend, Maurice Blanchot, and the exchange between them helps to raise the question of community in its most demanding form. Community is not treated by them only as a matter of intellectual debate but as a *practical* question, a question of how we live and how we die. Bataille is an essential figure in the thinking of community, which is never restricted to a theory opposed to praxis, because as Nancy remarks, 'No doubt Bataille has gone furthest into the crucial experience of the modern destiny of community.'[25] Community has been regularly invoked in contemporary politics, and a rhetoric of community has developed: of the decline of community, of the need to renew community, of community standards, and of the rights of communities for self-expression. This rhetoric of community has given rise to strategies for revital-ising communities and to the political theory of 'communitarianism'.[26] The tendency in this politics of community is to suppose that we already know what community is and that all that needs to be applied are certain measures to save or restore it. Bataille's thought of community is a practical interrogation of what is at stake in community, a rethinking of community itself.

Therefore, it is perhaps not surprising that neither his work nor that of Nancy is referenced by these contemporary debates, because they would call into question any politics of community which supposes a knowledge of community. It also suggests that the war and the subsequent Cold War did not settle the political debates initiated during the 1930s. Rather than the war violently resolving the political debates between proponents of fascism, democracy and communism, it violently put an end to those debates. The 1930s are not in fact over, in the sense that what was at stake, not least in relation to the question of community, is still to be thought. The continuing turning towards political thinkers of the 1930s, or thinkers who called the political into question, like Carl Schmitt, Martin Heidegger and Georges Bataille, are all indications that we are still living in the long 1930s. Nancy reopens these debates, where community is both a signifier and practice that was powerfully contested, by refusing to read Bataille as something belonging to the past.

Instead Nancy finds in Bataille an opening of the thought of community. Not only is it the opening of community but it is also a thinking of community as open, in contrast to contemporary readings of community as relatively closed and static forms. In this way Nancy is maintaining Bataille's resistance to the unitary conception of community which underpins fascism and, dis-turbingly enough, which continues to dominate the thought of community (even in some of the most 'democratic' or 'progressive' thinking of community). Nancy uses Bataille against models of community for which community is closed, where community is thought of as fusion or communion. This is what he calls a 'immanentism' because it thinks of community as immanent, present to itself, and so as closed to the outside.[27] To think community as immanent has two effects: firstly, it blocks a thinking of the opening that makes communities possible; and secondly, it tries to bring about a purely immanent community and this is an impossibility which leads to the destruction of community: 'Immanence, communal fusion, contains no other logic than that of the suicide of the community that is governed by it.'[28] The Nazi 'community' lived out this logic in the suicide of the *Führer* and the destruction of Germany, but it is implicit in any immanent model of community.

In Bataille can be found a thought of community as open: 'Bataille is without doubt the one who experienced first, or most acutely, the modern experience of community as neither a work to be produced, nor a lost communion, but rather as space itself, and the spacing of the experience of the outside, of the outside-of-self.'[29] Bataille does not reduce community to a work to be produced, and he resisted the idea of the 'labour of the negative' which is at work in Hegel, Marx and Kojève. Community is not reduced either to a nostalgia for communion, although we have seen how that desire persists in Bataille. In some sense the impossibility of communion animates Bataille's critical thinking of community, while still remaining in it as a dream. Bataille's resistance to communion is not only a resistance against fascism but also against contemporary revivals of community, because these revivals suppose that community can be produced rather than being an impossible possibility of an 'undefined throng of possible existences' (IE, 61). The lack of a thought of community as open is evident in how these 'revivals' of community are all too often accompanied by a resistance to 'immigrants' which, it is claimed, would 'destroy' or 'contaminate' community. Bataille absolutely resists this thought through his rethinking of community.

But he also too faces difficulty in conceiving of an open community, and Nancy is a careful enough reader to note the problems of some of Bataille's formulations of community as communication. Although communication is an act of opening, Bataille's description of 'a place of communication, of fusion of the subject and the object' (IE, 9) can reduce the communication of community. As Nancy notes, 'The "place of communication" can in the last analysis still be determined as presence-to-self: for example, as the presence-to-self of communication itself, something that would find an echo in certain ideologies of communication.'[30] Bataille is in danger of taking communication as a moment of fusion where community is produced as present, whereas his own reading of communication is of communication as the interruption and opening of community. This is the impossibility of community as what makes community possible and as that which makes it impossible to achieve communion. Bataille reached this thought of community through his impossible community with Nietzsche.

Nancy responds to the demand to read Bataille critically, to analyse his writings rather than trying to assimilate them. Blanchot also responds to this demand, taking up his debates with Bataille at the prompting of Nancy's work. What he finds echoed in Nancy's writing is 'the communist exigency'[31] which can be found in Bataille. This is a 'communism' that is thought through the being-in-common of community, a 'sovereign' (see Chapter 3) communism that resists reduction to the ideology of communism as a support for state power or the power of the party. As Bataille remarked, 'Today, sovereignty is no longer alive except in the perspectives of communism' (AS2/3, 261). Bataille's is a convulsive communism that is a convulsion of community. What Blanchot finds exemplary about Nancy's reading of Bataille is its recognition of the irreducibly political dimension of Bataille and of the political stakes of community. This politics of communism as community also involves Nietzsche, because Bataille plays Nietzsche off *against* communism. In particular, Nietzsche offers a freedom which can challenge the communist reduction of people to objects of *use* (AS2/3, 368).

Nietzsche retains this force because he has still not been read: 'His [Nietzsche's] mobile thought, concrete thought, tied to historical conditions, completely vanished with him' (AS2/3, 367). Bataille resists this disappearance by finding in Nietzsche a thought of freedom, of community, which is still at stake, and not least for communism, which has too often tended to destroy community. Blanchot takes up this reading again as an experience which disrupts the limited individual (including the Nietzschean *Übermensch*) and the limited community: 'Experience could not take place for the single being because its characteristic is to break up the particularity of a particular person and to expose the latter to someone else; to be therefore essentially for the other.'[32] He confirms our reading of inner experience as an opening to the outside, to community, rather than as an *internal* experience. The problem with Blanchot's reading, and to a lesser extent with Nancy's, is that it understands community on the basis of what Blanchot calls 'the heart of fraternity'.[33] This involves reading the freedom of community through a thematics of *brother*hood, a reading which is at once faithful to Bataille and faithful to a reduction of community which haunts all Western political thought.

For Blanchot, Bataille's 'entire work expresses friendship ...' (CR, 51), both the friendship that he felt for Bataille and a friendship which offers an open community. Derrida is critical of a thinking of friendship and community which rests on the figure of the brother: 'There is still perhaps some brotherhood in Bataille, Blanchot and Nancy, and I wonder, in the innermost recess of my admiring friendship, if it does not deserve a little loosening up, and if it should still guide the thinking of community, be it a community without community, or a brotherhood without brotherhood.'[34] Thinking friendship and community through the figure of the brother results in an exclusionary masculine model which has dominated Western philosophy and politics:

> the *double exclusion* that can be seen at work in all the great ethico-politico-philosophical discourses on friendship, namely, on the one hand, the exclusion of friendship between women, and, on the other, the exclusion of friendship between a man and a woman? This double exclusion of the feminine in the philosophical paradigm of friendship would thus confer on it the essential and essentially sublime figure of virile homosexuality. Within the familial schema, whose necessity I mentioned earlier, this exclusion privileges the figure of the brother, the name of the brother ...[35]

This exclusionary model of friendship and community, which ties Bataille to the tradition of Western philosophy and politics, is visible in his reliance on models of community that are dominated by men. Denis Hollier has speculated that Bataille's work at the time of the College of Sociology relies on a concept of virile unity that excludes women (CS, xvii) and Susan Rubin Suleiman has traced the persistence of this language of virility from the 1930s into *Inner Experience*.[36] As Derrida suggests this demands a loosening up of friendship and community with and against the readings of Bataille by Nancy and Blanchot. Bataille suggested that the reading of Nietzsche had not really begun and the same effect of disappearance belongs to Bataille's writings. To resist that disappearance is not to endorse all of Bataille's writings *uncritically* but to read them through the experience of freedom that dominates them. Bataille has to be taken further into community and friendship, and he can be taken further by the guiding thread of the impossible.

The impossible resists the incarnation of friendship and communion in the form of the brotherhood. It is not attached to the figure of the brother or to any incarnation in presence, and so it resists the making present of community in any form. Of course, the impossible is also the opening of the question of community in all its forms, a question that it does not presume to resolve. To purify community of all its 'contamination' for whatever political agenda is an activity that leads to the destruction of community. A community without foreign bodies is a dead community, a community that lacks any communication with its outside. It is in the negotiation with the foreign body that community is at stake, and the punitive rejection of 'immigrants' is a sign of the paucity

of the thought of community at present. We are very far from the
sovereign generosity of Nietzsche who 'is on the side of *those who
give* ...' (AS2/3, 370).

The impossibility of community can also return us to our
opening question – the relationship between Bataille and
philosophy. Bataille's reading of Nietzsche has led us to the
impossible as the opening of community, and it can also lead us
to impossibility as the opening of philosophy. In their different
ways both Nietzsche and Bataille are impossible for philosophy;
they are foreign bodies who cannot be accepted within the body of
philosophy without provoking a violent sickness. Philosophy;
responds with agitated gestures of appropriation that assimilate
them to the history of philosophy or rejections that exclude them
from philosophy altogether. However, Bataille contaminates
philosophy with impossibility by considering its *necessity* for
philosophy: 'This condition of impossibility is not the excuse for
undeniable deficiencies; it limits all real philosophy' (TR, 11–12).
Impossibility is not an excuse for poor thinking where the
impossible is casually invoked to justify our own inadequacies, but
it forms a *real limit*.

The impossible is not only a limit that prevents philosophy from
achieving the universal knowledge that it desires, it is also the limit
that provokes that desire. Philosophy begins from the impossible:
'Philosophy responds from the start to an irresolvable exigency'
(TR, 12). So, impossibility can never be removed from philosophy
as an impediment that blocks the path of knowledge, but it is the
dispersal of the path into the labyrinth of thought. Therefore the
impossible functions for philosophy analogously to the way it
functions for community, as a 'real limit' which both sets up a
limit and which is a limit as an opening possibility. This is why
the refusal of philosophy to recognise impossibility is also a refusal
of philosophical thought to recognise community. Philosophy, so
often read as the work of many solitary (male) individuals, resists
the effect of community, the being-in-common that touches on
all philosophy.

To read philosophy as impossible does not mean the end or
destruction of philosophy but a different thinking of philosophy.
Bataille, following Nietzsche, moves towards this when he suggests
a different *image* of philosophy, an image that subverts the philosophical image of philosophy: 'A philosophy is never a house; it is
a construction site' (TR, 11). Philosophy thinks of itself as a
completed architectural form, and in an article in *Documents*
Bataille had noted that whenever we find a taste for architectural
construction 'we can infer a prevailing taste for human or divine
authority' (EA, 35). The image of the house is an image of
completion that imposes an authoritative completion on thought

but a thought of the impossible undermines this image and reveals that philosophy is really a construction site. For philosophy this incompletion is only ever a stage in a movement towards completion, even if that completion be infinitely deferred. For Bataille philosophy can only be thought as this incompletion, as a construction site rather than a house and without the taste for authority that the architectural construction imposes on thought.

Inner experience was a rejection of external authority, and so a rejection of the authority of philosophy and the authority of community. While it lacks authority this experience of the impossible does demand different images of thought, different practices of reading and writing. For Derrida the impossible always leaves us with a question: 'The *impossible* meditated by Bataille will always have this form: how, after having exhausted the discourse of philosophy, can one inscribe in the lexicon and syntax of a language, our language, which was also the language of philosophy, that which nevertheless exceeds the oppositions of concepts governed by this communal logic? Necessary and impossible, this excess had to fold discourse into strange shapes' (CR, 103–4). The impossible exceeds the logic of oppositions on which the architecture of philosophy rests, which for Derrida is a *communal* logic. The philosophical image of philosophy also supposes a community, a closed construction of community. To respond to the demand of the question of the impossible requires that this communal logic, the discourse of philosophy, be folded into strange shapes.

Bataille's folding of the discourse of philosophy comes from his feeling of community with Nietzsche. In his community with Nietzsche the communal logic of philosophy is shaken, philosophy can no longer be sustained as a community of seekers of knowledge (IE, 24) without provoking hilarity. By forcing philosophy back into the waste products, the heterogeneity, which it tries to put to use, Bataille is disrupting the tendency of philosophy to appropriate those waste products in new intellectual constructions. Philosophy is not only an exercise of thought but it also guarantees an image of community, a communal logic, which is closed. To reopen community is to reopen philosophy, politics and the stakes of thinking today. Philosophy and community always stumble over impossibility, over the impossibility which they thought they had excluded to begin their appropriation and accumulation of resources. Bataille, together with Nietzsche, makes that stumbling a fall beyond appropriation. At this moment community is no longer a closed experience, no longer the accumulation of power or knowledge but is opened by a sovereign generosity which is the opening to a sovereign experience.

CHAPTER 3

Sovereignty

In his 'Autobiographical note', possibly written in 1958, Bataille remarked that his 'aspiration is that of a sovereign existence, free of all limitations of interest' (B, 116). Sovereign existence is an experience of freedom. However, Bataille's writings on sovereignty discuss it in terms that appear to be *opposed* to freedom: violence, power, *jouissance*, hierarchy and criminality. Bataille scandalises our democratic good conscience when he claims that 'social difference is at the basis of sovereignty' (AS2/3, 300). How can sovereignty be an experience of freedom when it appears that it can only exist within what Roger Callois calls 'the hierarchy of beings'?[1] I want to answer this question by returning to the extreme tension at work in Bataille's writings on sovereignty. Not only does sovereignty express the tension between a free existence and the social hierarchy, it also expresses the tension between a disordered experience and an ordered concept. This second tension is heightened because after the war Bataille will become more concerned with giving his writings an ordered form. Sovereignty runs like a fault line through this work, tracing an impossibility that cannot settle within a stable system.

This impossibility finds its most extreme form when Bataille writes about the sovereignty of Gilles de Rais in *The Trial of Gilles de Rais* (1959). Here we are confronted with sovereignty in all its magisterial obscenity, in crimes that leave us gasping for breath and revolted. Gilles de Rais was a medieval Lord, companion in arms of Joan of Arc, and a mass murderer. His crimes were serial acts of sexual abuse, torture and murder against young children and he would become the model for the legend of 'Bluebeard'. Children would first be kidnapped and taken into one of Rais's many castles, then they would be led to a death chamber where Rais and selected 'friends' had already begun drinking heavily. Once there Rais would strangle the child while sexually stimulating himself, sometimes reviving the child to consciousness before finally killing by stabbing. After the killing Rais would dissect the child's body because 'what mattered to him was less the sexual enjoyment than to see death at work. He liked to watch. He had the body cut open, the throat cut, the members carved to pieces; he relished seeing the blood' (TG, 14).

How can Bataille find *anything* in this infliction of pain and
suffering that would be a 'release towards a freedom that is direct'
(BR, 117)? How can he write of 'the sovereign monstrosity of Rais'
(TG, 20) or contend that Gilles de Rais lived 'a life never
dominated by calculation' (TG, 14)? Bataille seems to affirm
violence against the weak and helpless, contradicting his earlier
claim that 'As a child, the notion of torture made life miserable
for me' (ON, 97). What makes this all the more distressing is that
Bataille identifies with the torturer rather than the tortured, unlike
his meditation on the pain of the Chinese torture victim. However,
Bataille is only prepared to defend Gilles de Rais on the basis of
the excess of his crimes. The effect of this excess is that it disrupts
the usual role of the torturer: 'As a general rule the torturer does
not use the language of the violence exerted by him in the name
of an established authority; he uses the language of the authority,
and that gives him what looks like an excuse, a lofty justification'
(E, 187). Unlike the torturer, who conceals the violence he is using
beneath a reasonable justification ('maintaining security', 'fighting
subversion', 'defending democracy', etc.), the excesses of Gilles
de Rais's crimes lead us to an inarticulate expression of violence
in the cries and sobbing of a speech at the very limits of language.

Gilles de Rais's violence is also violence *against* language, a
violence that does not resort to lofty justifications or rationalisations
but instead is expressed in the immediacy of a *jouissance* that
violates bodies and language. It is a traumatic experience, not only
at the time of his crimes but also in the trauma it inflicts on
language itself. That trauma reaches us through Pierre Klossowski's
translations of the trial documents (that Bataille is introducing), but
the legal proceedings cannot contain the irruptive force of these
crimes: 'Few human beings have left behind traces permitting
them, after five centuries, to speak thus! To cry thus!' (TG, 23).
In *Beyond Good and Evil* Nietzsche wrote that 'A criminal's lawyers
are seldom artists enough to turn the beautiful terribleness of the
deed to the advantage of him who did it.'[2] What is most scandalous
and painful about *The Trial of Gilles de Rais* is the skill with which
Bataille articulates the crimes of Rais in terms of sovereignty.
Bataille is not only meditating on violence but also affirming
violence in its most extreme and distressing forms. Perhaps here,
at the limit of our acceptance of Bataille, is where we must
negotiate most carefully between the rejection and appropriation
of Bataille.

To reject Bataille is also to reject the possibility of understanding the crimes of Gilles de Rais. The act of rejection reinforces the
violence of those crimes by violently cutting us off from any contact
with them. Rais is confined to the domain of the monstrous and
this creates a distance between his crimes and us – although never

a 'safe' distance. This distance is undermined because this confinement also increases the power of those crimes; they come to exist as inexplicable, inhuman activities. Bataille tries, as he put it in the 'Programme (Relative to *Acéphale*)' (4 April 1936), to 'Take upon oneself perversion and crime, not as exclusive values, but as integrated within the human totality' (BR, 121). To exclude crime and perversion from the human totality is an act of violence against that totality that does not destroy crime and perversion. However, if we take on perversion and crime as exclusive values then we celebrate them as such and thereby increase their violence. What Bataille demands is that we integrate crime and perversion within the human totality, that we refuse to leave them outside. This taking within is a disturbing gesture that ruins the distance from violence of rejection and the identification with violence of appropriation.

The appropriation of Bataille also finds its limit in the sovereign reading of Gilles de Rais. Nick Land's *The Thirst for Annihilation* is an extended act of appropriation through identification with Bataille. It is a painfully earnest, although often philosophically astute, exercise in extended pathos. However, even Land's celebration of textual violence has reservations about Gilles de Rais, for which he feels the need to apologise: 'I hope that it is not mere timidity on my part that leads to this reservation. It would be the shoddiest domestication to suggest that some theoretical comfort were possible here.'[3] Most of all Land fears being timid, but why shouldn't we be timid, considering the violence at work here? The appropriation of Bataille is caught off-guard by the scandal of Bataille and, as we saw with Sade, those who react by rejection are more aware of what is at stake. To reject Bataille is to reject violence, but this does not lessen the power of violence, it increases it; to appropriate Bataille means to accept violence but then only to celebrate it and thereby increase it. Sovereignty shatters the limits of these gestures, so the question of sovereignty is also a question of violence that is irreducible: 'Violence is as stubbornly there just as much as death' (E, 187).

Bataille is not alone in reflecting on violence, especially within 'Continental' thought. It is thinkers from this tradition who have confronted the question of violence most directly. For example, André Breton writes that 'The simplest Surrealist act consists of dashing down into the street, pistol in hand, and, firing blindly, as fast as you can pull the trigger, into the crowd. Anyone who, at least once in his life, has not dreamed of thus putting an end to the petty system of debasement and cretinization in effect has a well-defined place in that crowd, with his belly at barrel level.'[4] Another example would be the violence of Michel Foucault's dossier on an infamous nineteenth-century parricide *I, Pierre*

Rivière, having slaughtered my mother, my sister, and my brother ...,[5] which owes so much to Bataille's dossier on Gilles de Rais. Étienne Balibar has argued that the disturbing implication of violence is that we can 'imagine that *nothing* is to be thought, really, at least nothing decisive, *outside* violence, if thinking or writing does not become itself "violent", or *mimetic* of some act of violence?'[6] To really think violence is to be involved in a becoming violence, and how can we resist this becoming an apology for violence?

Reflections on violence – which is, incidentally, the title of a book by Georges Sorel,[7] have been a vital part of European, and particularly French, thought. Within Anglo-American thought violence has more often been the preoccupation of popular culture, particularly in the contemporary cult of the serial killer. This cult often involves a pseudo-intellectual analysis of violence where religious themes of evil and nineteenth-century social Darwinism are revived in new forms. It is by no means confined to so-called 'low' popular culture, and violent criminality is an object of voyeuristic fascination for a 'middle-brow' (or petit bourgeois) culture. While intellectuals are often condemned as apologists or supporters of violence, the role of this 'popular' culture of violence has been undiscussed, except in occasional outbreaks of moral panic or hypocrisy. All too often Bataille is assimilated to this popular culture of violence, not least to give his work a 'transgressive' image. Bataille's discussion of Gilles de Rais is not the first example of the cult of the serial killer but the first deconstruction of the celebration of violent criminality.

In particular Bataille is fascinated with the way in which violence breaks down the integrity of the body or of things, and in the way that violence breaks limits. This tendency of violence to be connected to opening, the relation of violence to violation, makes it essential to any thought of freedom. It also challenges the confinement of violence within 'safe' limits, because those limits are themselves acts of violence and those limits are open to violence. In this way Bataille reveals the excessive nature of any act of violence, because all violence involves violence to boundaries, membranes and integrity. Violence is at once excessive as it steps outside those bounds, and it also exists within even the most innocuous activities. Any act that crosses a limit as the word crosses our lips involves violence. Sovereignty is the interrogation of this general violence beginning from the most extreme in Gilles de Rais.

Gilles de Rais faces us with the violence, and freedom, of the broken limit. Bataille expresses a terrified awe before his acts of violence, which are so excessive that they question the limits of human existence. In the extraordinary violence of Gilles de Rais we can experience the vertigo of this shattering of boundaries, and this transgression leaves us with 'the sense, perhaps misleading, of a summit' (TG, 13). We touch upon the summit in these secret crimes carried out during the sleep of reason. Bataille tries to unfold the 'logic' at work in these crimes, which cannot be understood by reason. Rais is beyond reason but for Bataille this is where analysis must begin, at the limits of reason and logic. He does not pass judgement on Rais, although he points out that 'there is nothing seductive about cutting children's throats' (TG, 41). Instead, we must understand how these crimes come about as the effect of wider forces which condensed in Rais, but which he could not control: 'His crimes arose from the immense disorder that was unwinding him – unwinding him, and unhinging him' (TG, 14).

This 'immense disorder' is not an internal psychopathology but a social process, an *excessive* social process that cannot be grasped within the terms of an historical sociology. Bataille analyses the factors that make up this disorder: the violence of military life during the period, the tolerance for barbarity in warfare, and the family background of Gilles de Rais. The most important effect at work, the one that dislocates and deranges Rais from his time, is the transition from a feudal era of expenditure to the beginnings of an accumulative and rationalist order. It is because 'Gilles de Rais belongs primarily to his time' (TG, 25) that he cannot escape this immense disorder and instead he expresses the disorder of the collapsing feudal order in his crimes. He is exceptional but only as the extreme example of the feudal lord who 'lived in a contradictory chaos of calculation, violence, good humour, bloody disorder, mortal anguish, and the absence of anxiety ...' (TG, 25).

The public expenditures on ceremonies, which every lord had to provide, became festivals in which Rais liquidated his fortune with amazing rapidity. His extreme public expenditure had its hidden private counterpart in the violence of his expenditure of children's bodies, taking to the extreme the right of the feudal lord to dispose of the lives of his peasants. These expenditures are not 'rational' either by the standards of his time or of ours, and it is his lack of calculation that marks Rais as sovereign. It is also this lack of calculation that prevents him from understanding the historical changes he is living through: although he is 'capable of base cruelties, he is incapable of calculation' (TG, 27). He cannot understand that warfare, which had brought him power and which he had treated as a game, was the cause of the transition to a rational society. The new demands of mass warfare restricted the role of knights and demanded more and more complex logistics. As Bataille put it in *The Theory of Religion*, 'The military order put an end to the malaises that corresponded to an orgy of consumption' (TR, 65). It organised violence in a form which can be controlled and directed, and so it left the spontaneous, personal violence of Rais as an historical aberration.

Not only does this make Rais's life a historical tragedy but it is also the source of its fascination. Rais incarnates a dazzling expenditure to which we no longer have access. For Bataille the closest modern analogies are literary writers, and his study of Gilles de Rais is parallel to his studies of literary writers collected in *Literature and Evil*. The questions of sovereignty, communication, liberty and evil that reverberate through *Literature and Evil* find their echo in Bataille's introduction to *The Trial of Gilles de Rais*. Both works are concerned with the relation of childhood to adulthood, not only as a process of maturation but also as the violent transformation of the freedom and excess of the child into the constraint and calculation of the adult. The writer has the personal experience of remaining in touch with a childhood as the time of 'young savages' with an 'innocent sovereignty' (LE, 18). Gilles de Rais has the historical experience of living between a time of excess and a time of accumulation. He remains childish but a child 'in the manner of savages' (TG, 33).

To celebrate Rais is to celebrate the power invested in him by the society in which he lived: 'This world had sanctioned the cruel difference that left these throats defenceless' (TG, 47). Bataille ties the lightness of the freedom of sovereignty to a particular existence, and to its social power. He finds in Rais's excesses the 'question of living sovereignly' (TG, 34), but then sovereignty is reduced to one particular life. In this reduction the tension between sovereignty as freedom and as dependent on social hierarchy reaches its limit. As we will see in Bataille's more detailed and more 'academic' reflections on sovereignty, this reduction can be resisted. Sovereignty cannot be confined to an individual, and so it also contests the limits of Bataille's own authoritative account. Sovereignty is the contestation of authority, a reversal of our traditional concepts of sovereignty. From sovereignty we can begin a critique of the reduction of sovereignty and of Bataille's celebration of Rais as an example of sovereignty.

In the third volume of *The Accursed Share* entitled 'Sovereignty' Bataille writes that 'Sovereignty has many forms; it is only rarely condensed into a person and even then it is diffuse' (AS2/3, 221; BR, 318). Is Gilles de Rais one of these rare condensations of sovereignty? Can we find sovereignty in him, even if it is diffuse? Bataille tries constantly to produce sovereignty, to describe it, to analyse it and to give it an existence; but sovereignty does not play the role of a concept that dominates a certain domain. Instead sovereignty exists as an anti-concept or, to draw on Bataille's arguments about the 'headless' (atheology and *Acéphale*), it is an 'a-concept'. This would be a headless concept, one without authority and prone to a fundamental irregularity. The sign of the sovereign operation is that it actively displaces the mastery implicit in any concept, as Derrida remarks, 'sovereignty *does not govern itself*' (CR, 116). So, sovereignty is always dislodging itself from conceptual security at the same time that it is always resting within a concept.

By presenting sovereignty incarnated in an individual Bataille risks turning this limit-experience into a *limited* experience. So, with Gilles de Rais, Bataille is trying to explore a sovereign existence but the freedom of this sovereign existence becomes confined to one person and to his social and historical context. Sovereignty is in danger of being pathologised, criminalised or legalised, something that Bataille is trying to resist. At the same time the violence of sovereignty is confined to moments of extreme violence, whereas Bataille is suggesting that in any limit there is violence involved, violence which is also an opening to freedom. The tension of sovereignty emerges when Bataille describes it as diffuse, because this diffusion splits sovereignty: he condenses the diffusion of sovereignty into an individual – which is an ontological reading of 'being as *sovereignty*' (BR, 116) – but this diffusion resists being condensed into an individual or into being, as it exists at the limit of the concept of a subject.

Derrida notes that 'One could even abstract from Bataille's text an entire zone throughout which sovereignty remains inside a classical philosophy of the *subject* and, above all, inside the *voluntarism* which Heidegger has shown still to be confused, in Hegel and Nietzsche, with the essence of metaphysics' (CR, 119). This is the tendency of Bataille to make sovereignty the property of a subject or an act of a subject, like Gilles de Rais. Although this is an 'entire zone' of Bataille's text it does not saturate the entirety of his writings. I want to draw on resources in Bataille's text which allow us to resist the reactionary interpretation of sovereignty as the call for a new master, or a new *Führer*. They also resist the restriction of sovereignty to the figure of the violent criminal, the outlaw, or to the contemporary cult of the serial killer. Violence, as we have seen, certainly is an undeniable feature of sovereignty and the freedom that it promises. By removing sovereignty from its ontological interpretation we also reinterpret violence, and we can begin to understand the violence at work in the imposition of identity. This is all the more important because of the current dominance on the left of 'identity politics', where the violent imposition of identity is not considered because it is in the name of a politics of liberation.

To reflect on these questions requires that we return to Bataille's attempts to describe the summit and sovereignty, the two terms that he uses to suggest the power of Rais's crimes. Both the summit and sovereignty are very similar terms in Bataille's lexicon, and both have the features of irregularity and headlessness which make them difficult to describe. They exist at the very edge of meaning because they both have a meaning and they also exhaust that meaning in their own operation. Furthermore, they have a close relationship to violence and, like inner experience, contest language. The history of these terms in Bataille's writings makes them far more complex than they appear in his account of Gilles de Rais, and these complex histories complicate Bataille's account of Gilles de Rais. To trace these histories involves returning to philosophical questions from Bataille's readings of Nietzsche and Hegel, and in turn this demands a close attention to the continuity of Bataille's writings and the way that Bataille often supposes a familiarity with arguments he has developed elsewhere. We will begin with the summit.

On the Summit

Bataille's most extensive discussion of the summit can be found in *On Nietzsche*, where he considers it to be a place 'beyond good and evil' (Nietzsche). The reason that Bataille finds a sense of the summit in the crimes of Gilles de Rais may be because these crimes are the immediate expression of violent passions and are not subordinated to calculation. They are not carried out as a means to an end, as a crime for monetary or political gain would be, but as an end in themselves. We experience a sense of the summit from them because the excess of these crimes places them beyond good and evil. The problem is that this 'sense of the summit' must encounter the summit as the limit of sense. To return to *On Nietzsche* is to return to the summit as *beyond* sense: 'Definition betrays desire. Its aim is the inaccessible summit. But the summit eludes any attempt to think about it. It's *what is*. Never *what should be*' (ON, 91). Bataille wavers, the summit is inaccessible but it is also what is, a definition is both resisted and offered, sense withdrawn and given.

He is trying to save a sense of the summit that he has put outside of language, reason, morality and philosophy by giving the summit an ontological sense, as being, as what is. Through the being of Gilles de Rais we get a sense of the summit as an experience of being. This sense of the summit is in conflict with the summit as inaccessible and *unstable*: 'To speak of the summit is to put ourselves in a position of instability' (ON, 42). The summit cannot achieve the consistency of being, either with a capital B or of a particular being (i.e. Gilles de Rais) because of this fundamental instability. For Bataille the subject cannot contain instability, because any effect of subjectivity has its origin in instability. As Bataille wrote elsewhere the 'I' only arises out of an 'infinite improbability' (VE, 130). Not only is the individual unstable but also 'Being is in fact found NOWHERE ...' (VE, 173). In *On Nietzsche* Bataille is resisting the loss of the summit by clinging on to it as Being, but he had already ruled out that possibility.

The summit expresses a violent tension between its instability and Bataille's imposition of an ontological sense on to this instability. We can understand this tension as the result of the structure of the summit, a structure that undoes itself. When Bataille describes the summit as 'the impossible limit' (ON, 39) it is no longer a place that can be occupied or a space of Being. Instead it is a bar to any occupation of the summit or to any existence on the summit. This barring of the summit not only makes decline inevitable, but it also makes it impossible to oppose the summit to decline. This disorientation of the summit will alter the sense of the summit that Bataille finds in Gilles de Rais. That sense can no longer be a positive sense of what the summit is, because the summit is an *impossible* limit. Therefore, any sense of the summit is a restriction of the summit, a restriction of the impossible to sense.

Bataille shatters the opposition of the summit to the decline when he writes that '*Just as in the last analysis the summit is simply inaccessible, from the start, decline is inevitable*' (ON, 39). If the summit is inaccessible, impossible, then we can no longer have an opposition between the summit and the decline, *all we have is the decline*. The summit, as the impossible limit, is an effect of the decline. It is only through the decline that we can posit the idea of the summit. However, without a summit to oppose itself to, the idea of a decline is also made unstable. If there is only a decline then that decline can no longer be organised as a descent from the summit. The dislocation of the summit dislocates the decline, and that is perhaps why Bataille only indicates the possibility of *chancing* upon the summit. No longer can we ascend to the summit or decline from it as the summit and the decline become *indistinguishable*.

Bataille's ontological interpretation of the summit is a symptom of his desire for the summit, his desire to produce the summit. It is also the way in which he avoids his own disorientation of the structure of the summit and the decline. By finding a sense of the summit in Gilles de Rais, Bataille tries to arrest the indistinguishable blurring of the summit and the decline. At the same time as he gives the summit a sense he also betrays it, and Bataille's writings are a tangled labyrinth that cannot be regulated by him. To understand the summit requires that we remove it from the safety of ontology and expose it to the general effect of the decline, a decline that is without orientation.

Bataille's early essay 'The "Old Mole" and the Prefix *Sur* in the Words *Surhomme* [Superman] and *Surrealist*' (1929–30?) (VE, 32–44) can help to remove the summit from his ontological interpretation because it is a self-criticism in advance of his own desire for the summit as being. It was written as a critique of Nietzsche's and surrealism's tendency to indulge in a 'simple subversion' (VE, 37) which exalts power and desires the heights. Bataille argues that any attempt to reach the heights is doomed to an inevitable fall back down into the dirt. He criticises the desire for the high as an evasion of this inevitable decline. Although it is a slightly simplistic critique of Nietzsche, and perhaps also of surrealism, it is a powerful critique of Bataille's own tendency in *On Nietzsche* to hold on to the summit despite claiming that decline is inevitable. Bataille has forgotten his own critique of the idealist tendencies in Nietzsche and he has reproduced them in his own desire for the summit. In fact the early essay suggests that, if anything, the 'summit' is to be found in the *fall*, the shattering experience of the loss of self-control. There is a paradox whereby decline and summit become blurred in the movement of decline.

How can we understand this tension between Bataille's desire for the summit and the collapse of the summit? If we understand the summit as impossible then the desire for it can be understood as an *effect* of this impossibility. By interpreting Bataille in this way the summit is the impossible limit that tries to arrest the disorientation of decline, and at the same time the summit is the impossible limit that is the sign of that disorientation. The double effect of the impossible limit is to produce the summit as an object of desire and to make it impossible ever to reach the object of desire. The explosive tension of Bataille's writings emerges in the impossible moment of the summit, as it will through sovereignty. The summit is, in many ways, a thought that is moving towards sovereignty.

The loss of the summit through the disorientation of a decline which is out of control takes us back to Bataille's earliest insights into the parodic circulation of foundations (VE, 5) and to his Nietzschean intuition that 'it is the *foundation* of things that has fallen into a bottomless void' (VE, 222). In Nietzsche the madman's announcement of the death of God has a similar effect of disorientation:

What did we do when we unchained this earth from its sun? Whither is it moving now? Whither are we moving now? Away from all suns? Are we not perpetually falling? Backward, sideward, forward, in all directions? Is there any up or down left?[8]

Bataille's own desire for access to the summit, to find an existence on the summit, is a resistance to this radical disorientation. It also means that if Gilles de Rais can give us any sense of a summit it would have to be found in the excess that threatens his security as a subject rather than in his embodiment of the summit or of sovereignty.

There is evidence for this in Bataille's remark that 'if he [Gilles] reveals a grandeur beyond his baseness it is in the calm of collapse' (TG, 22). The 'fault' or 'error' of Gilles de Rais would be to believe himself to be sovereign, to believe that he has the power of life or death over others as an absolute right. The pitifulness of his confessions before his judges and God during his trial and execution would then reflect his inability to lose his belief in a sovereign power. Rais would have been involved in a battle with God for this power over death, and his attempts to raise the devil would be part of this attempted seduction of God. Rais 'acted out' (in the psychoanalytic sense) his belief that he could control the life and death of his victims to resist the sovereign existence of collapse. In fact it would be his inability to control the violence he unleashed, and its return back upon him in his contrition, confession and execution that would signify the 'summit'.

It is in his fall from his high social position rather than in his possession of social power, that Rais touches on the summit and sovereignty. The reactionary interpretation of sovereignty as nostalgia for social power or the call to put into place a leader cannot be sustained in the face of this collapse. The fascist leader is only another example of avoiding sovereign freedom by trying to maintain a sovereign power in an individual. Bataille argues that the fascist leader attempts to control or concentrate the freedom of sovereignty in his person: 'But this concentration in a single person intervenes as an element that sets the fascist formation apart within the heterogeneous realm: by the very fact that the affective effervescence leads to unity, it constituted, as *authority*, an agency directed *against* men' (VE, 143–4; BR, 129). In trying to control this sovereign freedom the fascist leader gains a sublime authority but also destroys that freedom by directing this authority against others.

This argument can help us to render more concrete the connection that Bataille makes between the crimes of Gilles de Rais and the crimes of the Nazis. While Rais does not represent a modern calculating exercise of totalitarian power he does attempt the same condensation of sovereign power, although in himself and not in a leader. He is trying to save the social power that is slipping away from him and he directs it not against men but against children, those children who would have become his peasants and servants. Rais is therefore eroding his social power as he tries to save it and within this spiral his fantasies of power become more obscene and grandiose, until he is finally engaged in a struggle with God. God would be the transcendental interpretation of sovereignty that Rais both wants to destroy and possess. In contrast Nazi crimes are a calculated terror, either to secure the purity of what they regard as the 'master race' or to instil fear into their subject populations. For Rais this effect of terror is secondary to the desire to encounter death, which Kojève called 'the absolute master'.[9]

The similarity of the crimes of Rais and those of the Nazis lies in their extreme violence, the obscene incarnation of a power over life and death, and in their condensation of that power in an individual. The difference lies in Rais's lack of calculation, his expenditure of power rather than its accumulation. Moreover, Rais is fascinated by an encounter with death through the other rather than by the extermination of the other to preserve his purity. Despite this there is an intimate connection between this sovereign exercise of power and the modern total state of Nazism. Foucault comments that 'Nazism was doubtless the most cunning and most naïve (and the former because of the latter) combination of the fantasies of blood and the paroxysms of a disciplinary power'.[10] Nazism took up what Foucault calls '*the symbolics of blood*'[11] from medieval and early modern societies and combined it with the modern developments of bio-power (which brings life into the domain of political calculation).

In doing so it combined a practice of bloody excessive power with a bio-power that dominated and organised subjects and populations. By applying one to the other it produced a massively violent extermination which attacked the sovereignty of free existence. This helps to explain why Rais could appear to be so close, as well as so distant, to the Nazis, and also why Nazism is a contradictory phenomenon that presents itself as both modern and atavistic. To interpret the summit not as *the* summit but as an 'impossible limit' is to detach sovereignty from its condensation in a leader, and to resist both a 'symbolics of blood' and the disciplinary organisation of modern 'bio-power'.[12] An interpretation of the summit as an impossible limit gives us access to an experience of radical disorientation. Bataille has taken us back to a labyrinth where Ariadne's thread has been broken, and the labyrinth itself is unstable.

This is not only a spatial but also a temporal disorientation. In fact, for Bataille, it is impossible to completely separate the spatial from the temporal, in particular because, as we will see, spatial arrangements also dictate an experience of time. They also both undergo radical disorientation in Bataille's description of the summit, and Gill has interpreted the temporal effects of the summit in very similar terms to the spatial effects I have noted: 'So both times at once. At the same time. A "moment of fissure", and a sliding away. Summit and decline simultaneously.'[13] It is not possible to secure the summit either in space or in time but only in its collapse, which itself collapses the distinction between space and time.

Bataille makes explicit these connections between the death of God, the disorientation of space and therefore of time, in a text from 1938 called 'The Obelisk' (VE, 213–22). Bataille quotes Nietzsche's announcement of the death of God through the voice of the madman, but what interests Bataille is the space in which this announcement is made – the public square. In particular because it is the *Place de la Concorde*, the public square where Louis XVI was executed and in which an obelisk has now been placed. The obelisk is the 'calmest negation' (VE, 215) of the death of God because it arrests the disorientation caused by the loss of a transcendental signifier with its 'sovereign permanence' (VE, 215). This is not simply an arresting of spatial disorientation but also of temporal disorientation, in particular the void opened up by the death of the sovereign, firstly as king and then as God. The obelisk is an attempt by man 'to set the most stable limits on the deleterious movement of time' (VE, 216), it is an attempt to control both space and time. As the anthropologist Marc Augé makes clear, 'The monument, as the Latin etymology of the word indicates, is an attempt at the tangible expression of permanence or, at the very least duration. Gods need shrines, as sovereigns need thrones and palaces, to place them above temporal contingencies.'[14]

The obelisk can never completely succeed in expressing permanence because it is itself contingent, it has been erected upon a void that it can conceal but which also threatens it with an essential instability. It is open to what Bataille calls a 'reversal of signs' (VE, 217), a violent reinterpretation that alters it from an object of sovereign permanence to an object caught up in the mobility of sovereign freedom. There are two moments here that are heterogeneous to one another in the erecting of the obelisk – the gathering and ordering of time and space around a centre and the potential dispersal of that centre by movements of time and space. Bataille notes that it is the philosophy of Hegel that will attempt to hold these two moments together and so to privilege the moment of gathering over the moment of dispersal. It is the 'heavy Hegelian process' (VE, 219) that attempts to save sovereignty as a sovereign permanence by integrating the movements of gathering and dispersion: 'Thus he gave the movement of time the *centripetal* structure that characterises sovereignty, Being, or God. Time, on the other hand, dissolving each centre that has formed, is fatally known as *centrifugal* – since it is known in a being whose centre is already there' (VE, 219).

For Bataille, Hegel cannot completely control the centrifugal movement of time that he makes central, and the obelisk never succeeds in arresting time because 'the obelisk marks the location of the guillotine – an empty space, open to the rapid flow of traffic' (VE, 221). The obelisk is no longer the figure of sovereignty as 'the purified head, whose unshakeable commands lead men ...' (VE, 221) but sovereignty as a 'derisive and enigmatic figure placed at the entrance to a labyrinth ...' (VE, 222). Sovereignty without a head, the figure of *Acéphale*, is already visible in the description of the summit. What is also visible is the important role that Hegel plays for Bataille, as the philosopher who places time, sovereignty and death at the centre of philosophy, always trying only to preserve the centre of philosophy against the disorientation that Nietzsche would later reveal. Bataille identifies with Nietzsche and takes up again his thought of disorientation and dispersal. The impossibility that Bataille's writing confronts is in its encounter with a disorientation that cannot be mapped or be subject to temporal ordering.

By connecting Bataille's comment that the crimes of Gilles de Rais give us a 'sense of the summit' to the development of his thought of the summit, the 'sense' of the summit is profoundly changed. All that Rais's crimes can give us is a 'sense' of the summit, and that sense is a restriction of the summit to a particular person and to *sense*. The summit actually does not conform to an economy of sense because in the experience of the summit there is a spatial and temporal disorientation which ruins sense. At this moment we cannot distinguish the summit from the decline or find a place on the summit. It is even possible that the decline is the only summit we have, because the summit is impossible. The summit is no longer an accumulation of power but an experience of expenditure without reserve. This interpretation of the summit must be connected to sovereignty, with which it shares so much, in order to reject Bataille's identification of Rais with a sovereign power.

Sovereign Existence

Bataille presents his most disarming definition of sovereignty in the third volume of *The Accursed Share*, when he states that 'Sovereignty is NOTHING' (AS2/3, 256). The supposed 'object' of the book slips away from us and is withdrawn from an organised exposition. Bataille both writes and erases sovereignty by making it NOTHING or by making it *impossible* in an exercise of thought in extreme tension. As with the summit Bataille trembles at maintaining this tension because of his desire for a sovereign existence. He wants to produce the impossibility of sovereignty, to make it present in an act that destroys the freedom of sovereignty. Identifying sovereignty with subjectivity does this: 'The sovereign, epitomising the *subject*, is the one by whom and for the moment, the miraculous *moment*, is the ocean into which the stream of labour disappear' (AS2/3, 241). The thought of sovereignty proves too much for this attempted limitation because no sooner has Bataille restricted sovereignty to subjectivity than sovereignty is expressing its force of freedom by rupturing the concept of subjectivity.

After being made sovereign subjectivity is no longer what is held within the subject but 'it is *communicated* from subject to *subject* through a sensible, emotional contact ...' (AS2/3, 242). Bataille is still trying to hold on to communication between subjects through this 'contagious subjectivity' (AS2/3, 243), although his own thought of communication pulls the rug out from under the subject. Communication causes a flowing away of which the subject can only ever be an effect, a temporary dam. In fact there is good reason for us to identify sovereignty with communication rather than with subjectivity. We would then use the disordered meditations of *Inner Experience* against the historical framework of the third volume of *The Accursed Share*. Bataille's clinging on to his historical framework would not be a sign of his clarity or academic rigour but of his refusal to engage with the disruptive violence of sovereignty. To counter this the mobility of his war thought can be used against the historical framework of the post-war work.

In *Guilty* Bataille wrote, 'Fear carries me onward. Fear or horror, of the stakes involved in systematic thought' (G, 16). The movement onward would be the movement of sovereignty as NOTHING, and of sovereignty as that which refuses to settle within subjectivity. To follow this movement is to arrive where Bataille states that 'Basically, sovereignty never has anything personal about it' (AS2/3, 311). His hesitations in describing sovereignty can be understood as the effect of this thinking of sovereignty as a 'slipping away' (AS2/3, 203), which means that it also slips away from Bataille. He concludes that 'Sovereignty, on the other hand, is the object which eludes us all, which nobody has seized and which nobody can seize for this reason: we cannot possess it, like an object, but we are doomed to seek it' (LE, 193–4). It is this impossibility of sovereignty that forces us to seek it, but while sovеignty is NOTHING it is also a 'nothing' that displaces the philosophical model of the subject. Sovereignty is

detached from an ontological interpretation, including that of
Bataille: 'Never can we *be* sovereign' (LE, 194).

Sovereignty is NOTHING, a nothing that is a slipping away of
the subject. This slipping away is not secondary because it does
not happen to a subject who is secure or has integrity, instead it
reveals the unstable status of the subject. What Bataille calls
'contagious subjectivity' is the alteration of the subject from a
secure being to a momentary arrest of the flow of falling back. It
has profound repercussions for philosophy and for history, and in
particular where they share concepts of the subject and history.
Hegel is one of the most historical of philosophers and Bataille's
sovereignty is a displacement of Hegel's philosophical history.
Derrida has argued most strongly for Bataille's displacement of
Hegel in his essay 'From Restricted to General Economy: A
Hegelianism without Reserve' (CR, 102–38). In particular, he
examines how Bataille's sovereignty is a translation of Hegel's
concept of mastery which transforms that concept.

Bataille forces the master–slave dialectic from Hegel's *Phenomenology* to undergo a series of 'essential displacements' (CR, 105).
The result is that Bataille undoes Hegel's attempt to organise and
orient a philosophical history and a philosophical subjectivity. By
taking Bataille back to Hegel it becomes possible to understand
the depth of Bataille's displacement of the classical concepts of the
subject and of history so 'it must indeed be concluded that what
is exceeded by sovereignty is not only the "subject", but history
itself' (CR, 121). Guided by Derrida it is possible to examine more
closely Bataille's textual engagement with both Hegel and Kojève.
Bataille's displacement of the master–slave dialectic is dependent
on Kojève's own displacement of Hegel. Kojève argues that '"consciousness" (*Bewusstein*) is the general term for man in the
Phenomenology',[15] and in this way he changes Hegel's account of
the origin of self-consciousness into an anthropological story of
the birth of man. Kojève has not misread Hegel but he has detected
the fact that the *Phenomenology* is a fissured text between being a
science of the experience of consciousness and a science of man,
and he exploits this 'minor' anthropological moment in the *Phenomenology* to make his reading.

It is this capacity to pick out the minor element of a text and
use it to displace the major structure of that text that will influence
Bataille's practice of reading. However, the problem with Kojève's
reading is that it makes this minor part of the text the repressed
truth of Hegel. The minor reverses position with the major and
Hegel's *Phenomenology* becomes anthropology and is given a new
dominant sense. In response Bataille will take this anthropology
to its limit (also see Chapter 4). The limit of Kojève's narrative is
the master, who is an organising figure but one who must disappear

in that narrative. Kojève makes the master–slave dialectic central in two ways, by using it to account for the origin of man and to account for history. In transforming mastery into sovereignty Bataille will put this use of sovereign freedom into question.

The master–slave dialectic is necessary for the birth of man because it tears him out from nature. In nature negation takes place but it does not lead to any transformation of the world, and Bataille faithfully summarises Kojève's lesson when he writes:

> ... No doubt the individual fly dies, but today's flies are the same as those of last year. Last year's have died? ... Perhaps, but *nothing* has disappeared. The flies remain, equal to themselves like the waves of the sea. (BR, 284)

When negation only negates the positive it remains positive itself, and nothing actually changes. For man to become man he must negate actively and the only object he can negate actively is the active desire of another man to negate. Desire is directed against desire in the form of a demand for recognition (*Anerkennung*) that can only be met through violent conflict.

The negating demand for recognition has to be greater than the desire for biological preservation to take man out of nature: 'It is by voluntarily accepting the danger of death in a struggle for pure prestige that man appears for the first time in the natural world.'[16] Kojève's anthropological reading of Hegel's master–slave dialectic limits it to being a *potential* fight to the death. For both Hegel and Kojève the encounter with death cannot lead to the death of one or both of the combatants because that would be the end of the dialectic. If one of the combatants were to die then the other would not receive recognition, and they would both have failed to achieve mastery. If both combatants die then there is no one left to supply recognition. So, this life or death struggle can actually only ever be what Derrida calls an 'economy of life' (CR, 106). Bataille finds this funny because the potential death of one or both combatants mocks the master–slave dialectic in advance, whatever its result. For Hegel and Kojève this possibility is controlled as 'abstract negation' which is a destructive threat to the dialectic that can never be fully realised. For Bataille it is one sign of the limit of the dialectic in the face of a death that refuses to be absorbed within an economy of life, a death that rises up as a bloody head and shatters us with laughter.

In contradiction to the battle of the master–slave dialectic, which ends with the victory of the master over the slave and the production of two stable existential positions, Bataille explores the death that threatens to undo this 'labour of the negative'. Kojève and Hegel unleash negativity, death, only to draw it back within the dialectic. Bataille takes negativity and death more seriously, to the point where he breaks down in laughter at the philosopher. In the 'Letter to X' Bataille argues that the result of Kojève's 'end of history' is not the completion of the dialectic but 'unemployed negativity' (BR, 297). At the end of Kojève's argument is the problem that is already embedded in its beginning: its failure to control negativity. It is this that will fundamentally alter the position of the master and justify Bataille's translation of the master as sovereignty. It also demonstrates how closely sovereignty is connected to the question of violence, as Bataille is revealing the attempt by philosophy to control violence and the necessity of its failure. The violence of the master–slave dialectic must be a violence that makes sense, a violence that leads to the production of sense in the form of man and history. What it has to resist is a senseless violence, a violence that lays waste without recognition, and a violence that Bataille found intimated in Gilles de Rais.

Both Hegel and Kojève must keep negativity under control at each stage of their philosophical history, from its beginnings in the master–slave dialectic to its closure in the end of history. This is why the master–slave dialectic must produce the positions of master and slave in order to produce history. For Kojève 'History must be the history of the interaction between mastery and slavery',[17] because the master–slave dialectic does not only account for the origin of man but also for the unfolding of his history. In this history the initial victory of the master is dialectically reversed into the eventual triumph of the slave: 'The future and History hence belong not to the warlike master, who either dies or preserves himself in identity to himself, but to the working slave.'[18] This is because although the master had the initial triumph over death in defeating the slave, the slave was actually defeated because of his fear of death. The result is that the master has not encountered death in all its terrifying reality as the 'absolute master', (Kojève) but the slave has. This is the first power of the slave over the master: the slave recognises the reality of death. The second power that he holds over the master is that in defeating the slave the master forces him to work. This labour means that while the master is idle the slave labours at transforming the world.

The slave's transforming labour eventually gives it the power to 'take up once more the liberating Fight for recognition that he refused in the beginning for fear of death'.[19] In contradiction to the idleness and decadence of the master, the slave is educated through work or, as Hegel argues, 'Through work and labour, however, this consciousness of the bondsman [slave] comes to itself.'[20] Marx too remains within this dialectic of labour when he argues for the education of the proletariat through 'the stern but steeling school of *labour*'.[21] In Marx, Hegel and Kojève it is the labour of the slave

that makes history and the labour of the slave that will give him
final victory. As we will see, in contrast, Bataille is always concerned
with play, the sacred, and waste dislodging the metaphysics of
production at the heart of philosophy and politics. Bataille opposes
the model of history as a history made by the slave, and how this
historical model dictates the defeat and disappearance of master.[22]
It is on 'this dissymmetry, this absolute privilege given to the slave,
that Bataille did not cease to meditate' (Derrida in CR, 106).

In the initial struggle of the master–slave dialectic Bataille
explored the death that threatened to derail the production of man,
which the dialectic tried to control as abstract negation. Now
Bataille is interested in the limit of this historical dialectic in the
figure of the useless master discarded by history. What connects
these moments that the dialectic rules out or subsumes is that they
are both destructive and unproductive. Unemployed negativity is
Bataille's name for a negativity that escapes the dialectic and
escapes being determined by the dialectic as abstract negation.
From the productive labour of the slave building a new world
Bataille turns toward the spectacular consumption of the master
as the model for expenditure without regard to utility (as we saw,
this is what fascinated Bataille about Gilles de Rais and it recurs
in his work on general economy discussed in Chapter 5). What
begins to be clearer is that Bataille is not advancing a reactionary
appreciation of slavery or of the aristocracy, or of the violent
criminality of Rais, but a *displacement* of the Hegelian concept of
mastery with the 'a-concept' of sovereignty.

Sovereignty resists the gathering necessary to the dialectic, the
Aufheben that is central to Hegel and to Kojève. It haunts the philosophical narrative with a force of negativity that cannot be
integrated into that narrative, and which that narrative only fully
confronts as its end. The end of this narrative takes different forms
in Hegel and Kojève. In Hegel it is the recollection (*Erinnerung*) of
all the previous historical embodiments of spirit: 'This last
embodiment of spirit – spirit which at once gives its complete and
true content the form of self, and thereby realises its notion, and
in so doing remains within its own notion – this is *Absolute
Knowledge*.'[23] The culmination of the *Phenomenology* for Hegel is
the gathering of substance as subject and the absorption of all
surplus negativity within knowledge. Bataille laughs a sovereign
laughter because '*absolute knowledge is definitive non-knowledge*' (IE,
108); the closure that Hegel wants to achieve is ruined because
the circle of absolute knowledge does not close. Rather it leaves
us where we were, a cause for laughter at the philosopher's expense.
The conclusion that the philosopher has reached has got us

nowhere and leaves us with the sovereign experience of disorientation that Nietzsche first explored and which Bataille exacerbated.

Sovereignty does not integrate into absolute knowledge but is the non-knowledge that undermines it. In the end Hegel could not surrender to the ecstatic experience of sovereignty: 'It seems to me however, that Hegel, shrinking back from the way of ecstasy (from the only direct resolution of anguish) *had* to take refuge in a sometimes effective (when he wrote or spoke), but essentially vain, attempt at equilibrium and harmony with the existing, active, official world' (IE, 110). Contrary to the common Marxist explanation that Hegel was a civil servant for the Prussian state because of the essentially reactionary nature of his philosophy, Bataille draws a more difficult lesson. The achievement of absolute knowledge had left Hegel on the verge of madness; he felt he was 'becoming dead' (IE, 110) or felt 'the more profound horror of being God' (IE, 110). His reaction was to try to take refuge in the world, to reconcile his philosophy with that world and to elaborate philosophy as a work of mourning. Bataille regards this as the result of Hegel's own lucidity, but what Hegel could not recognise was that in trying to gather everything in absolute knowledge it became fatally contaminated by non-knowledge and subject to a possible mimicry that would undermine the position of philosophy (IE, 108). In the end Hegel could not surrender the labour of the negative for the play of transgression, as we will see in the next chapter.

Kojève's narrative fares no better in its attempt at a conclusion which is imposed in his anthropological reading as 'the end of history'. Kojève also sees the end as the achievement of the subject, but this time as the complete human being: 'History will be completed at the moment when the synthesis of the master and the slave is realised, that synthesis that is the whole man, the Citizen of the universal and homogeneous state created by Napoleon.'[24] Napoleon had given the possibility of the universal state and Kojève, as a Marxist of the right, would scandalise his audience in the 1930s by arguing that 'the man of the end of history was not Napoleon but Stalin'.[25] What Napoleon had given as a possibility Stalin would realise in actuality. This end of history did not remain the end of history and, with what Derrida calls a 'naively joking baroquism',[26] Kojève would go on to suggest new ends of history, firstly looking to the 'classless' USA as the state which has ended history, and then to a supposedly 'post-historical' Japan. Which end is the real end, the end that brings an end to the end of history?

Kojève's playful taste for multiple ends of history has even been continued with a great deal of seriousness by Francis Fukuyama who claims that liberal democracy is the final state of the end of history.[27] This does not solve the problem of bringing an end to the end of history, and instead the power of Kojève's lectures is that they put the problem of negativity and sovereignty in relief. They can no longer remain within an historical or philosophical subject, but somehow escape from both. This is what made Kojève's interpretation of Hegel so profoundly ambiguous: it was a powerful interpretation but, because of its power, it also reached the limits of Hegel. For Mikkel Borch-Jacobsen, Kojève confronted his listeners with the problem that 'the complete fulfilment of desire (that is, of history, of philosophy), far from satisfying desire once and for all, exacerbates it instead, beyond all limit, for then and only then does the desperate question arise of what one can possibly desire once everything has been accomplished'.[28] For Bataille this question of what we desire after desire is the impossible question of sovereignty.

Bataille wrote, 'I grant (as a likely supposition) that from now on history is ended (except for the denouement)' (BR, 296; CS, 90). In that denouement is played out the exacerbation of a desire without any object, an 'unemployed negativity'. The end of history is no longer a moment of gathering together or stabilisation, either of thought or in reality, but the confrontation with negativity. The person of the end of history 'is confronted by his [sic] own negativity as if by a wall' (BR, 298; CS, 91). This is not a terminal point of thought but rather the denouement is also a new opening, and in a paradoxical fashion the end of history offers multiple possibilities for the future. The unemployed or recognised negativity of the end of history is liberated from the purpose of action or meaning and 'brings into play representations extremely charged with emotive value (such as physical destruction or erotic obscenity, an object of laughter, of physical excitation, of fear and of tears)' (BR, 298; CS, 91). Bataille's writing finds its beginning at the end of history because the end of history is the closure of philosophy but not in the sense that philosophy thinks. Instead of philosophy achieving its dream of completion the closure of philosophy puts us at the limit of philosophy in a way which opens new possibilities of thought.

For Nietzsche the struggle against philosophy 'has created in Europe a magnificent tension of the spirit such as has never existed on earth before: with so tense a bow one can now shoot for the most distant targets'.[29] The tension of Bataille's thought of sovereignty can be interpreted as an expression of the tension of this struggle, especially of the struggle against philosophical subjectivity. We have tried to interpret and maintain that tension because to resolve it is to lessen the effects of Bataille's writings. At the same time the resolution of violence and sovereignty as a subject is a betrayal of sovereignty and a refusal to think sovereign freedom. Sovereignty is always a bursting out of limitations, a transgression that haunts the limit as an internal possibility. This is its tension, a tension that resists being held within any intellectual framework and, as Bennington has pointed out, 'This is why happily, *there is no sovereignty*, and why Bataille's best lesson is just that.'[30]

CHAPTER 4

The Tears of Eros

The lesson of sovereignty is that it is impossible, but this is not the end of thinking, it is the beginning. Bataille begins from thinking impossibility and he begins to think impossibility through a thought of difference. His writings on the erotic will spur us to a thinking of impossibility as an effect of difference. For Bataille sexuality is inextricably connected to violence and death, and this explains the title of Bataille's last work, *The Tears of Eros*. Our relationship to sexuality can never be a happy one; it must always involve anguish (*angoisse*) because 'In essence, the domain of eroticism is the domain of violence, of violation' (E, 16). Bataille attempts to explain the necessity of this anguish in *Eroticism*, which defines the 'formula' of eroticism as 'assenting to life up to the point of death' (E, 11). It is in this work that Bataille begins to articulate the connections between violence, death and sexuality in terms of transgression. Transgression has become an emerging theme in contemporary culture, especially in relation to 'alternative' sexualities. However, any interrogation of transgression as an operation or of Bataille's development of transgression to describe sexuality has rarely been dealt with. Understanding the power of Bataille's thought of transgression is essential to developing that thought beyond the domain of sexuality. This raises the critical question of the status of Bataille's fictional writings, which closely connect transgression to sexuality. They make clear the formula of eroticism and provoke the tears of Eros, but they also conform to a reading of transgression that opens beyond the sexual. It is in this play of transgression between sexuality, death, violence and an irreducible exteriority that Bataille's thought flows.

Initially in *Eroticism* Bataille explains these connections through a consideration of sexual reproduction. For Bataille reproduction involves shifts between discontinuous states, in which beings are separate, to continuous states, in which beings are connected together. He explains this by contrasting reproduction in the most elementary of creatures with reproduction in complex organisms. In the case of elementary organisms they reproduce asexually by splitting into two. This involves the transition from a discontinuous state, in which there is one being, to a continuous state, in which that one being is split into two, and finally back to a discontinuous state of two beings. These shifts involve the 'death' or non-existence of the first organism, now doubled into two different beings and the violent act of the splitting of that organism. In this sense it lays bare the mechanisms of eroticism and, in particular, how the state of continuity is one that is fundamentally linked to an opening and flowing of the organism which is both violent and deadly. In the case of these elementary organisms reproduction is literally deadly; the single organism ceases to exist in the act of becoming two when it is stretched to breaking point.

Bataille traces the same pattern in reproduction for complex organisms, including human beings. Now the question is of sexual reproduction, but they follow the same process of transition from discontinuous to continuous and back to discontinuous. In this case we begin with two separate beings in a state of discontinuity and it is in the act of sexual reproduction that they achieve '*one instant* of continuity' (E, 14). After this moment of connection they return to a state of discontinuity and separation as two separate beings. The sexual act is an experience of continuity, that is an experience of the loss or dissolution of the boundaries of our body. This loss of the boundary of the body is an act of violence, even if we experience it in the tenderest caress, and in this loss of discontinuity it prefigures death, when our body will lose its integrity and return to the earth. Bataille argues that 'only violence can bring everything to a state of flux in this way, only violence and the nameless disquiet bound up with it' (E, 17).

What Bataille is trying to establish is that already in reproduction, the most 'functional' moment of sexuality, there are effects that cannot be reduced to the natural. Instead, 'On the most fundamental level there are transitions from continuous to discontinuous or from discontinuous to continuous' (E, 15), and the play of the *difference* between these states produces the feeling of eroticism. Bataille takes this model further to argue that human beings have a 'tormenting desire' (E, 15) for the state of 'lost continuity' (E, 15). Bataille connects this continuity to an experience of the sacred as an immanent plane of fusion (TR, 35). Therefore, 'The whole business of eroticism is to destroy the self-contained character of the participants as they are in their normal lives' (E, 17), and the result of this destruction is a contact with an experience of the sacred. The difficulty with this extension of the model is Bataille's positing of continuity as primary, because if it was a state of pure continuity from where would discontinuities arise? I want to suggest instead an interpretation of Bataille which is not concerned with the desire to return to this lost state but with the play of difference between the two states.

In fact, it is out of the play of difference between these two states that it becomes possible to posit the limits of continuity and discontinuity as limits that are *fictional*.[1] This would mean that absolute continuity and absolute discontinuity would both be *impossible* and instead life would exist in the flow and turbulence that Bataille finds in the *difference* of these two states. As he writes in *Guilty*, life is 'a constant destabilisation of the equilibrium without which it wouldn't be' (G, 15–16). Bataille, of course, suggests that absolute continuity as such would be death, and we could argue the same for absolute discontinuity: to be cut off completely from other organisms and the environment would be deadly. However, while continuity may not be primary as a state in which we could exist Bataille is correct to note its primacy as an effect of opening and of communication between bodies. Without this opening discontinuous bodies would not be possible, and these discontinuous bodies exist as discontinuous by denying their continuity, the difference that inhabits them. As Derrida has argued 'the experience of the *continuum* is also the experience of absolute difference' (CR, 115) and Bataille suggests that fundamental continuity be thought of 'like the waves of a stormy sea' (E, 22), which is an inscription of difference in continuity. The necessity of difference undoes the opposition between discontinuous and continuous and forces a different thinking of difference beginning from impossibility.

Bataille expands this intuition through analysing the play of transgression and taboo, which broadly correspond to continuity and discontinuity. Transgression is 'a movement which always exceeds the bounds, that can never be anything but partially reduced to order' (E, 40), and this breaking of the boundary connects it to continuity. The taboo is the boundary and as Bataille points out, using the example of the biblical commandments, it often regulates sexuality and death and thereby forms the limits of a discontinuous existence. While transgression and taboo closely correspond to continuity and discontinuity they are not as easy to regard as separate states, and Bataille is more sensitive to the necessary coexistence and mutual dependency of transgression and taboo. At the same time they remain irreconcilable, and it is the constant clash of transgression and taboo which drives eroticism to its 'ultimate intensity' (E, 40). Bataille resists the idea that transgression could lead to the complete lifting of all taboos on sexuality and the return to some idyllic state of nature. That prospect is a myth that refuses to negotiate with the violence and anguish involved in sexuality, and so a project of sexual liberation based on a natural sexuality will actually increase sexual misery. This is because transgression can never eliminate all taboos: 'But a transgression is not the same as a back-to-nature movement; it suspends a taboo without suppressing it' (E, 36). While Bataille resists a project of sexual liberation his thought of transgression is actually an expansion of sexual freedom that is sensitive to the violence that all sexuality involves.

Bataille likens this play of transgression and taboo to the Hegelian dialectic, specifically to the operation of the untranslatable *aufheben*: 'transcend without suppressing' (E, 36 n. 1). For Derrida, 'Here, we must interpret Bataille against Bataille, or rather, must interpret one stratum of his work from another stratum' (CR, 127) because 'Bataille is even less Hegelian than he thinks' (CR, 128). Bataille is conceding too much too quickly by assimilating the play of the difference between transgression and taboo to a dialectical operation. Just as a reading of transgression as a movement back to nature threatens to eliminate the necessary tension between transgression and taboo that generates sexuality so a dialectical reading threatens to eliminate the play of transgression in taboo in a dialectical 'synthesis' or *aufheben* that will bring these forces into equilibrium. When Bataille makes clear that transgression and taboo require each other and that they are irreconcilable he is resisting any possibility of an equilibrium of the difference between these two forces: 'Transgression piled upon transgression will never abolish the taboo, just as though the taboo were never anything but the means of cursing gloriously whatever it forbids' (E, 48). This difference between transgression and taboo cannot be held together in a stable arrangement nor can it be reconciled dialectically.

These forces are never balanced because transgression has a certain dominance over taboo as the force that makes taboo possible. In the very movement of transgression towards 'infinite excess' (E, 40) it solidifies the taboo as it reveals the fragility of the taboo. As Bataille puts it, the taboo can only 'curse gloriously whatever it forbids'. What is forbidden must be possible, for example incest or murder, or there would be no need of the taboo. If it were naturally impossible for us to murder or commit incest then neither possibility would arise. That we do have taboos on these acts makes those taboos secondary to the transgressions they rule out. Of course, at the same time, transgression can only operate as a movement across the boundary of the taboo so, although it may be a 'primary impulse' (E, 40), it too is secondary to the limit it crosses. In the complex difference between transgression and taboo which is primary and which is secondary is undecidable and they swirl around each other in the turbulence that Bataille always regards as a play of differences. It is one of the decisive arguments of this book that Bataille's work traces this movement from a thought of the impossible to a thought of the impossible as an *effect* of difference.

For Bataille life exists in this difference: 'Life is a swelling tumult continuously on the verge of explosion' (E, 59). Life is this tumult that the difference between taboo and transgression produces and the explosions are the effect of transgression as the opening of taboos. Humans try to restrict this tumult, especially in the organisation of labour, which requires the deferment of enjoyment to allow accumulation. However, to organise enjoyment through the limit of taboos is at the same time to make possible the transgressions that already fissure those taboos. It is not possible to line up taboo on the side of rationality and transgression on the side of irrationality because the inextricable relation between taboo and transgression gives them both 'a certain illogicality' (E, 63). Once again, contrary to the hope of Hegel, difference cannot be regulated by logic (as Hegel attempted in *The Science of Logic*). Furthermore, for Bataille transgression has a certain privilege as the opening of this tumult, this play of difference, because it is the 'primary impulse' and the 'explosion' that is life (which at the same time touches on death).

This is why Bataille is obviously more interested in transgression than taboos, and he analyses transgression as a social phenomenon that has two forms. The first is an organised transgression, which describes the fact that transgressions do not destroy social life but are necessary for it. So, festivals, ceremonies and sacrifices are often forms of 'communal negativity' which are fundamentally stable: 'The frequency – and the regularity – of transgressions do not affect the intangible stability of the prohibition since they are its expected complement ...' (E, 65). The other form of transgression happens when these socially organised transgressions go off the rails, because 'once a limited licence has been allowed, unlimited urges towards violence may break forth' (E, 65). This is the possibility of what Bataille calls an 'unlimited transgression' (E, 65) that threatens the fabric of the social order and we could use the example, although Bataille does not, of moments of revolt before they become stabilised in the form of a revolution.

The difficulty is that, however useful this distinction between organised and unlimited transgression is for the description of social phenomena, it *cannot* maintain its own stability in the face of transgression. If transgression is the act of crossing boundaries then the boundary between the two types of transgression is also vulnerable. Bataille himself makes this clear by firstly noting that unlimited transgression only emerges from organised transgression, and we can reverse this to say that any unlimited transgression can also become an organised transgression. Bataille's own writing itself follows this movement of crossing and returning that is the play of transgression and taboo, and finds itself constantly on the limits of sense. Once again Bataille is developing and exploring an a-concept because transgression not only describes an act of crossing and rupture but also crosses and ruptures itself. It has no secure conceptual identity and just like sovereignty it is ungovernable, headless, but not simply nonsensical. Instead it spreads out beyond itself and ruptures all concepts generally; it is a movement that wears out concepts.

It cancels itself out because pure transgression and pure taboo are *impossible* just as are organised transgression and unlimited transgression. Bataille is operating within limits that are fictional and it makes no sense to talk of transgression without taboo, because a pure transgression would destroy the possibility of transgression. Without boundaries to cross, or laws or rules to break, transgression would not exist. Moreover, if there were to be a pure taboo that would make no sense either; it would be unthinkable because it would not even appear as a taboo. By stressing the inextricable relation of these forces Bataille also resists the idea that we could oppose irruptive forces to their corresponding limitations because, as with transgression and taboo, they are bound up together. As with transgression though, the irruptive forces are a force of opening and any corresponding limitation is formed from those irruptive forces as it limits them. There cannot be a pure irruptive force or a pure limitation, just as there cannot be a pure transgression or a pure taboo.

If life exists in the tumult between these impossible limits then both these limits are deadly – pure transgression or pure taboo would be an end to life. As we have seen, the same arguments apply to organised and unlimited transgression: organised transgression is never so organised that it cannot break out of its limits and unlimited transgression is never so unlimited that it can do without organisation. It may be wiser therefore to speak about transgression, if we can respect the tensions of this experience in the way that Bataille's refinements try to. If these limits are impossible and deadly then life is a play of difference and these impossible limits are effects of difference too. Here Bataille is returning to his articulation of heterogeneity that we saw him develop in the essay on Sade and which he also explored in 'The Psychological Structure of Fascism' (1933–34) (VE, 137–60; BR, 122–46). Transgression opens a heterogeneous economy of an irreducible difference; it also opens possibilities of writing on transgression as heterogeneous that Bataille will exploit in his fiction.

Fictions of Transgression

As Bataille states, 'It [transgression] opens the door on to what lies beyond the limits usually observed, but it maintains these limits just the same' (E, 67). Bataille's fiction also exists within this play of difference in which limits are shattered and re-formed, solidified and displaced, over and over again. His fictional writings exhibit the tension of trying to write transgression, which is also to write taboo. He does this by making explicit the connection between violence, sexuality and religious experience that is articulated by transgression. In particular this connection is made *explicit* in the most literal sense of the word by displaying bodies in a state of violent *jouissance*. In this way Bataille's fiction exists on the unstable limit between pornography and eroticism, a limit that is at once legal, political and social. Many of Bataille's texts were published under pseudonyms, such as Lord Auch for the *Story of the Eye* and Pierre Angélique for *Madame Edwarda*, to avoid legal prosecution (and the selection of these pseudonyms and their effects on Bataille's writing would deserve a study in itself). If during his lifetime Bataille risked legal prosecution, since his death he has been condemned as a pornographer by the radical feminist writer, Andrea Dworkin.[2]

Andrea Dworkin's reading of the *Story of the Eye* is violently reductive, breaking down Bataille's writing into the staging of perverse scenarios. It redescribes Bataille's writing and inserts it into the context of hard-core pornography constructed as an assault against women. The very violence of this reading and the horrified affect that Dworkin feels before Bataille is, in a strange way, a sort of respect for Bataille's writing. What it completely omits is any connection to Bataille's wider work or any recognition that Bataille also might be trying to think through the intimate connections between violence and sexuality that Dworkin is so concerned with. Dworkin's desire to categorise and condemn, to draw up firm boundaries and taboos, at once makes her feel the violence of transgression more and fail to appreciate the porous boundary between her own work and Bataille's. It is Leo Bersani who, in another context, has noted the very strange proximity between the hatred of sex in the work of Andrea Dworkin and Bataille's recognition of the essential violence of sexuality.[3] At the very least this should suggest that the relationship between Bataille's fiction and feminism is more complicated than that of condemnation. It also indicates the complex situation of texts which find themselves overrun by the effects of a transgression that they are trying to describe or categorise. What Dworkin's reading fails to recognise is this effect, both in Bataille and in how it rebounds on her own text, and so Bataille's work demands a reading that is more sensitive to transgression. I want to begin that reading here and at the same time to respect the (multiple) affects that Bataille's texts can provoke (disgust, arousal, horror, amusement, boredom, etc.)

The explicit sexuality of Bataille's fiction, with its intensity, violence and naivety, place it in a heterogeneous relation to literature by displaying what literature usually rejects and conceals. Although these texts are heterogeneous to literature as it is usually thought and heterogeneous among themselves, they also have immediately recognisable features. What makes Bataille's works of fiction distinctive is their directness, brevity and intensity. It soon becomes possible to recognise very easily a piece of work written by Bataille and it is easily possible to imagine intentional or unintentional parodies of his work. This directness of Bataille's writing can be described as a writing that is denuded, a writing that is naked and, like the state of nakedness, it is a writing that both excites and embarrasses. For Bataille stripping naked 'is a state of communication revealing a quest for a possible continuance of being beyond the confines of the self' (E, 17). In this state Bataille's writing subjects itself to dispossession, exposure and loss of control. This is what makes it open to reading and yet also resistant to any reading that would try to create a distance from the intimacy it offers. In his fiction Bataille is at his most accessible and most elusive, explicit and secret, open and concealed.

To describe what Bataille's fictions share is to run the risk of reducing the heterogeneity between those fictions: *Story of the Eye*, *Blue of Noon*, *The Dead Man*, *Madame Edwarda*, *My Mother* and *L'Abbé C.* However, the extent to which they do share common features is also striking. Firstly, they are very often autobiographical with a narrator figure who appears to be a thinly disguised Bataille. So, in *Blue of Noon* (*Le bleu du ciel*), the central character, Troppmann, is a dissolute libertine on the fringes of the political left in Paris in the 1930s, as was Bataille. Susan Rubin Suleiman points out that this name can be transformed into 'Trop-*peu*-mann', not enough of man, signifying the impotence of the character in the face of political and sexual crisis.[4] Although the novel was written in 1935 it was not published until 1957, perhaps not only because of its pornographic nature but also because of its caustic satire on the revolutionary left of which Bataille was a part at the time. The novel dates from the time of Bataille's involvement with Counter-Attack and from his traumatic affair with 'Laure' (Colette Peignot).[5] In the novel the character of Dorothea/'Dirty' appears to be close to Laure while the politically militant woman, Lazare, is said to be modelled on Simone Weil.

If this indicates the autobiographical resources Bataille draws on it also suggests certain recurring characters who dominate Bataille's fictions. We have noted the relation of the narrator to Bataille, but the narrator also often doubles as the libertine who experiences personal and sexual dissolution. This is true of Troppmann in *Blue of Noon*, Pierre in *My Mother*, and Charles who narrates most of *L'Abbé C*. Along with the dissolute libertine there are two other characters who regularly recur in Bataille's fiction: the woman who possesses an ecstatic female *jouissance* and the figure of innocence who is the object of both horror and fascination. The woman of *jouissance* is Simone in the *Story of the Eye*, Eponine in *L'Abbé C*., Mary in *The Dead Man*, the mother in *My Mother*, Dirty in *Blue of Noon*, and Madame Edwarda in the eponymous novel. The figure of innocence is more elusive and may well be corrupted or corruptible, but we have Marcelle in *Story of the Eye*, Robert in *L'Abbé C*., and Lazare in *Blue of Noon*.

Bataille's fictions share a style, they share certain characters, and they share the exploration of eroticism and transgression. However, each is also singular in is articulation and heterogeneous to Bataille's other fictions. His fictional writings move between their grouping under Bataille's proper name as an ensemble and the specificity of each text. That is why I want to consider the articulation of one of Bataille's fictions, *L'Abbé C*., in more detail. This is a slightly unusual choice because it is perhaps the least sexually explicit of Bataille's writings and one of the least commented on. Despite this lack of explicit sexual content it is very explicit about the connection between eroticism and religion. This is explored in a more subtle way than the violent anticlericalism of the *Story of the Eye*, with its obscene parody of the mass and the murder of a priest at its climax (which is also a sexual climax). Instead *L'Abbé C*. explores Bataille's contention that 'The saint turns from the voluptuary in alarm; she does not know that his unacknowledgeable passions and her own are really one' (E, 7). This passionate connection between the saint and the voluptuary is figured through the identical twin brothers who provide the central narratives, Charles the libertine and Robert the pious priest, so pious he is nicknamed *L'Abbé*.

The unfolding of the narratives of the brothers is presented posthumously by a third narrator who has known the brothers and been entrusted with the presentation of the stories. The novel begins from the contrast between the two brothers: 'Robert fascinated me: he was the comic double of Charles: Charles broken down, disguised under a cassock' (AC, 13–14). These twin brothers obviously owe something to the paired sisters Justine and Juliette in Sade's eponymous novels, in which Justine demonstrates the misfortunes of virtue and Juliette the profits of vice.[6] However, Bataille is not as schematic as Sade is, and he is truly post-Sadian because his novel is organised around the fact that 'this absolute contrast was tantamount to a perfect identity' (AC, 77). Bataille's novel is a very strange experience because of the shifts in the identities of the two brothers which causes a blurring of identity reflected in their physical resemblance, which means that they are often mistaken for each other. This reversal and blurring unfolds in the exchange of narrators throughout the novel, where the shifting viewpoints of the writing reflect the shifting of identity.

In the first narrative by Charles we encounter a scene where he attempts to corrupt the pious Robert by leading him to a tower where Eponine, a scandalous and promiscuous woman, is waiting. In their perilous ascent of the tower Charles is haunted by the possibility of 'emancipation in a dizzy fall' (AC, 41), which is the possibility of the collapse that will collapse the identities of all the characters. The dominance of collapse in Bataille's fiction indicates that, although he had a certain fascination with virility in his political and sociological writings of the 1930s, his fictions are remarkably lacking in virility, especially considering they are quasi-pornographic. As we saw with Troppmann in *Blue of Noon* the libertine in Bataille is always in a state of collapse or, often, drunken intoxication. Denis Hollier describes *Blue of Noon* as a 'novel of impotence',[7] both sexual and political, and this description could be extended to Bataille's other fictions. The powerlessness of the male libertine is often in contrast to the erotic power of the female libertines, such as Dirty or Eponine. In his fiction Bataille reverses the conventional erotic dialectic he subscribes to in *Eroticism* where 'In the process of dissolution, the male partner has generally an active role, while the female partner is passive' (E, 17).

Of course, there is a current in misogynist discourse where women are given power but only as figures of horror that terrify men, what in psychoanalysis is called the 'phallic mother' who threatens the man with castration. Is Bataille's narrator (and perhaps even Bataille himself) an 'Obstinate and obsessed believer in an almighty feminine libido that would be the equivalent of a maternal phallus?'[8] Certainly Bataille works on this image of the woman, not least in the incestuous obscenity of the novel *My Mother*, but he also takes his distance from this image through a general thought of collapse and excess that shatters identities. By the end of *L'Abbé C.* Eponine, the possible figure of a 'virile' female *jouissance*, has also 'sunk as low as anyone can get!' (AC, 85). *L'Abbé C.* is not concerned with the possibility of a virile identity for either a man or a woman; instead, it plays out the collapse of identity in all its central characters. In this collapse the psychoanalytic categories that would attempt to catch hold of this experience are dragged into a turbulent sovereign displacement of identity.

One of the turning points in this narrative of collapsing identities comes when Eponine confronts Charles with the fact that he is just like his pious brother, 'You make me sick with your pompous voice and your fancy, polished language!' (AC, 64). At this point Charles encounters another of Eponine's lovers, the butcher, a man of a lower social class and also a man of violence. His rejection by Eponine and his encounter with the butcher push Charles further into the experience of collapse, which is also an experience of transgression: 'The worst of it was to be at the point where, by a quirk of fate, everything has been carried to the limit and to feel, at the same time, abandoned by life' (AC, 67). The experience of transgression is an experience of *jouissance* taken to the limit, a pleasure that is so excessive as to bring him to the point of death. In the rupture of the limit by transgression Charles is no longer left within the sexual in a restricted sense but 'I had the vacuous immensity of time before me' (AC, 68). Here the novel reflects Bataille's own description of transgression as an opening out on to an exteriority, here thought of as time. It is also an experience associated with the destitution of Charles as a character, his failure as a lover and the danger that the character feels in the merging of his identity with his brother.

In the next chapter of the novel this collapse of identity is extended and mirrored by the physical collapse of Robert. Robert is already ill but he still proceeds to celebrate mass without realising that Eponine is attending with two prostitute friends, Rosie and Raymonde. This causes Robert to feel disorientated: 'Then he cast his eyes toward Eponine and, since she was herself overcome with fear, he fell: his body suddenly went limp, slid to the floor, and tumbled down the steps of the altar' (AC, 76). The collapse of Charles is doubled by the collapse of his brother, and where Charles passes from the sexual to the religious feeling Robert moves from the religious to the sexual. In these collapses there occurs a fall, an exchange of identities, and finally a deadly play with the impulses of transgression. The collapse of Robert into a fever is actually a deception and later Charles discovers that Robert went to visit Eponine and the two prostitutes. There 'Robert, in his drunkenness, was like a mystic' (AC, 123) and he spends weeks in an orgy with Eponine and the two prostitutes (the subject of Robert's narrative) before he is finally arrested by the Gestapo. Robert's fall continues because under torture he incriminates Eponine and Charles rather than his comrades from the Resistance. This act is at once cowardly and brave and Robert can only explain his refusal to give his comrades' names as the result of his being 'more at odds with myself' (AC, 157).

Not only is Robert at odds with himself but Bataille's is a writing which is at odds with itself and at odds with literature. It is distanced from itself by the device of being structured as a series of narratives written by two brothers gathered together by an editor after their deaths. In this way the narratives are embedded and distanced, but at the same time strangely intimate. They also reflect on the act of writing, most explicitly in the foreword by Charles to Robert's narrative where Bataille (as Charles) writes,

> The only way to atone for the sin of writing is to annihilate what is written. But the author can only do that; destruction leaves that which is essential intact. I can, however, tie negation so closely to affirmation that my pen gradually effaces what it has written. In doing so it accomplishes, in a word, what is generally accomplished by 'time' – which, from among its multifarious edifices, allows only the traces of death to subsist. I believe that the secret of literature is there, and a book is not a thing of beauty unless it is skilfully adorned with the indifference of ruins. (AC, 128)

The words of the character Charles or the writer Bataille? The play of identity and collapse in the writing, as the play of transgression, makes a new form of writing possible. This is not a 'transgressive' writing, which would present transgression as such, that Bataille regards as impossible. Rather it is a writing that is at odds with itself, a writing that effaces itself in the effect of difference.

In this play of identity and piety, innocence and debauchery, image as truth and fiction, Bataille is closest to Pierre Klossowski. As well as friendship they both share a parallel exploration of the erotic at the level of the theoretical and fictional, and a fascination with the intimate connection between sexuality and the religious. Perhaps the writing that is closest to *L'Abbé C.* is Klossowski's novels *Roberte Ce Soir* and *The Revocation of the Edict of Nantes*.[9] In these novels Klossowski is more theologically subtle than Bataille in his exploration of the relationship of the soul to the body, but he is like Bataille in his obsession with a perverse sexual freedom and a writing of scandalous images. Klossowski's novels are also focused on a triad: Octave, a professor of scholastics, his young and beautiful wife, Roberte, and their nephew, Antoine. Octave formulates the 'laws of hospitality' by which his wife is to be made sexually available to any guest to the house, Antoine is fascinated by his aunt, while Roberte is at once austerely moral and wanton. The result is a theological pornography that is often more comic than Bataille's intensity. For example, when Roberte seduces a visiting bank clerk (in accordance with the laws of hospitality) and is having sex in an alcove, the telephone in the alcove rings and Octave has to untangle it from their writhing bodies and hold a conversation with a church canon.[10]

This difference in tone suggests that despite their closeness there is also a certain distance between Bataille and Klossowski. Bataille could dismissively refer to 'the Christian Klossowski' (LE, 116) in his study of Sade in *Literature and Evil*. After Bataille's death Klossowski contributed an essay to the special issue of *Critique Hommage à Georges Bataille* (1963), translated into English as 'Of the Simulacrum in Georges Bataille's Communication',[11] which is an exemplary reading but which also subtly assimilates Bataille to Klossowski. The closeness between Bataille and Klossowski may be what produces the distance between them, as their own identities come to be threatened by the play of transgression that they both describe in different ways. This is not to say that they are the same – they both articulate the force of transgression in particular ways but this force also throws them together. This makes it all the more important to understand the singularity of Bataille's articulation of transgression, in particular in the connection between Bataille's fictional writings and his studies of transgression.

L'Abbé C. is literature in a state of collapse, and this is the effect of the impulse of transgression that runs through the text and leaves its open. Bataille is always obsessed with openings and most of all *bodily* openings. As we have seen he is obsessed with the opening of the eye, but also the mouth open in the act of screaming (EA, 62; VE, 59) or the erupting 'solar anus' (VE, 5–9). For Bataille 'Bodies open out to a state of continuity through secret channels that give us a feeling of obscenity' (E, 17), and these 'secret channels' open up the body in a violent and shattering experience. In *L'Abbé C.* these 'secret channels' also open the body through a sexual impulse to the religious and to the 'vacuous immensity of time'. Bataille's writing, written as the ruins that are the result of the passing of time, is a writing that is obscurely worked over by what he called 'infinite excess'. This ruination of writing by time is opened by transgression, and the opening of transgression always opens *beyond* the body.

The Disintegration of Philosophy

If transgression is a game, and we have suggested already that it is a play of difference, then 'In the world of play philosophy disintegrates' (E, 275) and the novels are in touch with this disintegration. In his fictional writing Bataille explores the disintegration of personal identity, political allegiances and all calls to action in the tumult of transgressive impulses. Bataille's narrator heroes become the men of 'unemployed negativity' which he described in his 'Letter to X' (BR, 296–300). They experience 'the negativity of a man with nothing left to do, and not that of man who prefers to talk' (BR, 297). The man of unemployed negativity is only left with the task of exploring negativity and his exploration of negativity brings into play what is at stake in all of Bataille's writings but is extremely charged in his fiction. The reference to negativity also returns Bataille's writing to problems of philosophy, in particular the formulation of negativity made by Hegel. By drawing on the opening that Bataille's fiction makes through its use of transgression we can also use it to open philosophy.

Michel Foucault offers a sketch of the relation of transgression to the history of philosophy in his essay 'A Preface to Transgression' (CR, 24–40). While it is true that, as Nick Land writes, 'As an overt theme, "transgression" is nothing like as dominant within Bataille's writings as is often suggested, and it is only with extraordinary arbitrariness that he can be described as a "philosopher of transgression"',[12] it is also true that transgression is a force of *opening* that is dominant in all of Bataille's writings. Transgression as a term may be confined to *Eroticism* and is not explored in any depth in any of his other writings, but it connects with a number of Bataille's concerns in his fiction and in his more academic writings on the erotic. The difficulty is that his fictions tend to restrict transgression to the sexually explicit and the blasphemous to the point where transgression can become indistinguishable from a sense of sin.

As we saw in the Introduction it is possible to impose a religious identity on Bataille, and he himself even invites that identity at times. Klossowski offers an idiosyncratic religious interpretation of transgression, but for Bataille transgression is an impulse that is irreducible to religion. It is what permits the interpretation of Bataille as a Catholic writer but also what denies him a religious identity. This conflict is most explicit in his fiction, where transgression is both restricted to the religious and expands beyond the religious (and we might wonder whether it is ever possible not to remain in this double bind). This makes it all the more necessary to hold on to the moment of opening in the fiction by connecting it both to Bataille's exploration of transgression and to the effects of that transgression on philosophy. Bataille himself explicitly linked these tasks, with the preface to *Madame Edwarda* appearing as a chapter in *Eroticism* (E, 265–71) and texts like *Guilty* and *The Impossible* operating on the border between fiction and philosophy in an undecidable way. To extend and explain this strategy involves recognition of the 'unemployed negativity' which exists in the fiction and a rebounding of the forces generated by the fictions on to philosophy.

I am following this eruption of forces from the initial movement of transgression to Bataille's fiction as series of meditations on transgression, and then back to the effect of transgression on philosophy. As Michel Foucault puts it 'sexuality is a fissure' (CR, 25), and we slip through this fissure into the experience of transgression. If that experience is initially articulated by Bataille in the field of sexuality it is also a crucial experience of thought and as Foucault states, 'Perhaps one day it will seem as decisive for our culture, as much a part of its soil, as the experience of contradiction was at an earlier time for dialectical thought' (CR, 27). Transgression displaces the religious and the philosophical as universal discourses. Foucault raises the stakes of transgression by specifying this irrecuperable movement: 'Transgression, then, is not related to the limit as black to white, the prohibited to the lawful, the outside to the inside, or as the open area of a building to its enclosed spaces. Rather, their relationship takes the form of a spiral which no simple infraction can exhaust' (CR, 28).

The 'spiral' is an attempt to think the movement of transgression in terms of its paradoxical structure of crossing and return which cannot be exhausted by description in terms of an infraction. Instead, the spiral of transgression is another way into the labyrinth of thought. It indicates that transgression puts itself and the limit into play in a way that cannot be spatially organised in terms of two separate spaces, nor organised temporally in terms of before and after. It scrambles these points of co-ordination, as did sovereignty, in a whirl of movement where the points are both retained and lose their solidity. Although originally located in the field of sexuality, this play of the limit and transgression in the spiral exceeds sexuality. For Foucault it opens again the question of reason and its limits which was first introduced by Kant: 'Undoubtedly, it can be said that it comes to us through that opening made by Kant in Western philosophy when he articulated, in a manner which is still enigmatic, metaphysical discourse and its reflection on the limits of reason' (CR, 30).

For Kant a reflection on the limits of reason was essential to philosophy because philosophy goes beyond the limits of experience to formulate universal rules. Once it passes beyond the limits of experience philosophy is drawn into conflicts which can have no decisive resolution: 'Since the principles of which it is making use transcend the limits of experience, they are no longer subject to any empirical test. The battlefield of these endless controversies is called metaphysics.'[13] In response to these endless, and irresolvable, conflicts a scepticism arose which claimed that the only valid field for reason was experience. The result was a crisis: 'Her [metaphysics] government, under the administration of the *dogmatists*, was at first *despotic*. But inasmuch as the legislation still bore traces of the ancient barbarism, her empire gradually through internecine wars gave way to complete anarchy; and the *sceptics*, a species of nomads, despising all settled modes of life, broke up from time to time all civil society.'[14] Dogmatists and sceptics exist on either side of the limit: dogmatists beyond the limit which means that their claims can never be assessed by reason and in this sense they ruled despotically; while sceptics are inside the limit, insisting that nothing lays beyond experience and so vulnerable to the variation of that experience, anarchy.

What this crisis of philosophy amounts to for Kant is a failure to consider the limits of reason, and his response to the violent conflicts between the two opposing sides of the limit is to find 'the true mean'[15] between dogmatism and scepticism. This 'true mean' is a critical philosophy which can think the limits of reason while not lapsing into scepticism. Kant draws a limit between the empirical and the transcendental, and between the world of appearance – the phenomenal – and its limit – the noumenal or things-in-themselves. The transcendental contains both the categories, which are the universal conditions of possibility of experience, and the ideas of reason. For Kant it is necessary that the transcendental be related to experience because this prevents us 'wandering inadvertently beyond objects of experience into the field of chimeras'.[16] The two 'sides' of the limit have to be held together, not simply drawing a limit but reading the limit as both division and connection, which resists the reduction of reason to experience and reason becoming a transcendent beyond experience. This is a remarkably fragile and delicate way of thinking the limit.

Kant argues that the categories of the understanding, which are transcendental and *a priori*, not only make experience possible but also mean that we are not confined within experience: 'In the consciousness of our existence there is contained something *a priori*, which can serve to determine our existence – the complete determination of which is only possible in sensible terms – as being related, in respect of a certain inner faculty, to a non-sensible intelligible world.'[17] The limit of experience also touches on the outside, the ideas of reason and the voice of moral conscience which regulate our conduct. Kant takes reason to the limit to find a reason that can regulate us; in contrast Bataille takes reason to the limit to derange reason and shatter its law-giving powers: 'Without the support of reason we don't reach "dark incandescence".'[18] What is odd is that both Bataille and Kant have a thought of the limit as an opening and also as a difference that is unstable. This is why Foucault connects these two thinkers together, despite the fact that they are so radically different in

their lives (Kant led a notoriously regulated and routine life) and
their styles of thinking.

Kant opened the thinking of the limit in philosophy but then he
folded this limit back into the anthropological question of man. In
The Order of Things Foucault describes how Kant's 'three critical
questions (What can I know? What must I do? What am I
permitted to hope?) then found themselves referred to a fourth
and inscribed, as it were, 'to its account': *Was ist der Mensch?*'[19]
By moving from the question 'what is the limit?' to the question
'what is man?', Kant absorbed and obscured the distinction
between the empirical and transcendental *within* the human
being. What Bataille did in *Eroticism* was to unfold this folding of
the limit within the human by reopening the limit of the body.
Bataille poses the diversity of the data of anthropology as a
discipline against a philosophical anthropology which constructs
an image of man as a singular being. However, that opening has
to be a double gesture because not only has the problem of the
limit been closed within a Kantian anthropology but it has also
been closed within a Hegelian dialectics, and we have been left in
'the confused sleep of dialectics and of anthropology' (Foucault
in CR, 30).

This is all the more ironic because Hegel's dialectical reading
of the limit had developed from a very powerful critique of Kant
and in particular the tendency in Kant to limit the limit. Hegel's
devastating rejoinder to Kant is to argue that 'It is asserted that
the limitation *cannot* be transcended. To make such an assertion
is to be unaware that the very fact that something is determined as
a limitation implies that limitation is already transcended.'[20]
Hegel argues that for Kant to set a limit requires that he already
has to know what is beyond the limit and that this means that the
limit of reason is actually no such thing. Kant sets up the
distinction between a reason employed legitimately within the
limit and an unknowable beyond the limit. Hegel's response is to
regard this 'unknowable' beyond as knowable by reason *as*
unknowable. Rather than the limit between them forming an
uncrossable boundary it places them in a contradiction whereby
reason can expand itself and draw in what lies beyond its limit.
This is very close to the effect of transgression on the limit; in the
same way that transgression both opens the limit and makes the
limit possible it also exceeds it. In this sense then Hegel is
reopening the problem of the limit that Kant has already closed
off in anthropology.

The problem with Hegel's dialectical reading of the limit is
twofold: firstly, it underestimates the sensitivity of Kant's thought
of the limit, and secondly, it conducts its own closure of the limit.
I want to concentrate more on this second problem because it

demonstrates how a limit can be opened and then rapidly closed in a way that is very close to transgression but importantly different from it. It is different in the way it treats difference because in treating the difference between the two sides of the limit as contradiction Hegel can introduce a stability that transgression will destroy. The difference between the two sides of the limit is absorbed within the dialectical reading: 'Difference as such is already *implicitly* contradiction; for it is the *unity* of sides which are, only in so far as they are *not one* – and it is the *separation* of sides which are, only as separated *in the same relation*.'[21] By reading difference as contradiction Hegel can hold the two sides of the limit together in a relatively stable arrangement. This is because for Hegel, 'The resolved contradiction is therefore ground, essence as unity of the positive and negative.'[22]

Hegel moves from a difference which destabilises the limit to a difference determined as the difference between the two sides of the limit, and finally to this difference being a contradiction between the two sides. By determining difference as contradiction Hegel admits difference but only as a difference that is on the way to being resolved as a new ground. This is the dialectical operation on the limit in which Kant's opening is held further open, it is expanded beyond the limit, only to be drawn back into a more complete *unity*. If Bataille exists between Kant and Hegel he exists between these two concepts of the limit and of difference with the a-concept of transgression. Transgression awakens Kant from his anthropological slumber and at the same time resists the dialectical reading of the limit through transgression. In reopening the problem of the limit that Kant had closed it follows in the footsteps of Hegel's critique of Kant but, once again, Hegel 'did not know to what extent he was right' (BR, 289). Hegel did not follow the movement beyond the limit *far enough*; he could not trace it as a spiral of transgression but only as the forward dialectical movement of reason. Hegel violently imposed a meaning of the difference that he uncovered in Kant, turning it into a difference between two sides rather than a difference that could disorientate the very idea of the limit, 'sides', and contradiction. The difference put into play by transgression in the act of crossing the taboo is one that does not settle into a dialectical arrangement, or one that does so only at the cost of a violence which destroys the very effect of that movement.

Bataille himself misunderstood the play of transgression and taboo when he reduced it to a dialectical operation, but he revealed how much he had learned from Hegel in trying to articulate a thought of transgression and difference. That is what makes Bataille's relationship to Hegel at once so close and so distant. It is also what resists the usual terms of description of relationships between thinkers; Bataille is not making a critique of Hegel but neither is he simply extending Hegel's work. He is neither a disciple of Hegel nor is he an anti-Hegelian; he evades these categorisations. He takes Hegel further by plunging him into the movement of transgression, to the point where reason becomes lost on the spiral of transgression. Here the limit is radically displaced from philosophy, whether Kantian or Hegelian, as philosophy itself disintegrates in the play of trans-gression. The displacement of the limit through a difference that cannot be controlled by philosophy is also what displaces the dominance of philosophy as a discourse and exposes it to the effects of other discourses, literature for example. In Bataille's 'literary' texts there is a circulation of difference at work which threatens the order of philosophy as well as threatening the stability of literature itself.

Foucault's spatial description of transgression should not lead us to conclude that transgression is only a spatial effect. The movement of transgression not only disrupts spatial orderings but also temporal orderings. This effect is visible in transgression's resistance to historical location; in Bataille's writing it is inserted between Kant and Hegel but also revealed as implicit in their works. Transgression is what opens their thought and for Bataille it is the opening of thought as a movement which is also the opening of space and time. By opening space and time through difference Bataille's thought of difference disorients space and time, as we saw with his Nietzschean disorientation of the summit. This will have a profound influence on poststructuralism as a thought of difference, and it allows us to read Bataille and poststructuralism as thinking a difference that resists spatial or temporal categorisation. The resistance to categorisation extends to the categorisation of poststructuralism as an intellectual movement with clear temporal and spatial limits and of Bataille as belonging to that movement as a precursor.

Jacques Derrida coined the neologism *différance* to describe a difference that marks a difference and a deferral, that is both 'spatial' and 'temporal', and also marks 'the becoming-time of space and the becoming-space of time'.[23] This re-inscription of difference is closely dependent on Bataille's inscription of a difference that resists reduction to the Hegelian dialectic. Post-structuralism initially drew on this thinking of difference but as it has become constituted as a 'discipline' or a 'method' this thought of difference is in danger of being minimised, as Bataille is minimised by being confined to the prehistory of poststructural-ism. The tendency has often been to reduce difference to a difference between different identities rather than a difference being heterogeneous to identity, and as being what leads to the collapse of identity. Bataille can help us reopen this heterogeneous difference which still lies in all identities and will not settle into the difference between identities.

This problematic reduction of difference is even visible within Foucault's analysis of Bataille's writings. Despite the fact that Foucault's writings open the possibilities of seeing Bataille as a reader of difference, they also close these possibilities when they attempt to locate his thought historically. In the 1963 essay 'A Preface to Transgression', Bataille's thought lies in the *future*: 'The language in which transgression will find its space and the illumination of its being lies almost entirely in the future' (CR, 27). However, in the first volume of *The History of Sexuality* (1976) Foucault now implies that Bataille is bound to the past. No longer is transgression a thought of the future but Bataille's description of sexuality involves 'a symbolics of blood' that belongs to the pre-modern: 'To conceive of the category of the sexual in terms of the law, death, blood, and sovereignty – whatever the references to Sade and Bataille, and however one might gauge their "subversive" influence – is in the last analysis a historical "retro-version".'[24] By trying to provide a historical location for Bataille's thought Foucault is forced into a paradox: what was once the thought of the future is now the thought of the past. This paradox, the failure of temporal and historical grounding that Foucault tries to impose on Bataille, can allow us to read Bataille differently through a difference that does not belong to this linear ordering of time: past/present/future.

Transgression and difference open the possibility of another time: 'Ecstatic time can only find itself in the vision of things that puerile chance causes brusquely to appear: cadavers, nudity, explosions, spilled blood, abysses, sunbursts, and thunder' (VE, 200). This is not an alternative model of time but a possibility that ruptures the order of time without reordering itself. It is an experience of chance that Bataille regarded as central to existence itself. Time is usually read as an ordering of causal chains which are opposed to chance or which integrate chance within historical narratives. Bataille's fictional narratives explode this ordered narration through their inscription of chance and difference. For Bataille time emerges in all its violence as a disorder which cannot be organised: 'Because of the Revolution, divine authority ceases to found power; authority no longer belongs to God, *but to time*, whose free exuberance puts kings to death, to time incarnated today in the explosive tumult of peoples' (VE, 200, italics added). The 'model' of time is the rupture of revolution, the destruction of any model.

Bataille's is close to Benjamin's considerations in the 'Theses on the Philosophy of History'. Benjamin presents revolution as the rupture of 'homogenous, empty time'[25] and he writes that 'The awareness that they are about to make the continuum of history explode is characteristic of the revolutionary classes at the moment of their action'.[26] Like Benjamin, Bataille resists historicism, making him out of step with our time where historicism has become a dominant mode in many disciplines, in particular in the humanities. It may be that thinkers like Benjamin and Bataille are becoming objects of interest because of their resistance to the dominance of historicism. Historicism tries to assimilate them by locating their resistance historically and thereby neutralising this resistance, but both Benjamin and Bataille inscribe a rupture that is irreducible to historicism. Bataille breaks up time from 'within' through a difference that cannot be assimilated to history and, therefore, he can never be completely historicised. He traces the limit of the historical in an experience of transgression that crosses over that limit.

Transgression draws us into a thought of difference by the force of opening that it inscribes. Bataille is one of the first to outline a difference that cannot be structured by an opposition or absorbed within logic. The impact of this difference reverberates in post-structuralism but also has to be uncovered there to activate it as a thought of difference. That is why we must read Bataille *with* poststructuralism, to experience transgression as what disorients us by displacing God, the universals of philosophy and even knowledge itself. This is a result of the effects of non-logical difference, which produce the turbulent movements of Bataille's writings. To fail to read difference in Bataille is to fail to read Bataille. Transgression connects impossibility to difference and it also opens the problem of time, not least the time of Bataille's own writings. In the next chapter these questions of difference and the time of Bataille's writings will be taken further so we can consider the fate of Bataille's writings. The guiding question will be, to what extent can we consider Bataille to be, as Leslie Hill describes Blanchot, our 'extreme contemporary'?[27]

CHAPTER 5

The Accursed Share

To the end of his life Bataille remained 'the sorcerer's apprentice' conjuring forces that were always out of his control, provoking turbulent affects that would sweep him away in their tide. It is 'the accursed share' (*la part maudite*) which is his final re-description of these forces: 'tracing the exhausting detours of exuberance' (AS1, 13). The accursed share was the excess energy, the remainder, and an irrecuperable difference, which could not be controlled within any system: 'Like an unbroken animal that cannot be trained, it is this energy that destroys us; it is we who pay the price of the inevitable explosion' (AS1, 24; BR, 185). Bataille's most substantial work would be devoted to it – the three volumes of *The Accursed Share*, which he considered to be the most important statement of his thought. Despite the fragmentary and sometimes sketchy nature of Bataille's writings he also has a powerful impulse to create totalities, and *The Accursed Share* is the most complete example of this impulse. It repeats and gathers a great deal of Bataille's earlier writings within a framework that constantly tries to describe what the accursed share is. This is what makes it from the beginning a divided work, because as Bataille remarks 'the announcement of a vast project is always its betrayal' (AS, 10). To try to put difference in the frame is to betray difference as that which opens the frame to the outside.

Jean-Joseph Goux offers an accurate assessment when he remarks that '*La Part Maudite*, Bataille's most systematic and long-considered work, provokes in the reader an inescapable feeling of mingled enthusiasm and disappointment' (CR, 196). As a work it was a failure in commercial terms; the first volume sold few copies and the later two volumes would not be published during his lifetime. It did not have the intellectual success that Bataille had hoped either. It was lost in the rise of Sartrean existentialism to intellectual dominance. Sartre had already indicated his hostility to Bataille in a review of *Inner Experience* when he labelled Bataille 'the new mystic'.[1] Sartrean humanism could not tolerate Bataille's impersonality or his tracing of an exuberance that does not belong to any human subject. However, *The Accursed Share* was not only a failure because of a hostile intellectual context, but also because of the failure of the work itself.

It is a divided work: divided between a desire for completion, power and mastery and the necessity of collapse, ruin and loss; divided between an intellectual exhilaration and a pedantic establishing of academic credentials; divided between its failure at the time and its posthumous success. Bataille recognised the difficult, divided and unsatisfactory nature of *The Accursed Share*, remarking that the very range of the books' concerns means that 'The result is that such a book, being of interest to everyone, could well be of interest to no one' (AS1, 10). The divisions went further than the range of the book, but lie in the profound difficulty for Bataille to find a framework to describe what is irreducible to any framework: the accursed share. Derrida has pointed out that Bataille is limited by his own 'conjectural approximations' (CR, 135 n68) for the accursed share. Bataille is constantly trying to find *examples* of the accursed share, to prove that the accursed share exists and is not just a fantasy.

However, to provide examples of the accursed share limits the effects of the accursed share by reducing it to a limited example. The 'conjectural approximations' in which Bataille indulges are, as we will see, severely limited in terms of what Bataille is trying to trace in the accursed share. They risk reducing the difference of the accursed share by inscribing it into the identity of an example. As the accursed share is the sign of a difference that resists identity, a difference that emerges from the concrete but is irreducible to an example, then any exemplification will also be a limitation. In fact, as we will see, the accursed share has no examples as such and Bataille is attempting to present a thought of that which is without example. This is a thought that cannot be contained within any framework or even within thought itself.

Bataille names it *general economy*, as 'the notion of a "general economy" in which the "expenditure" (the "consumption") of wealth, rather than production, was the primary object' (AS1, 9). General economy is a differential economy that displaces the frameworks into which Bataille tries to hold it by tracing the detours of an excessive force which transgresses the limit of the frame. The accursed share disrupts the discourse it is being sketched out by and for Bataille 'the object of my research cannot be distinguished *from the subject at its boiling point*' (AS1, 10), but how to present this thought in a book, and a theoretical book at that? This is the problem of writing a book *about* general economy which itself will be an example *of* general economy.

Bataille struggles with the problem of writing about general economy, and this can be seen in the different frameworks he deploys in trying to grasp what is always slipping out of his control. From his early political account to his later scientific account of the accursed share Bataille is led by the *impossibility* of producing an account of it into a thought of difference which would try to explain this impossibility. It is by sketching a thought of difference that he will have a decisive influence, and this influence is reflected in his fate and in the fate of the accursed share. If the accursed share is out of Bataille's control then it is also out of the control of all those who try to write on Bataille. Although there are many interpretations of it, the accursed share eludes these interpretations. Once again we should be reminded of how closely Bataille linked the fate of his work to that of Nietzsche's because in both cases the freedom of the writing lends itself the grossest misinterpretations. That is why both Bataille's and Nietzsche's writings actually demand a cautious reading to do justice to the freedom of the writing rather than destroying that freedom by imposing a stable interpretation on it. In this reading we must follow Bataille through the 'exhausting detours' of expenditure to realise that the detour is the very structure of general economy, the very effect of the accursed share.

The Notion of Expenditure

The first step to take is to go back to the essay which sets out the research programme Bataille would develop in *The Accursed Share*, 'The Notion of Expenditure' (January 1933) (VE, 116–29; BR, 167–81). This precise summary of Bataille's economic thought is far more accessible than the sometimes clumsy search for intellectual foundations in *The Accursed Share*. 'The Notion of Expenditure' is charged with the revolutionary fervour of the time and Bataille's faith in mass insurrection. So, rather than being a work of 'political economy', as *The Accursed Share* claims to be, 'The Notion of Expenditure' is a work of revolutionary critique. Perhaps Bataille's energetic reflections on the crisis of value were influenced as much by the 1929 Wall Street crash and the subsequent world depression as they were by the anthropological data on which Bataille drew. When Bataille wrote 'A human society can have … an *interest* in considerable losses, in catastrophes that, *while conforming to well-defined needs*, provoke tumultuous depressions, crises of dread, and, in the final analysis, a certain orgiastic state' (VE, 117; BR, 168) he could just as well have been describing the economic crises of the 1920s and 1930s as the massive expenditures of so-called 'primitive' societies.

Bataille wanted to take these crises further and to encourage the transformation of the psychological states induced by these crises from dread to an 'orgiastic state'. This was a political task because it involved the critique of a political and economic system in which a financial crisis simply increased wealth for some and

poverty for others. This is where the decisive difference lay
between modern societies and the so-called 'primitive' societies.
In those 'primitive' societies a crisis leads to the 'delirium of the
festival' (VE, 122; BR, 173) where social divisions are affirmed
but economic divisions shattered by mass gift giving: *potlatch*.
Wealth would be expended and lost in a round of exchanges
where each giver had to give more to demonstrate their superior
status. By contrast the crises of the capitalist world simply spurred
further accumulation and increased economic divisions. As this
economic division became sharper Bataille saw the possibility of
the working class using a modern *potlatch* as a political weapon.

Deprived of economic wealth the working class could only
assert its social power by humiliating the bourgeoisie through the
appropriation of its wealth *and* its immediate expenditure. Unlike
the bourgeoisie where 'wealth is now displayed behind closed
doors, in accordance with depressing and boring conventions'
(VE, 124; BR, 175) the proletariat can restore the generosity and
nobility which have disappeared from modern life. Although this
was consciously expressed in Marxist terms Bataille saw this
seizing of the means of production not as the prelude to a better
and more productive socialist society but as the occasion for a
festival of expenditure: 'Class struggle, on the contrary, becomes
the grandest form of social expenditure when it is taken up again
and developed, this time on the part of the workers, and on such
a scale that it threatens the very existence of the masters' (VE,
126; BR, 178). Bataille would have agreed with the Italian
communist Amadeo Bordiga (1889–1970) that 'One does not
build communism',[2] as for him at that time communism was an
experience of violent consumption.

Instead of exploring communism as accumulation Bataille
chooses to examine it as a principle of loss; therefore communism
is no longer a better or more rationally organised economic form
than capitalism (as so many Marxists have argued) but a more
irrational one. Marxism can no longer be reduced to being the
mirror image of capitalism or restricted to being a new form of
political economy. Bataille's communism is a heterogeneous
communism of what is *excluded* by capitalism: 'It excludes in
principle *non-productive expenditure*' (VE, 117; BR, 168). Of
course, non-productive expenditure can be seen as another name
for the accursed share, from which Bataille will try to lift the curse
of exclusion in his later work. Already in 'The Notion of
Expenditure' Bataille tries to develop an initial characterisation of
this excluded non-productive expenditure by marking out its
difference. The first distinction he draws is the one between
production and consumption, and, as we have seen, Bataille is
already trying to displace the emphasis that both capitalism and

socialism place on production. However, it is not enough to move towards consumption because there are two forms of consumption. There is productive consumption, broadly speaking consumption which serves the reproduction of the system or the consumption necessary to survival rather than life. This form of consumption is actually directed towards production, it is subject to the delay and detours necessary to reproduction. There is, however, another form of consumption, unproductive expenditure which is an end in itself.

Unproductive expenditure is the principle of loss which is excluded by modern society but which still lives on within it, revealed in the traces and remnants of the great exercises of expenditure of the past and of 'primitive' societies. Bataille gives a number of examples of the survival of processes of sumptuary expenditure, for instance in the continuing fascination we have with jewels. These functionally useless items, except for decoration, lead to massive expenditures both in their recovery from the earth and in their sale. For Bataille they have the profound unconscious meaning of 'cursed matter that flows from a wound' (VE, 119; BR, 170). Jewels, especially the great diamonds, are often rumoured to be cursed or possessed of a malign power to excite greed and violence. Wilkie Collins's *The Moonstone* (1868) is the classic fictional exploration of this 'cursed matter' with its story of a fabulous and uncanny diamond circulating through multiple acts of theft and betrayal before it finally returns to that locus of fantasies of a 'primitive' Orient – India.[3] Bataille's other examples include games, both the expense of putting on sporting events and the gambling and excessive consumption they provoke (a tendency which has increased since Bataille wrote), art and sacrifice. In each example Bataille finds that we still remain attached to this principle of loss, of non-productive expenditures which remain more and more confined to the margins of existence.

This marginal existence of the principle of loss conceals the fact that in reality non-productive expenditures are not a minor economic phenomenon but the very origin of economy. Bataille's turn to 'primitive' societies is not a romantic projection of the 'noble savage' who exemplifies unproductive expenditure but an act of what Goux calls 'ethnological decentring' (CR, 196). By returning to a different possibility of economy Bataille dislodges our tendency to project capitalism as the eternal model of economy. Instead, through examining the past economic institution of *potlatch* described by anthropologists we discover that 'The secondary character of production and acquisition in relation to expenditure appears most clearly in primitive economic institutions, since exchange is still treated as a sumptuary loss of ceded objects: thus at its *base* exchange presents itself as a process of expenditure, over which a process of acquisition has developed' (VE, 121; BR, 172). For Bataille economy, and especially modern restricted economics in its capitalist form, is secondary to the primacy of this process of expenditure and loss.

Economy originates not in accumulation but in *loss*, which is visible in 'the archaic form of exchange' (VE, 121; BR, 172), *potlatch*. Drawing on the work of Marcel Mauss in *The Gift*[4] Bataille describes *potlatch* as an act of gift-giving which is a challenge and demands a greater gift in return. This practice, found among North-western Native American tribes, is a form of exchange that is based on loss or as Bataille would claim *'limitless loss'* (VE, 123; BR, 174). However, Bataille recognises that while this competitive gift-giving may lead to material loss it is also organised around a gain in social power: 'It is the constitution of a positive property of loss – from which spring nobility, honour, and rank in a hierarchy – that gives the institution its significant value' (VE, 122; BR, 173). The chief or the tribe which gives the larger gift and outbids its rival gains power over them, so loss already appears to exist within a dialectic of accumulation. Bataille resists this reading by stressing that loss comes first and is primary to the process as its trigger. He also stresses that this social dominance based on loss, the giving away of wealth, resists the accumulation of absolute economic power over others and their destitution. Finally, Bataille is interested in how this process can always go out of control and lead to mass destruction, as when a tribe destroys its entire village to place its rival in an inescapable debt to it. No matter how much the *potlatch* can lead to the accumulation of status and wealth it is always inhabited by the ghost of absolute loss.

At the same time the principle of loss is also at the basis of the restriction of economy to accumulation, and we cannot strictly separate *potlatch* from accumulation. The difference that defines unproductive expenditure is actually not as stable as Bataille's confident assertions sometimes claim. It is because *potlatch* cannot be separated from accumulation that it haunts accumulation as an unlimited loss. However, accumulative capitalism both represses and limits the principle of loss and of origin of economy in that loss. We have reached the situation where 'Today the great and free forms of unproductive expenditure have disappeared' (VE, 124; BR, 175). An economy which is open to loss and organised through the principle of loss, which as Bataille would later say is in touch with general economy, has been eroded and replaced by a market economy oriented towards accumulation. Even in feudal times, as Bataille found with Gilles de Rais, there was still expenditure by the aristocracy on spectacle and war which wasted immense amounts of wealth. With the rise of capitalism and its ethic of accumulation there is now a far more restricted expenditure, and Bataille argues that the bourgeoisie has decided 'only to *spend for itself*' (VE, 124; BR, 176). This erosion of free expenditure is clearly visible in the erosion of gift-giving in contemporary life.

Adorno has explored this decline of the principle of gift-giving in very Bataillean terms in an entry called 'Articles may not be exchanged' from *Minima Moralia* (1951). For Adorno the fact that 'We are forgetting how to give presents'[5] can best be seen in the invention of special gift items and more particularly in the right to exchange an unwanted gift, 'which signifies to the recipient: take this, it's all yours, do what you like with it; if you don't want it, that's all the same to me, get something else instead'.[6] This decline of gift-giving under modern capitalism is not a trivial matter because, when the capacity for giving is lost in people, 'In them wither the irreplaceable faculties which cannot flourish in the isolated cell of pure inwardness, but only in live contact with the warmth of things.'[7] Bataille would agree that the intimacy of a free exchange based on loss, risk, and a challenge that involves the donor giving himself or herself with the gift, has been lost. Writing after the experience of the Shoah and witnessing the rise of capitalist consumerism in the United States Adorno was, understandably, pessimistic about any possibility of the rediscovery of this warmth. Bataille, writing in a time of capitalist crisis and revolutionary fervour, was optimistic about the political possibility of restoring gift-giving. As we saw he regarded *potlatch* as the very possibility of a new form of revolution, a revolution of festival and expenditure.

Bataille strongly believed that the process of the bourgeoisie spending for itself would lead to the increasing immiseration of the proletariat and the necessity of revolution. Although he had already noted that the bourgeoisie was engaging in limited processes of amelioration ('welfare'), Bataille thought that these attempts to limit and heal the social division of class simply would lead to further humiliation and eventually an outburst of revolutionary expenditure. They remained pathetic stopgap measures which refused to confront the proletariat in a game of agonistic exchange but instead patronised it and left it dependent. This limited amelioration would also always leave an abject segment of the population which could confront bourgeois dominance. Bataille argued that in the United States, where experiments in welfare had gone furthest at the time, African-Americans were left in this abject position and so offered the best possibility of political rebellion (VE, 102).

Bataille's political reading of the gift as a gesture of class struggle, as a gesture that would resist the poverty of everyday life (in all its forms), exerted a subterranean political influence. Greil Marcus has traced the influence of Bataille's 'gnostic materialism' (VE, 45–52; BR, 160–4) through the radical groups, the Lettrist International (LI) and the Situationist International (1957–72). The LI would name its journal *Potlatch* and call for the sort of total festival revolution of which Bataille had dreamed. Marcus suggests that 'Bataille was laying down a challenge; twenty-one years later, the LI picked it up.'[8] Bataille's revolutionary *potlatch* is also at work in the Situationist International, the revolutionary group most renowned and reviled for its role in the May '68 events in France.[9] The events are closest to Bataille's vision of the revolution as 'an outlet for collective impulses' (VE, 101), but Bataille's influence on the Situationists goes further.

It can be seen most clearly in the Situationist analysis of the Watts riots which broke out in Los Angeles in 1965, published as 'The Decline and Fall of the Spectacle-Commodity Economy' (1966). The violence and looting which characterised the riot drew opprobrium from both left and right but, for the Situationists, marked the radical clarity of the most excluded element of American society – African-Americans. They wrote that in the moment of the riot 'real desires begin to be expressed in festival, in playful self-assertion, in the *potlatch* of destruction'.[10] At the most extreme radicalisation of the Popular Front in 1936 Bataille wrote of 'human reality in the street' (VE, 164), in Watts it was *potlatch* in the streets. From 1936 to 1965 to 1991, and another riot (or rebellion) erupted in Los Angeles with more 'senseless' violence, looting and mass destruction. What seemed most irrational to many commentators on the events was the self-destructive nature of what happened as people destroyed their own communities rather than strike out at the affluent areas around them. Here, however, could be read another sign of the *potlatch*, where in the act of self-destruction a challenge is thrown down for the dominant powers to respond to. Of course, the challenge was not picked up, at least not directly, and the poor were left to face the further militarisation of policing, the flight of employment and services, and their own destructive impulses were turned inwards to self-destruction (gangs and drugs).

What I want to suggest is that this political reading of expenditure and the gift, both by Bataille in the first place and by those who consciously or not followed after him, is both powerful and limited. It gives Bataille's writing clarity and all the force of a violent demand for revolution. Also, it remains a necessary critique of capitalism and a contribution to the future possibilities of communism (all the more so with the disintegration of the existing accumulative models of communism). However, already by the end of the 'The Notion of Expenditure' Bataille is suggesting a shift away from political concerns to the more general problems posed by expenditure, including the problem of *how* it is possible to write about it. If 'human life cannot in any way be limited to the closed systems assigned to it by reasonable conceptions' (VE, 128; BR, 180) then it cannot be limited either to the closed systems of politics. Expenditure will continue to have political and economic effects but it cannot be determined and controlled politically. Bataille is starting to elaborate a different way of thinking of the energies of expenditure, one in terms of '*states of excitation*' (VE, 128; BR, 180) or in terms of matter 'defined as the *nonlogical difference* ...' (VE, 129; BR, 180). These are hints of a new thinking of expenditure and a new thinking of difference that is out of political, logical, philosophical or economic control. It is at the limit of any 'closed system', heterogeneous to any system, and will be taken up again after the war in *The Accursed Share*.

The Solar Economy

In Bataille's political detour we have already seen how he multiplies distinctions to analyse what he would come to call the accursed share: the distinction between production and consumption, and then the distinction within consumption itself between productive and unproductive expenditure. Although his political account requires the stability of these distinctions the origin of economy also blurs these distinctions through the instability of a nonlogical difference. *The Accursed Share* begins with its own set of distinctions, which indicate its departure from 'The Notion of Expenditure'. Instead of non-productive expenditure being the result of a principle of loss originating in a human drive best exemplified in 'primitive' societies, non-productive expenditure is now the result of a 'circuit of cosmic energy' (AS1, 26; BR, 186–7). Bataille is distinguishing between the limits of the 'closed system' of the terrestrial biosphere and an excess that lies outside those limits: 'Solar energy is the source of life's exuberant development' (AS1, 28; BR, 189). The opposition is now between the limited space of the earth and the unlimited gift of the sun rather than between the bourgeoisie and the proletariat or between accumulation and *potlatch*.

Bataille's 'theory' (which never achieves theoretical closure) is a weird combination of the scientific knowledge of the time and the sun-worshipping sacrifices of the Aztecs that he wrote about in detail (AS1, 45–61). It is an unstable agglomeration of science, myth, ethnography, economy and philosophy which goes back at least to Bataille's 'excremental fantasy' of the pineal eye. There, as we saw in Chapter 1, Bataille traced the connection between the sun, the upturned eye and the anus (VE, 79–90). In the 1920s and 1930s this would form the basis for Bataille's ecstatic personal myth: 'And when I scream I AM THE SUN an integral erection results, because the verb *to be* is the vehicle of amorous frenzy' (VE, 5). Bataille had already distanced himself from taking this fantasy seriously in the 1930s, and *The Accursed Share* can also be regarded as part of this same process. Now the powerful place of the sun in Bataille's thought is justified in terms of a '*cosmically expanded* energy ecology' (Habermas, CR, 186), rather than through the appearance of the pineal eye. The sun always has a key force for Bataille and it is surprising that, to my knowledge, there has been no account of its changing effects in Bataille's work.

Although Bataille is now attempting a more 'scientific' analysis of the sun as a source of energy, *The Accursed Share* still retains some of the strangeness of the myth of the pineal eye. Certainly Bataille's 'cosmically expanded energy ecology' has few parallels in modern European thought, except for the later work of the renegade psychoanalyst Wilhelm Reich (1897–1957). Reich believed he had discovered a cosmically circulating form of energy – orgone. Although Reich had attempted to subject orgone to scientific measurement and testing it also had a semi-mystical character. Blockages of orgone or deadly orgone energy (DOR) were responsible for all individual, social and natural pathologies and Reich attempted to design machines to destroy DOR. However, Reich descended into paranoia and madness, partly due to persecution, harassment and eventual imprisonment by the US government during the 'red scares' of the 1950s.[11]

What Bataille and Reich share is the attempt to think energy at a cosmic level operating through all phenomena, and they both link this energy to sexuality (probably because they are both indebted to Freud's energy-based model of libido). However, despite these similarities there are critical differences between Bataille and Reich which are decisive. The first is that Bataille does not consider the accursed share as another form of energy which could be subject to scientific measurement, rather the accursed share is an excess of energy which applies to any system. Bataille does not share Reich's search for a scientific inscription or recording of energy, which may have contributed to Reich's paranoia as he sought out proof of this energy which 'existed' as the hidden meaning of all energy. Bataille and Reich also differ on the nature of the relation between energy and the sexual. For Reich the model of free-flowing energy is an orgasmic heterosex-

ual relationship, but because Bataille is interested in the excess of
energy he analyses unproductive 'perverse' sexuality which does
not lead to reproduction. These differences are visible in Bataille's
very different style of writing and research which does not give in
to the paranoia which destroyed Reich but analyses the accursed
share as that which 'requires thinking on a level with a play of
forces based on the laws that govern us' (AS1, 12).

Bataille offers a novel theory which is both specific to particular
energy systems and affects all energy systems, a 'general
economy'. It is a very different work from 'The Notion of
Expenditure', which was written in a time of crisis and responded
to the vertigo of expenditure with political action. *The Accursed
Share* is a book of a different time, of the aftermath of war and the
post-war reconstruction of Europe by the United States rather
than of immediate crisis. The difference is evident when Bataille
looks favourably on the Marshall Plan, whereby the USA gave aid
to Western Europe, as a model for 'expenditures without return'
(AS1, 169–90). Here Bataille demonstrates his political naivety
with one of his most unlikely 'conjectural approximations'
(Derrida) of the accursed share. The Marshall Plan was a 'gift'
which involved certain conditions, not least because it operated as
means of support for European states that might be tempted to
enter the Soviet sphere of influence. Already the Cold War was as
much an economic as a political conflict, something that Bataille
did not recognise. *The Accursed Share* is at its most disappointing
in its concrete political proposals, which reveal Bataille's failure to
analyse the political effects of the 'gift'.

However, there is one interesting connection between Bataille's
new theory and the emerging post-war economic system. At
Bretton Woods in 1944 the idea of a *world* economy gained shape
with the founding of the International Monetary Fund (IMF) and
the World Bank. Bataille's description of energy flows was
structured by the idea of a *closed* world economic system which
can only draw 'free' energy from outside itself. This could be
understood as an ambivalent resistance and reaction to this
emerging global economy. Bataille is implicitly suggesting that an
economic model based on the world is a limited model and he
regards the earth's 'biosphere' as a finite system (AS1, 29; BR,
189). Moreover, his thought is transfixed by the limits of
terrestrial space, so his work may also be a distorted reflection of
the world market. Nowhere does Bataille engage directly with
these questions, and I am not suggesting that he is reducible to
the ideological model of the world market. Later I will explore
how Bataille's 'economic' thought resists such reductions.

To this closed system of the earth's surface Bataille opposes the
free expenditure of the sun. It is the sun which is now the model

for the 'gift without return': 'The radiation of the sun, which dispenses energy – wealth – without any return' (AS1, 28; 189). It is this gift of energy which explains the excess energy circulating on the surface of the earth. The presence of this excess energy is what leads to the demand that this excess be dealt with, precisely because it cannot be completely absorbed within the existing system:

> The living organism, in a situation determined by the play of energy on the surface of the globe ordinarily receives more energy than is necessary for maintaining life; the excess energy (wealth) can be used for the growth of a system (e.g. an organism); if the system can no longer grow, or if the excess cannot be completely absorbed in its growth, it must necessarily be lost without profit; it must be spent, willingly or not, gloriously or catastrophically. (AS1, 21; BR, 184)

And, of course, Bataille is suggesting it would be better spent willingly and gloriously than unwillingly and catastrophically. The situation which produces the accursed share depends on two pre-suppositions: the unlimited energy of the sun and some limit to growth. For Bataille that real limit of growth 'is the size of terrestrial space' (AS1, 29; BR, 189); as organisms which will eventually run out of space cover the surface of the globe, this lack of space will limit their capacity for growth and so an excess will result.

Eventually 'the pressure exerted by the exuberance of life' (AS1, 38; BR, 196) will find its limit and crash through that limit with a surplus of useless energy. Bennington has pointed out that Bataille's opposition of the freely giving sun and the limited space of the earth cannot be sustained because the sun can only appear as freely giving from the restricted space of the earth. This would mean that general economy is actually only possible because of the restrictions of the earth's surface, and thereby that general economy is really a restricted economy.[12] These presuppositions of a finite terrestrial space and the infinite energy of the sun are limits which are ruined by the circulations of energy that Bataille traces. Bennington suggests that Bataille is caught up in the tangles which structure these two opposed limits, a tangled 'stricture' which ties the opposition together and ruins the possibility of either a pure gift or a purely limited space.[13] Bataille's own text bears this out as this rather simplistic initial set-up is complicated by the 'wild exuberance' (AS1, 33; BR, 192) of this 'circuit of cosmic energy' (AS1, 26; BR, 186–7). Rather than an opposition between the freely giving sun as general economy and the finite space of the earth as restricted economy Bataille suggests that general economy is a differential economy, existing in and through the unstable differences between forces.

Bataille is concerned with '*a play of forces*' and it is the play of these forces which generates the accursed share rather than one supposedly stable energy source. In his desire to *prove* the existence of the accursed share Bataille has reduced the accursed share to a perception from a restricted economy. But his writing also offers a different possibility, a different account of general economy as emerging through difference, the difference that restricted economies cannot control. A great deal turns on the interpretation of Bataille's statement that 'Changing from the perspectives of *restrictive* economy to those of *general* economy actually accomplishes a Copernican transformation: a reversal of thinking – and of ethics' (AS1, 25; BR, 186). Is this transformation a transformation from one type of economy to another, from restricted economy to general economy, or is it a transformation of perspective on to one economy?

I think that Bataille desired the first transformation from one type of economy to another. The sun figures in this desire as the *impossible* place of pure general economy, impossible to exist on or to gaze upon directly for human beings. The impossibility of inhabiting this position is, I think, recognition by Bataille of the impossibility of general economy as a pure economy. It cannot be another type of economy based on the sun but instead it is the Other of economy. So, while Bataille desires general economy as a pure 'gift without return', as the source and terminus of the accursed share, he also has a different thinking of general economy as a transformative force. General economy would no longer be a place to be occupied outside of restricted economy but a fleeting and effervescent effect of the swirling turbulence of energy flows that constantly puncture limits, create openings and new limits.

Bataille makes explicit the impossibility of ever making distinct the difference between general and restricted economy, or productive and unproductive expenditure: 'Real life, composed of all sorts of expenditures, knows nothing of purely productive expenditure; in actuality, it knows nothing of purely non-productive expenditure either' (AS1, 12). The contamination cuts both ways; there is no stability to productive expenditure or to non-productive expenditure and they are mixed up in an undecidable fashion. We have no choice between two different economies, but only the economy in which the productive is haunted by becoming non-productive and the non-productive by becoming productive, with shifts and changes between them that have to be analysed in an open assessment of the current play of forces; an assessment which must be open and radically

contingent because it is always subject to further alteration
through the play of excess which it traces. This change of
perspectives on economy will be very influential on poststructuralism; Derrida remarks that 'General economy also supposes
something other than productivity and, in the economic process,
it even incorporates (without being capable of integrating it) a
certain unproductiveness or even non-productivity – something
heterogeneous both to productivity and unproductiveness.'[14]
This heterogeneous economy is an economy indebted, not just in
name, to Bataille's Copernican transformation of our concept of
economy.

It is striking how Bataille plays with difference and how that
difference constantly plays with Bataille's attempts to establish
distinctions, to produce postulates and to set up theoretical
machinery to describe general economy. The later work is actually
in some sense more open to this play of difference than the earlier
work. The political demands made by 'The Notion of
Expenditure' call for a clear division and difference between the
bourgeoisie and the proletariat:

> The first phase of a revolution is *separation*, in other words, a
> process leading to the position of two groups of forces, each one
> characterised by the necessity of excluding the other. The second
> phase is the violent *expulsion* of the group that has possessed the
> power by the revolutionary group. (VE, 100; BR, 156)

In this political model it is class difference which is the difference
that makes the difference. Whatever its merits as a revolutionary
programme, and it has many compared to the revolutions that
have often been offered to the working class, it still faces the
problem that it is trying to control and limit a force out of control.

The end of 'The Notion of Expenditure', with its suggestions
of a 'nonlogical difference' and the need 'to accede to the insub-
ordinate function of free expenditure' (VE, 129; BR, 181),
implicitly signalled the limits of any political control of
expenditure. It would also provide a criticism in advance of those
who would try to turn an economics of the gift into a social
programme, a temptation that Bataille gave into in his comments
on the Marshall Plan and one which was later taken up by
economists working with the Mitterand government in the 1980s.
Bataille's own political model undercuts itself through an
emphasis on difference which cannot be stabilised within a
political difference. Bataille's later 'scientific' model still takes up
the opposition between a limited giving and a pure gift without
return, with the roles no longer being played by the bourgeoisie
and the proletariat but the earth and the sun. The difference is
that the later model is not so stable because it does not cling to

this distinction. It is more open to 'nonlogical difference' and to energy interchanges and contaminations than the political model. The fate of the accursed share will turn on the interpretation of this 'nonlogical difference'. It will also decide the fate of Bataille and the extent to which he is our 'extreme contemporary'.

The Fate of the Accursed Share

The play of the accursed share dominates not only Bataille's writing but also that of those who try to interpret his texts. Bataille was never trying to describe an idiosyncratic effect of his own writing but a *general* economy, one that no writing, or any other action, could reckon without and could never entirely reckon with. This means that to write about Bataille is to be forced to engage with the effects of general economy that is not dominated by either Bataille or his readers. General economy is an economy of difference that is irreducible either to a universal law or to a particular context or, to use the terminology of philosophy, it is neither transcendental nor empirical. Instead general economy is specific to a particular play of forces, so it is never an abstract universal, but it is always tracing the excess of this play of forces, and so it can never be reduced to the empirical description of this play of forces. This is an economy of difference where difference does not settle into a stable structure of opposition. The fact that Bataille himself sometimes tries to describe general economy in terms of a structure of opposition – restricted v. general, productive v. unproductive, pure gift v. exchange – indicates how difficult it is to maintain this thought of a 'nonlogical difference'. The fate of the accursed share in Bataille's own writing is mirrored in the interpretations to which his writing has been subjected.

General economy is immediately related to restricted economy, it cannot be extracted from restricted economy and Bataille constantly reads the accursed share in its relation (or non-relation) to economic data. This close connection between general economy and existing economies always makes it possible to reduce general economy to a set of economic relations. It also means that the data that Bataille uses to provide 'approximations' of the accursed share is easily reversible and instead the accursed share can become another economic fact. In a very powerful essay called 'General Economics and Postmodern Capitalism' (CR, 196–213) Jean-Joseph Goux questions the historical limits of Bataille's interpretations of economics. He argues that contrary to Bataille's view of capitalism as inherently accumulative and of 'primitive societies' as inherently wasteful 'No society has "wasted" as much as contemporary capitalism' (CR, 199).

For Goux, Bataille's interpretations are determined by the experience of capitalism which he lived through and he did not recognise the tendencies by which capitalism would move from a model of production and accumulation to a 'society of consumption'. Rather than capitalism being a rational system the increasing complexity of the system throws rational economic justifications into crisis, and 'Bataille does not seem to have foreseen this conflict born of abundance and the extraordinary sophistication of production' (CR, 207). The recent application of mathematical models from chaos theory to describe economic systems and behaviours is an indication both of attempts to control and understand these processes and that these processes exceed 'rational' models. In fact rather than being a restricted economy capitalism is coming to resemble more and more general economy. Drawing on Goux's argument Fred Botting and Scott Wilson have argued that 'the world is becoming *more* like a Bataillean universe rather than less' (CR, 18). Here Bataille is claimed as our extreme contemporary; what he described has now come to be and he is treated like a successful futurologist.

Bataille's failure is that he did not predict shifts in capitalism from a model of accumulation to a model of consumption, his 'success' is that now general economy *appears* to correspond to contemporary economic facts. The price of this 'success' is that Bataille has been subject to an ironic dialectical reversal: the unproductive expenditure that he used as a principle to criticise capitalism has now been absorbed as a principle of capitalism. Goux uses this to criticise Bataille, arguing that at best Bataille can offer a 'new grid' (CR, 211) to understand this mutation of capitalism. This, of course, suggests that Bataille remains folded within contemporary capitalism, even as its extreme contemporary. Botting and Wilson draw on Goux but reach a different conclusion: because the world is becoming more Bataillean, Bataille is more critically relevant today. In a similar way Baudrillard has also argued that 'Bataille would have been impassioned by the present evolution of capital in this era of floating currencies, of values seeking their own level (which is not their transmutation), and the drift of finalities (which is neither sovereign uselessness nor the absurd gratuitousness of laughter and death)' (CR, 193). For Baudrillard then, Bataille would have been 'impassioned' by this historical mutation of capitalism, the fulfilment of his desires in another form.

Whether the reaction is positive or negative in both cases Bataille's general economy is reduced to a capitalist economy. Bataille has been absorbed by a mutation of capitalism that he did not foresee, and the liberating possibilities of his work have become reduced to a proliferating series of market choices. The

power of these arguments is that they stress how general economy
has to be discussed as an analysis of particular forces – it cannot
be detached from economies as they are. Furthermore, it brings
out the instability of the distinction between general and
restricted economy. In fact Bataille's attempts to describe general
economy as such are what lead to the reduction of general
economy to contemporary capitalism. This argument, in both of
its forms, also has profound limits. It is true that Bataille did not
predict the rise of consumer capitalism but the 'limitless loss' that
is heterogeneous to economy cannot be reduced to the losses of
capitalism. For Bataille the issue is not simply whether a society
is wasteful and destructive but *how* it goes about dealing with the
accursed share.

He argues that it is the rate of development of capitalist society
that leads to the massive destruction of twentieth-century warfare;
what Bataille calls the 'industrial plethora' is 'the plethora that
both wars [World Wars I and II] exuded' (AS1, 25; BR, 186).
These global conflicts are symptoms of the failure of capitalist
economies to deal with the excess of the accursed share, except
catastrophically. Within contemporary capitalist systems this
'plethora' and the concomitant waste and loss are still organised
as functions of the system. Goux's reading sees the accursed share
as an element of capital, becoming the necessary element of risk
and chance in market calculations. However, it could also be
argued that this is a refusal to deal with the accursed share at all.
Capitalism is not just a restricted economy in terms of accumulation but also in terms of the range of its expenditures, and
Bataille's point that the bourgeoisie spends 'within itself' does not
seem any less true than when he first made it. The gift of *potlatch*
is exactly that, a gift, not the gamble of an investment or the
selling of goods in new and unstable markets.

The accursed share cannot be definitively purified from any
taint of capital, because it is that which is not pure and because it
is at the origin of *any* capitalisation. The agonistic exchanges of
potlatch not only threaten the organisation of economy but they
also make economy possible. Perhaps what Goux is noting,
although he does not make this explicit, is the *impossibility* of
Bataille extracting a pure accursed share outside of the restricted
economies he wishes to condemn. The result of this impossibility
is not to destroy Bataille's work or reduce it to a particularly
sophisticated ideology for a 'postmodern capitalism'. Instead the
accursed share demands a more complex reading, one which does
not reduce it back into the play of forces from which it emerges or
reduce it to new elements of the system that is has disrupted.

The accursed share, and with it Bataille, has another
symmetrical fate: to float above any system as an abstract universal,

a metaphysical principle to be added to the debris of philosophy. These two positions are actually in very close proximity, and it is not surprising that, beginning from premises very similar to those of Goux, Baudrillard should be led to this opposite position. As we have seen Baudrillard also recognises that Bataille's work has been superseded by changes in economic and social systems, but instead of using this to criticise Bataille as tied to the past Baudrillard attempts to 'modernise' Bataille and bring out his relevance for the present. To do this Baudrillard has tried to recontextualise Bataille's thought by shifting the model of gift exchange away from a model based in nature and back to the social model to be found in Mauss.

He argues that 'one can reproach Bataille for having "naturalised" Mauss' (CR, 194) by which he means that Bataille has unnecessarily turned gift exchange into a natural process to account for the 'accursed share'. The accursed share is better accounted for in terms of the model of social exchange to be found in Mauss, a kind of re-sociologisation of Bataille. For Baudrillard: 'The "excess of energy" does not come from the sun (from nature) but from a continual higher bidding in exchange – the symbolic process that can be found in the work of Mauss, not that of the gift (that is the naturalist mystique into which Bataille falls), but that of the counter-gift' (CR, 194). He returns Bataille to the French sociological tradition with which Bataille always had such an ambivalent relationship,[15] and no matter how 'radical' this radical sociology is it is still a matter of exchanging one framework for another. Although Baudrillard may appear to remove Bataille from his grounding of the gift in nature he will actually be led from sociology to a metaphysical grounding of the gift that will turn the accursed share into a philosophical principle.

What forms the core of Baudrillard's reading of Bataille is the idea of symbolic exchange, a type of exchange that would be exterior to the exchanges characteristic of capitalism.[16] Baudrillard is trying to save the critical principle that Goux believes is lost, because contemporary capitalism demands a different response than that of Bataille. In the 1970s Baudrillard focused on death as the inassimilable which could not be organised by exchange and which exchange had to refuse to secure itself. While still reiterating his criticisms of Bataille's 'naturalism' he believed that 'Nevertheless, something remains in Bataille's excessive and luxuriant vision of death that removes it from psychoanalysis and its individual and psychical domain. This something provides the opportunity to disturb every economy, shattering not only the objective mirror of political economy, but also the inverse psychical mirror of repression, the unconscious and libidinal economy' (CR, 143). We can see how Baudrillard, who was strongly influenced by the events of May '68, was hostile to attempts to explain those events in terms of psychoanalysis or Marxism. His idea of the symbolic challenge evolved not only theoretically but also out of the events, as a model for a challenge that disturbs every economy.

What is remarkable is that, despite supposedly profound changes in his views, Baudrillard has still held on to much the same reading of Bataille. In a more recent work called *The Transparency of Evil*, published in France in 1990 and in English translation in 1993, Baudrillard reactivates the accursed share. He argues that:

> In a society which seeks – by prophylactic measures, by annihilating its own natural referents, by whitewashing violence, by exterminating all germs and *all of the accursed share*, by performing cosmetic surgery on the negative – to concern itself solely with quantified management and with the discourse of the Good, in a society where it is no longer possible to speak Evil, Evil has metamorphosed into all the viral and terroristic forms that obsess us. [Italics mine][17]

Baudrillard introduces the 'theorem of the accursed share': 'Anything that purges the accursed share in itself signs its own death warrant'.[18] Baudrillard does not refer to Bataille directly, although his aphoristic, repetitive and often amusing pensées hardly refer directly to anyone any more. But there is a strong continuity in his use and his assimilation of Bataille.

Baudrillard no longer needs to make critical comments about the 'naturalism' of the accursed share, because now the accursed share is more a possession of his than of Bataille. At the same time that Baudrillard rehabilitates the accursed share as a critical tool he also turns it into a metaphysical principle. The accursed share becomes an eternal capitalised 'Evil', that is the ruin and destruction of every system. This destroys the accursed share as the effect of a particular play of forces having a finite existence which results from the excess that a system cannot control. The accursed share has gained a firmer identity but only by becoming a principle or system in itself. This is not to deny that Baudrillard has a valid critical point about how the more the accursed share is controlled the more virulent its effects become, although Bataille had already made exactly this point; but this critical point becomes lost when the principle of critique becomes a floating metaphysical dogma. If Goux reduced the accursed share to the effects of a particular context, the existing 'restricted economies' which Bataille studied, then Baudrillard inflates the accursed share to an almost parodically cosmic principle ('Evil'). It is all the more ironic that Baudrillard had begun by criticising Bataille for turning nature into a metaphysical principle.

These two gestures, these two fates of the accursed share, can be understood as effects of the accursed share and its differential economy. In Bataille's work the accursed share swings between oppositions but is never finally determined by them. Instead it undermines oppositions by connecting them through the turbulence of general economy. 'Nonlogical difference' is how Bataille describes this difference which does not settle into a binary opposition, and this difference is central to understanding of the accursed share. Goux and Baudrillard both, in their own ways, reduce this turbulent play of forces to the structure of an alternative: the accursed share is either inside capitalism or outside it. These two responses are symptomatic of the difficulty of the accursed share, although both Goux and Baudrillard provide some of the most interesting discussion of the accursed share in modern European thought. By far the most common symptom of the difficulty of the accursed share is simply to reject it as incoherent. However, this rejection will always fail because the accursed share inscribes an excess into *every* system (including those which reject it).

The differential economy of the accursed share resists the way in which Goux and Baudrillard (and those like Botting and Wilson who use Bataille in a similar way) make Bataille into our extreme contemporary. While Goux sees Bataille as being passed over by current events Baudrillard sees him as keeping up with the present. As we saw with Foucault's comments about Bataille belonging both to the past and the future it is very difficult to determine the 'time' of Bataille. Attempts to apply his thought to contemporary events are in danger of not proving it to be relevant to today but of making it a symptom of the present. This is what Goux warns us of, that Bataille's general economy can easily become an ideology of a particular form of modern (or, as some would say, 'postmodern') capitalism: a capitalism wasteful, ecstatic, always extending itself, colonising new areas of experience, an 'avant-garde' capitalism even. It is a common enough criticism of thinkers like Bataille that they can provide no real critical interventions and simply offer impossible escape routes from the present. Once again this is a failure to understand the movement of the accursed share, which does not conform to this opposition between being within present conditions and being outside, but which is instead a movement of opening.

This opening is an opening to the future, so Bataille can never simply remain of the present. In order to discover this movement of the accursed share in Bataille a critical reading is required. Bennington has provided the beginnings of this critical reading with his consideration of the *limits* of Bataille's general economy. For Bennington Bataille is constantly torn apart by the fact that as he tries to organise general economy by certain limits (like the pure expenditure of the sun or the finite surface of the earth) those limits themselves touch on what they are opposed to and are supposed to separate. This means that when a limit is set up it does not only divide but it also connects, and for Bennington this is a logical result of the structure of any limit. However, he argues that Bataille 'tends to personalise and anthropologize this strictly logical problem as a subjective problem of writing (such a move is always a principle of the existential pathos infusing Bataille's work in general, leading him to derive what is ultimately an ethics from what is immediately a logic)'.[19]

Bennington is very critical of the pathos that Bataille reads into this problem of the limit, without perhaps recognising that his own limitation of the problem of the limit to being a logical problem is reductive of the subjective, existential, ethical and emotional effects that the limit can have. It also underestimates the ways in which Bataille develops his thought in a similar direction to the one that Bennington is suggesting, in particular if we place together the remark from the end of 'The Notion of Expenditure' concerning nonlogical difference with the arguments in *The Accursed Share* that there is never purely productive or unproductive expenditures and that differences exist as a finite 'play of forces'. When Bennington argues that 'In its most abstract form, this suggestion would say that "general economy" is not the other of "restricted economy", but is *no other than* restricted economy; that there is no general economy except as the economy of restricted economy; that general economy is the economy of its own restriction – and that is necessity and not luxury',[20] there is enough in Bataille's thought to think this. But isn't Bennington bending the stick too far? Why isn't restricted economy also becoming-general?

In his critical desire to resist the pathos of the accursed share Bennington is himself in danger of misreading it, and another fate of the accursed share is to place even the most powerful interpretations at risk. His own desire to emphasise the finitude and restriction of general economy risks turning it into a restricted economy. However, Bennington can also help us to understand the irreducible movement of the accursed share. At the end of his essay he suggests that 'we are always left in fact *in the middle*, in the rhythmic restriction of gift to exchange and of excess to surplus value or profit'.[21] To understand the accursed share as a rhythmic pulsation or turbulence, which is neither absorbed within a particular context nor floating above all contexts, resists its reduction. If the accursed share has a fate it lies in the possibilities which exist in this 'middle', as well as the possibility that it can always be reduced to a stable position. This involves a specificity of intervention, of what Bataille called an 'intransigent materialism' (VE, 51; BR, 164), into the play of forces. But this materialism is also intransigent because it is irreducible to that play of forces, it is always opening the limits that it traces. Here is where materialism and matter coincide with nonlogical difference, revising both materialism and our thought of difference.

We are back within the ebbs and flows of Bataille's thought, from its earliest tracings of the collapsing back into the image to transgression as 'a movement which always exceeds the bounds, that can never be anything but partially reduced to order' (E, 40). These ebbs and flows are impossible – impossible to bring to order and impossible to describe. They also flow around and through difference, the 'delays' and 'detours' of circulation that Bataille would like to have done with but which he also recognises as the very matter of his thought. The paths of energy are knotted into a labyrinth, the guiding thread becomes tangled and frays, multiplies in excess: 'The history of life on earth is mainly the effect of a wild exuberance' (AS1, 33; BR, 192). Detours and delays are the effects of an ecstatic exuberance which leaves Bataille exhausted, and his own thought is also 'mainly the effect of a wild exuberance' which can be traced back to an effect of difference.

This exuberance of thought, of writing, is in play in the differences that are irreducible to the context of their emergence, while at the same time never fully detachable from that context. Bataille resists appropriations which would reduce his thought to a sign of the times, whether that is the times in which he lived or the times in which we now find ourselves. His writing also resists appropriations that would rewrite his finite analysis and calculation of the incalculable accursed share into a metaphysical principle. This is where Bataille's writing constantly engages with, and destabilises, philosophy: the general is the ruin of the universal. The impossible and the difference actively resist becoming stable concepts for philosophy, what Derrida calls philosophemes.[22] They are both free enough to resist this process of appropriation and free enough to invite it: that is why Bataille's thought constantly demands a vigilance of reading. For all his suspicion of reading, of intellectual production, of systems of knowledge, of what is often called 'the academic', Bataille responds with the demand for a closer reading that uncovers the violent forces which constantly flow through and around texts while not reducing these forces to what could be grasped by a reading. It is in this irreducible opening that Bataille offers us a thought which is for the future.

Conclusion

Everything takes place in a fiery penumbra, its meaning subtly withdrawn.

Georges Bataille (G, 12)

All of Bataille's writing takes place in the withdrawal of meaning (*sens*) into the senseless, and this withdrawal resists the drawing of a conclusion. To draw a conclusion is to impose a sense of the senseless play of difference. If we conclude with the senseless as senseless then we still impose a sense on it *as* the senseless. Rather than the senseless being nonsense it is the origin of sense, it inhabits sense and ruins the imposition of sense. This is why Bataille writes in *The Impossible* that 'Nothing exists that doesn't have this *senseless sense* ...' (I, 20). To negotiate senseless sense is an act of reading which does not try to appropriate it under sense and which does not impose a conclusion. In his analysis of the reading of Sade, Bataille opposed a reading which appropriates to a reading which does not aim at possession but rather at a liberating *excretion*: 'The process of appropriation is thus characterised by a homogeneity (static equilibrium) of the author of the appropriation, and of objects as a final result, whereas excretion presents itself as the result of heterogeneity, and can move in the direction of an ever greater heterogeneity, liberating impulses whose ambivalence is more and more pronounced' (VE, 95; BR, 151).

This excretion is not simply the removal of the foreign body but a confrontation with its heterogeneity. Excretion is no longer a rejection which firmly divides us from the excreted, where excretion imposes a homogeneous division. It is not absorbed either within a dialectic of appropriation in which it would lead to a controlled pleasure. What Bataille finds in Sade is a heterogeneous economy where excretion circulates as an unstable heterogeneous process. Rather than the excretion of the foreign body removing the foreign body it actually liberates it, and liberates it to a heterogeneity that is out of control. Therefore to conclude this reading of Bataille means that we must not appropriate him as a stable object for us but read him through this economy of heterogeneity, of difference, which liberates heterogeneous impulses from the prison of homogeneity and appropriation.

What remains is the question of reading, of how we should read Bataille and of how Bataille reads. In *Guilty* Bataille writes: 'It's so impossible to read – most books anyway. I've lost the urge. What's depressing is the amount of work I have to do' (G, 11). This loss of the urge to read can be interpreted as the loss of a desire to impose a sense through reading, the loss of the urge to read towards the conclusion. At the conclusion we are, usually, rewarded with the unique sense of the work, and in French the unique sense (*sens unique*) means a 'one-way street'. Bataille does not read along a one-way street leading to sense but leads us (and reads us) into a labyrinth in which the one-way street is placed as a momentary dead-end. This displaces the position of sense through general economy, as an economy of senseless sense. Rather than beginning with reading which already possesses an orientation towards sense Bataille begins reading in an experience of disorientation, of impossibility. After announcing in *Guilty* that reading is impossible and that he has lost the urge to read, Bataille starts to read: 'On a crowded train standing up, I began reading Angela de Foligno's *Book of Visions*' (G, 11).

Standing up reading, Bataille reads a book written by a saint and devoted to divine communications, 'visions', which exist at the limit of readings. These divine images are, on the one hand, full of sense because they convey the divine meaning of God's love; on the other hand, the effect of these images is to overflow consciousness with a divine love that is richer than any sense, a prodigality without return. Bataille reads in this economy of divine sense an overflowing of sense to the senseless, which reinscribes the divine economy that would finally return all sense to God within a general economy without return. Reading here is a reading in the wake of the death of God as the withdrawal of meaning, a reading against the return of sense, a reading without return. Bataille continues by copying out the text, the most faithful reading but also the most distant. In absolute replication the text is altered, as in Borges's fable, 'Pierre Ménard, Author of the *Quixote*'.[1] Ménard's *Quixote* is exactly the same as Cervantes' but also totally different, because 'perfect repetition is absolute difference'.[2] Bataille inscribes the saint's writing but also reinscribes it within his life in a gesture that carries reading further, to the limit.

This is only one of Bataille's readings but, perhaps all of Bataille's works can be read as a series of readings: of Nietzsche, Kojève, Hegel, Freud, Marx and Mauss among others (one large volume of Bataille's complete works (vol. XI) consists of book reviews). The importance of this reading is that it is a '*privileged instant*' (VE, 241) because it plays out the crisis of reading. It is a reading which carries Bataille to the limit, reading the instants of excess that destroy reading: 'Luxury, mourning, war, cults, the construction of sumptuary monuments, games, spectacles, arts, perverse sexual activity (i.e., deflected from genital finality)' (VE, 118; BR, 169). What he reads in books are these instants which bring the book into incoherence, overflowing the margin of the book and putting it into touch with the instants of lived experience. There is no 'static equilibrium' of the author or the 'objects' read, instead an unstable heterogeneous circuit is set up which flows between the author, the reader and the text. A conclusion has to be based on this instability, liberated from the sense of conclusion as closure to read the conclusion as an *opening*.

As Bataille jots down his readings in *Guilty* he feels that 'These notes link me to my fellow human beings as a guideline, and everything else seems empty to me, though I wouldn't have wanted my friends reading them' (G, 17). The reading by his friends is a reading that Bataille resists; they can read him to make sense of him and they read to understand him. The familiarity of the friend does not lead to reading but distances the friend from reading. Bataille is different from his friends and more different than they can understand because they are his friends. A friend of Bataille can always make the mistake of presuming to have understood him, to know him, but 'I differ from my friends in not caring a damn for any convention taking my pleasure in the basest things' (I, 17). Bataille's pleasure in the basest things puts an end to familiarity because it is an encounter with heterogeneity, with difference, which destroys the conventions of familiarity and friendship. Blanchot argues that because Bataille's 'entire work expresses friendship' (CR, 51) it places it as a work apart from any other work. Bataille inscribes friendship in this work apart from any other work: a heterogeneity, a distance, which cannot be read by the friend. This transforms friendship from an experience of familiarity into an experience of *distance*. The friend can only be the stranger, and friendship is only friendship through an encounter with the stranger who is the friend.

The guideline Bataille's notes offer is broken, and so reading cannot be guided by a familiarity with Bataille but reading must be led 'in the direction of an ever greater heterogeneity'. This is to read Bataille against those readings which try to appropriate a sense out of his heterogeneity. In the act of appropriating Bataille to a sense, to an identity, these readings also witness the inevitable effects of heterogeneity. Bataille is given a sense but the senses proliferate in the chain of readings of Bataille. The heterogeneity that is gathered into sense reappears in the different senses given to Bataille: Bataille as Nietzschean, Bataille as Hegelian, Bataille as social theorist, Bataille as modernist writer, even Bataille as madman ('his often disturbing prose has led many to question his sanity').[3] These appropriations of Bataille both succeed and fail; they impose a sense on Bataille but that sense is only ever grafted on to senseless sense, on to heterogeneity.

The appropriation of Bataille under sense produces different senses of Bataille, which can then be translated into a competition over who has grasped the true sense of Bataille, who is entitled to claim his legacy and who is his real friend. The plural heterogeneity of his writings is put to work in academic competition and, through the appropriation of Bataille, the academic (or other reader) claims to be expert on Bataille. In the competition over who is the most faithful reader of Bataille the occupation of this position destroys the reading of Bataille as heterogeneous and his reading of everything as heterogeneous. To read Bataille as a reader is not to join in this competition, this game, by trying to trump the other readings with the truest and most faithful reading of Bataille. As we saw with Bataille's reading of Hegel through Kojève, Bataille resisted the way in which Kojève turned a heterogeneous reading of Hegel into a true reading of Hegel. This in itself means that Bataille needs be read to the limit of reading, particularly to where he resists appropriation by reading.

The resistance to reading makes the absolute appropriation of Bataille impossible, and it inscribes impossibility in any gesture of appropriation. While Bataille is always reading he does not take on the identity of a reader, he rejects reading as an *inadequate* response to his writing: 'One mustn't read me: I don't want to be covered with evasions' (IE, 199). What reading evades is a *lived experience* that would strip away all evasions and expose us to our origin in chance. For Bataille reading can never lead us to this experience, 'But that one should read me – should arrive at the ultimate degree of conviction – one will not be laid bare for all that' (IE, 13). The reading of Bataille which would be most convincing would not lay us bare to this experience, it would not expose us trembling to chance. All reading is condemned to failure and betrayal.

Julian Pefanis remarks about the 'delay'[4] in the reading of Bataille in the Anglo-American world, but the irony is that Bataille would be happy if we delayed reading him for ever. This is not an end to our reading of Bataille as a reader, because Bataille is not immune from reading no matter how much he regarded reading as an evasive response. For us to realise that reading Bataille is inadequate we have to read Bataille's instruction that we not read him! If we had never read Bataille at all then we would be the best readers of Bataille, but we would never know this unless we had read Bataille. The result is a double-bind: on the one hand, to read Bataille is not to read him and, on the other hand, not to read Bataille is to read him, but we would never know this without having read him in the first place. It is always too late to have done with reading because we have to have started reading to reject the art of reading, and Bataille called this impossible position the 'absurdity of reading' (IE, 37).

For Bataille reading is absurd because it evades 'lived experience' but 'lived experience' cannot be experienced as such *without reading*: 'Human eyes tolerate neither sun, coitus, cadavers, not obscurity, but with different reactions' (VE, 8). The things that we most want to read or to have contact with without reading are intolerable, even deadly. Therefore we are forced to read them at second hand, but we have to recognise that we can only suppose a first-hand experience of them from this 'secondary' reading. There is a necessity to reading that Bataille recognises and wants to be rid of, and this is what makes him such an acute reader. He is a reader who wants to have done with reading and so he reads to the very limit of reading. It is possible to read Bataille's claim, 'But that one should read me – should arrive at the ultimate degree of conviction – one will not be laid bare for all that' (IE, 13), not just as a rejection of reading, which it is, but also as a call for a different type of reading. It implicitly rejects all reading but it can be reread to argue that it rejects a reading that arrives 'at the ultimate degree of conviction', a reading that is grounded in truth and the homogeneity of a secure and stable conviction, and thereby identity.

A reading which does not appropriate, an excretory reading which tries to liberate heterogeneity is what I have tried to trace in these readings of Bataille. It is a reading which is always the reading of a remainder that has not been read and a remainder that cannot be read: 'the impossible', 'senseless sense', 'hetero-geneity', 'excess', 'the accursed share', etc. It reads towards the limit of reading, 'an impossible limit' (ON, 39), which reads from the impossible to difference. Impossibility is the beginning where we encounter our own failure, our own powerlessness, but 'This powerlessness defines an apex of possibility, or at least, *awareness of the impossibility* opens consciousness to all that it is possible for it to think' (TE, 10) (Italics mine). Powerlessness is where we begin reading from as opposed to a will-to-power, a will to impose a reading if we are to read at all. A reading which appropriates the will through identity is a powerful reading, but also the violent destruction of the liberty of the text. We saw that the most extreme effects of a reading based on the will-to-power as a will to identity were the Nazi and fascist readings of Nietzsche.

However, all readings involve appropriations, violence and power, but Bataille reads against the dream of an absolute appropriation and its imposition of a unitary community. His community with Nietzsche is not a community formed out of a common will-to-power but a community which is an experience of chance. The chance that opens community opens reading and the political violence of fascism and Nazism can partly be explained by its exploitation of this chance opening of community (in its self-presentation as a 'revolution' for a new 'national community'). It then violently eliminates this chance of community by 'purifying' this community to the point of self-destruction. Impossibility is the opening that cannot ever totally be closed because 'at every point, at each point, there is the impossibility of the final state' (TE, 11). It intercedes at every point, even the most closed one, and for Bataille it leads to the expression of 'a *mobile* thought, without seeking its definitive state' (TE, 11).

The mobility of Bataille's thought is what makes it touch upon so many disciplines, upon those categorisations within which we are content to let thought rest. As it touches it displaces the limit of these disciplines, putting them into contact through the heterogeneity and difference that no discipline can control. This is not a peaceful inter-disciplinarity in which pre-existing disciplines would be brought together to co-operate in producing knowledge, but a transgression of the limits which circumscribe these disciplines *as* disciplines. Bataille does not settle comfortably within the division of labour of modern academic life, or between academia and other organisations of knowledge: the media, journalism, popular culture, etc. The different attempts to appropriate Bataille in these different areas all encounter Bataille as a foreign body, and unlike Lacan's Real which 'is that which always comes back to the same place'[5] Bataille lacks a proper place.

Philosophy is the discipline which steps in to regulate all other disciplines, even if only implicitly, and to put everything in its place. I have constantly read Bataille in relation to philosophy, *not* because I am trying to provide a philosophical reading of Bataille but because I am trying to analyse how Bataille resists being put in his place by philosophy. In particular he resists the reading of difference by philosophy, which tries to take that which escapes discipline and appropriate it to a *theory* of difference. This appropriation of difference is present in Kant's tendency to stabilise difference as the opposing sides of a limit or in Hegel's attempt to sublate and hold together that opposition as ground. Instead, Bataille begins a non-oppositional reading of difference and this is why he has to be read with poststructuralism. Bataille has had a profound influence on poststructuralism and has been read in fascinating ways by its proponents. To divide Bataille from post-structuralism is to divide him from some of his best readers and to divide us from a reading of difference that emerges from Bataille and poststructuralism.

To read them together is to read them against the reduction of Bataille to a footnote in intellectual history and the reduction of poststructuralism to an intellectual movement or discipline. In the conversion of poststructuralism into a discipline or a method of textual analysis the effects of difference are repressed and contained within this disciplinary organisation. Bataille too loses his heterogeneity and is absorbed within the narratives of intellectual history. The very linear narratives that his fictions and other writings shatter in their fragmentary and dispersed arrangements are re-imposed by intellectual history. Of course, poststructuralism is itself a name for this process of stabilisation, presuming as it does a transition from one intellectual movement to another, specifically from structuralism to something called poststructuralism. It also presumes the identity of all those thinkers that it gathers together, despite their frequent mutual hostility, violent disagreements and different styles and modes of thought. The imposition of a history of poststructuralism, gathering up and identifying 'precursors' like Bataille, and locating them within a model of intellectual generations, destroys difference. This model implicitly supposes that 'precursors' like Bataille have been superseded by the 'next generation' of thinkers and that the next intellectual movement will in turn supersede them.

Robert Young has suggested that poststructuralism is an 'improper name'[6] which is vulnerable to being read within a model of intellectual history. However, because it is improper he also argues that it resists any reading which would claim to give it a 'proper' meaning. In fact poststructuralism as an improper name also names a thought which resists the identity and propriety on which this naming rests by suggesting that all 'proper names' have a certain impropriety. It is this constitutional impropriety that Bataille understands as heterogeneity and which we can use to resist the potential appropriation of that which has no place by new gestures of appropriation and placing. Heterogeneity, as difference, touches on everything and cannot be limited by an identity, including that of Bataille or poststructuralism. Neither Bataille nor poststructuralism possesses this difference and, although Bataille reads this difference in his own irreducible style, it cannot be made his property. The dispersal of this difference by Bataille to poststructuralism is one of the gifts of his work, a gift without return.

The alterity of difference to identity not only implies that difference does not belong to Bataille but that difference cannot be read as the result of Bataille's life. While he constantly contaminates the line drawn between life and work, to try to find the key to difference in the irregularities of Bataille's life is to appropriate difference to a biographical identity. Although Michel Surya has produced a biography of Bataille[7] it is not the final word on Bataille. To explain Bataille's writings as the product of a 'genius' or a 'madman' tells us nothing, not only because of the banality of these descriptions but also because they suppose that these writings can be appropriated to the sense of an identity. Identity cannot be gathered on the side of his works either; while the bringing together of his complete works in French and the continuing translation of his works into English are vital for research on Bataille, they cannot be supposed to lead to the truth of Bataille. That reading would be reductive and mutilate the experiences of 'life' and 'works', of what Bataille called lived experience. Instead Bataille remains as the 'foreign body' (VE, 92: BR, 148), even to himself.

Bataille is not only literally foreign to those of us who are not French but also foreign 'within' France, foreign 'within' his intellectual and personal milieu. By thinking heterogeneity Bataille remains heterogeneous to any identity, even to his 'own' identity. In this way he extends the concept of what it is to be foreign to being something which can never be made familiar, something which can never be assimilated. This lack of assimilation makes it difficult to read Bataille as belonging to a national identity although, as Deleuze pointed out, at times he can seem very French. He would still not conform to that identity, to being a part of French thought, and neither would he be a part of European thought. Bataille is the foreign body to these identities, a heterogeneous part that is always subject to exclusion by homogeneous identity (VE, 140; BR, 125). To read Bataille is not to secure him but to read to the opening of identity to heterogeneity, a difference that can never be organised within a personal, national, supra-national or metaphysical identity.

That difference is not gathered within poststructuralism but is read by those thinkers who are identified by that name and read by them *with* Bataille. In fact by putting Bataille back into poststructuralism it can be redefined against its 'becoming-institutional'. Bennington suggests a definition of poststructuralism as 'a non-Hegelian questioning of Kantian frontiers',[8] and this is exactly what we have seen in Bataille's exploration of Kant and Hegel. This is tied to the instability of difference that Kant and Hegel both open and close, and which Bataille's analysis of transgression repeats. That repetition alters by opening the frontier of Kant in a way that cannot be dialectically sublated by Hegel. By actively contesting philosophy it refuses philosophical reading or being confined to one particular discipline – literary theory, for example. Two of the most influential 'poststructuralist' readings of Bataille, Michel Foucault's 'A Preface to Transgression' and Jacques Derrida's 'From Restricted to General Economy: A Hegelianism without Reserve', explore this position of Bataille between Kant and Hegel: Foucault's essay faces towards Kant and Derrida's faces towards Hegel. They both find in Bataille a reading of difference that reopens the history of Western philosophy and makes all the more problematic the idea of progression implicit in the term poststructuralism and in any intellectual history.

Derrida argues that 'Even when taking into account their value as ruptures, it could be shown, in this respect, that the immense revolutions of Kant and Hegel only reawakened or revealed the most permanent philosophical determination of negativity (with all the concepts systematically entwined around it in Hegel: ideality, truth, meaning, time, history, etc.)' (CR, 110). Bataille would be the rupture in these ruptures, once again the foreign body but this time the foreign body articulating a negativity which does not remain within a philosophical determination, an unemployed negativity (BR, 296–300). This reading of negativity by Bataille is an excavation of philosophy that still remains to be thought, not least in all the effects it would have on the reading of poststructuralism. It is a reading of Bataille that is still beginning and as such has often been barely registered, or has been actively and violently repressed. All too often the reactions to Bataille and poststructuralism have demanded an end to the freedom of their thought of difference and a call to order, whether it be in the name of politics, ethics or good sense.

The senseless sense of difference undermines these calls to order by digging under their foundations. Bataille once borrowed Marx's metaphor of class struggle as the 'old mole' to describe a materialism that is 'an appeal to all that is offensive, indestructible, and even despicable, to all that overthrows, perverts, and ridicules spirit ...' (VE, 32). The old mole may disappear from sight but is always burrowing beneath and undermining the 'firm' ground of our 'intellectual edifice' (VE, 32). Bataille can be read with poststructuralism as a reading of difference, and this can be used against the attempt to stabilise poststructuralism as an intellectual movement or discipline, whether by those who identify themselves as poststructuralists or those who oppose it. He is the old mole of modern European thought, burrowing through the base matter of our intellectual waste products. This burrowing undermines the assumption of stable intellectual objects of analysis: 'Dead matter, the pure idea, and God in fact answer a question in the same way (in other words perfectly, and as flatly as the docile student in a classroom)...' (VE, 15; EA, 58). This is a rebuff to all those who regard Bataille or poststructuralism as dead in intellectual terms, or who would like them to be dead or stay dead.

It also refuses to be brought to order by a piety of thought, or the call to save concepts like the subject, ethics or politics from the effects of thought. Of course, Bataille's work is not just destructive, and we have seen how he constantly tries to develop new modes of political practice, new ethics and new ways for us to live together. But Bataille is not willing to lessen the effects of difference to achieve these aims or to live in denial over the fact that '*Heterogeneous* reality is that of a force or shock' (VE, 143). Thinking and reading to the limit is dangerous – it puts thought at risk with a freedom that cannot be subject to control. This is a disturbing thought where freedom is not simply something we possess as a positive value but where it violently exceeds and dispossesses us. For freedom to be freedom it cannot be the property of an individual or community, but this threatens us with a violation that we cannot control in advance. Bataille is not praising this violence and we are better off examining mainstream popular culture for hypocritical 'condemnations' of violence which remain fascinated by excess, including a popular journalism which has made moralism an art form.

Bataille explores the violence of difference in a reading of violence as a general economy. This requires careful and critical reading because it becomes easy to assimilate Bataille to a culture of violence, and all too often 'celebrations' of Bataille do just that. However, in breaking the (violently imposed) taboos on violence Bataille is not aiming to increase violence but to examine how these strict taboos generate their own violence. In this exploration Bataille touches on points of affective excess in his writings, which are heterogeneous in their refusal to be organised within a homogeneous accumulation of knowledge. This is where impossibility and difference are knotted around an affect which, as Bataille suggests of the sacred, both attracts and repulses us (CS, 103–24). Bataille deploys the heterogeneity of these affects to rupture the usual inscription of events within our philosophical, political and social structures. These effects of rupture cannot be gathered up in a new identity as, for example, the 'transgressive'. Transgression does not form an identity and it is the mistake of those who claim a transgressive identity to believe they can limit the play of transgression. The porous nature of individual or group identities based around transgression, usually in the form of transgressive sexualities, indicates how it resists being gathered in identity.

Heterogeneity and difference cannot be reduced to marketing tools, artistic identities or slogans, although they can always be mistaken for them. To take them to the limit is to resist their restriction within a limit, to resist the claim that we know what heterogeneity and difference are and what they can do. This resistance also involves a heterogeneous reading of Bataille, a reading of Bataille *against* Bataille. This does not mean that we have to judge Bataille as lacking from a position outside his works, from the 'safe' space of rejection. Instead it draws on the heterogeneous resources in his works which they cannot control, resources which expose Bataille, and us, to irruptive forces. Derrida has exemplified and described this strategy: 'Therefore, if we proceed prudently and all the while remain in Bataille's text, we can detach an interpretation from its reinterpretation and submit it to another interpretation bound to other propositions of the system' (CR, 137, n79). To read in this way, which I hope to have done here, is to make a reading that does not suppose either that I possess the truth of Bataille or that such a singular truth can be found. Unlike Bataille's reading of Nietzsche it resists identification with Bataille, and it also resists any possible communion with the spirit of Bataille.

It is a 'base materialist' reading, an active interpretative reading of heterogeneity, of base matter and of difference both derived from Bataille and which is 'in' Bataille. Furthermore, it is not a reading carried out alone but with others, especially with poststructuralism redefined as a reading of difference. It would be a fiction to suppose that we could present Bataille as he 'really' is or that we could offer a reading that would have no effect on his works. That would be impossible and it is only through recognising the violence of reading, including those readings which claim to be the most modest and most true presentations of Bataille, that we can reduce that violence. Therefore I have proposed an active and critical reading, but one which is sensitive to its own violence and that of other readers of Bataille. I have not tried to present Bataille as he is, to erase this reading before Bataille, but tried to develop openings into his work to be pursued. In this reading Bataille emerges as torn between his desire to read and his desire to have done with reading, he is at war with himself. This is part of the fascination of Bataille, a writer who reads some of the most difficult works (not least Hegel and Nietzsche) but who also violently tries to destroy reading. He is the reader who wants to have done with reading, the reader who reads not to gain intellectual authority but to experience 'un-knowing' (BR, 321–6). Bataille is a divided or fissured reader but this difference cannot be organised or stabilised and it demands a reading that liberates its heterogeneity. This is why Bataille has to be read against himself to resist his own reduction of difference.

Our reading of Bataille as a reader has encountered his hatred of reading, and our reading Bataille from the impossible to difference also has to encounter his own reduction of difference. At various points in his writings there remains a fascination with a world without difference, and these are not fleeting moments or aberrations but essential to Bataille's descriptions of experience. For him they are an object of desire, a secret dream that animates his writing and remains secreted within it. I want to read one example of this desire to start to examine his desire as an effect of difference, and to suggest why we might wish to read Bataille. The effect of this will be that reading is never simply a matter of knowledge but also a matter of persuasion, of performative force, of desire. Bataille's desire for a world without difference emerges clearly in the *Theory of Religion* with his desire for 'the unconscious intimacy of animals' (TE, 54). The sacred and animality are thought together as a primal experience of continuity, the obliteration of difference in a flow of communication that Bataille did not cease to desire. It is a desire which dominates both his readings – which seek an unconscious intimacy with what is read – and his writings – which seek an unconscious intimacy with the reader.

The world of animals is a world without difference because animals know nothing of negativity, and thereby know nothing of difference: they live 'in a world where nothing is posited beyond the present' (TE, 18). This experience of the world as immanent gives us a glimpse of the undivided realm of the sacred: 'This continuity, which for the animal could not be distinguished from anything else, which was in it and for it the only possible mode of being, offered man all the fascination of the sacred world, as against the poverty of the profane tool (of the discontinuous object)' (TE, 35). However, the experience of the sacred is *not the same* as animality because 'the animal accepted the immanence that submerged it without apparent protest, whereas man feels a kind of impotent horror in the sense of the sacred' (TE, 36). This is man's tragic condition: cast out of the immanence of animality the potential immanence of the sacred is both desired but also felt as a mortal threat to his individual identity. Of course, the religious overtones of the fall of man and the dominance of the male subject in this model are worth noting as points to criticise. By reading this model through difference we can detach it from these religious and phallocentric effects, locating it within a general economy of difference.

Bataille marks off the world of animality as radically separated from us, and the sacred can only model itself on that world but can never recapture it. Animal life is a 'disconcerting enigma' (TE, 21) that is 'closed to us' (TE, 20) because it exists without difference. The model has some difficulties though, difficulties which will suggest that animality is not as far from us as we think and that this distance is essential to the *fantasy* of a world without difference. The first difficulty is that Bataille's paradigm of the world of animality is the act by which one animal consumes another, and the act of eating seems to suppose a difference between eater and eaten rather than the smooth world of immanence. Bataille's solution is to accept that there is a difference here but that it is a *limited* form of difference because it is only a 'quantitative difference' (TE, 18). What makes this difference different? When one animal eats another 'there is no transcendence between the eater and eaten; there is a difference, of course, but this animal that eats the other cannot confront it in an affirmation of that difference' (TE, 17–18). In making this argument Bataille returns to the philosophical limitation of difference by Kojève and Hegel that he had elsewhere so effectively displaced.

Kojève drew a firm distinction between nature and humanity: in nature all desire is positive while for humanity desire can negate only when it is directed against another human desire. If a human being directed their desire against nature, to gather food for example, then the negativity of their desire would become limited by the positive state of nature: 'If, then, the Desire is directed towards a "natural", non-I, the I, too, will be "natural".'[9] Bataille remains within this model by regarding the consumption of one animal by another as lacking the affirmation of difference to be found in the conflict of two desires directed towards negating each other, in the master–slave dialectic. The difference between animals is lost because there is, for Bataille, no possibility of it being affirmed or *recognised*, as with the clash of human beings in the master–slave dialectic.

Now Bataille has admitted difference into the world without difference but only to argue that it is a difference that makes no difference. This runs up against his own nonlogical difference which refuses to remain limited or organised as either quantitative or qualitative difference. It is visible in Bataille's own attempts to organise difference to save the object of his desire. So, the consumption of one animal by another is only 'a higher wave overturning the other, weaker ones' (TE, 19), a little difference that can be dissolved because 'every animal is *in the world like water in water*' (TE, 19). This flowing of difference does not limit difference as Bataille hopes but brings this 'limited' difference into play with the turbulence of general economy. From a tracing of the circuits and flows of these 'quantitative differences', Bataille had already deduced the violent emergence of a 'qualitative difference': 'What general economy defines first is the explosive character of this world, carried to the extreme degree of explosive tension in the present time' (AS1, 40; BR, 197). The explosion explodes the distinctions and limits of difference that Bataille tries to produce, transforming the stability of limited difference into nonlogical difference.

Libertson has remarked that 'A multiplicity of dual oppositions structures Bataille's system',[10] which would locate Bataille within the tradition of Western metaphysics. One of the clearest examples of this dualism is the dualism of animality and humanity which seems to remain organised within the metaphysical binary where humanity has dominance over animality. These dual oppositions and Bataille's 'system' are undone by his thinking through of these oppositions by their instability as we have repeatedly seen, and this applies to this opposition as well. So, the opposition of animality as a world of limited difference to humanity as a world of affirmed difference collapses along the fault line of the *difference* between these worlds. What sort of difference is the difference that confines animality to a quantitative difference and humanity to qualitative difference? Is it a limited difference? But as a difference that imposes a limit it also imposes the opening of this limit, as we saw with the play of transgression and taboo. The division of taboo is already inhabited by the transgression that crosses through it, the difference that the division of taboo cannot control. Bataille's own opposition, his own 'system' (which I would argue never reaches the consistency of a system), is deranged by a difference that cannot be controlled and organised within it.

Bataille preserves his world without difference only by failing to think through difference, and here is where poststructuralism imposes itself as a reading which can read Bataille against Bataille, difference against the limitation of difference. That reading can draw on resources in Bataille, and this is what we often find in reading Bataille. The security of his own reading which seems to operate through concepts finds itself altered by the a-conceptual. Bataille pursues reading to the point of collapse, to the impossible where his writings open themselves up to difference. Here we can consider to what degree Bataille's own desire for a world without difference is parasitic on difference. This difference both generates his desire and destroys it. It places the difference between animality and humanity which seemed so secure within a general economy in which the world of animality as a world without difference becomes the 'poetic fallacy of animality' (TE, 19).

Bataille wants to preserve the animal world at a seductive distance where 'Something tender, secret, and painful draws out the intimacy which keeps vigil in us, extending its glimmer into that animal darkness' (TE, 23). We can be fascinated by the animal world but the animal world cannot be fascinated by us, because 'We cannot discern in it an ability to transcend itself' (TE, 23). While this has the merit of common sense it actually sets up an untenable limit, a limit as a division, as Bataille will admit. It is possible that animals may have a capacity to transcend themselves and so also affirm difference: 'We can at least *imagine* an embryo of that ability in animals, but we cannot discern it clearly enough' (TE, 23) (italics mine). What was a firm division and opposition has now become a problem of perception, and we can approach this problem of perception and the blurring of this division from the other side, from humanity to animality.

If animality is so divided from humanity then how can we know that it is a world without difference? For Bataille the answer lies in poetry as an opening between the two worlds: 'Poetry describes nothing that does not slip towards the unknowable' (TE, 21). As poetry slips towards the unknowable it can then carry us towards the unknowable world of animality. Through poetry 'The animal opens before me a depth that attracts me and is familiar to me' (TE, 22), so animality can fulfil its function as a model for the sacred. The animal world is a promise of what humanity has lost, the promise of a community that is a *communion*. Bataille has become the victim of the desire that he describes as the 'sticky temptation to poetry' (TE, 22). The strict division is overcome but at the cost of a reading which violently recomposes that opposition and where poetry is violently limited to a place on this limit. However, poetry is also unstable because it exists on this limit as its, supposedly, temporary dilation. When Bataille writes that we can *imagine* that animals could experience difference, isn't this imagination linked to an experience of poetry which connects and contaminates the division Bataille has tried to impose?

The sticky temptation to poetry produces Bataille's fantasy of animality as closed but also opens it to a different reading connected through difference. This would not involve dissolving the difference between animality and humanity by either making animality a *construction* of humanity or humanity into animality, but rethinking the connections and differences between them. It would more or less violently reread Bataille's violent imposition of the division through the poetic as the operator of an exchange that could not be controlled within the terms of Bataille's text. Poetry would not just be imagination or fantasy, but the possibility of an opening and an encounter. It would no longer be a one-way access from humanity to animality but an opening, a reading, which would always be at risk of a contact which it could not control. The dream of a world without difference is both made possible and impossible by poetry, because of the difference as opening it inscribes in difference as division.

This last reading of Bataille is necessary to demonstrate the heterogeneity of his writings and the way in which they demand reading. They are fissured by a desire, a desire for presence which they both act on and which they withdraw through difference. It is through an active reading that it becomes possible to account for the impossible desire for presence as an effect of difference, and how the desire for a world without difference emerges from difference. We can even regard the immanent world of animality as a different world of difference, a world not dominated by the recognised negativity which is central to Hegelian philosophy. Rather it is a world of flowing differences emerging from the differences between forces, and this thought could join with Bataille's energy ecology of nature from *The Accursed Share*. The violence of Bataille's writing is that it opens up the possibility of a thought of difference, not by imposing difference on a world that lacks difference but by forcing it into the open by 'making a new laceration within a lacerated nature' (VE, 80).

This mobile difference exists at the limit of reading as the retracing and opening of that limit, as the beginning of reading, as a laceration that marks the already lacerated. To begin reading is to be 'open to all previous or *subsequent* movements' (TR, 12), open to the future that is opened at the limit of reading. Reading, reading Bataille and also reading others *with* Bataille, is never only a theoretical matter. The theoretical imposes a sense, a coherence, that Bataille does not simply lack but which his writings put into question. The opening that Bataille leaves us with cannot be concluded or grasped by the theoretical but it is always an event of desire that exposes the theoretical to desire: 'It is decisively important in this movement that the search, intellectually undertaken at the promptings of unsatisfied desire, has always preceded theory's delineation of the object sought' (VE, 241). The search begins first, the result of an unsatisfied desire generated by the impossible effects of difference. Theoretical delineation of what we are seeking, Georges Bataille for example, is always taking place *after* desire as the origin of the intellectual operation.

That is why I want to stress that reading Bataille, and reading for Bataille, is an experience of desire which cannot be appropriated theoretically. Desire takes us back to Bataille's resistance to the conclusion of reading and to our own desire to read Bataille. This desire has to remain unsatisfied, not just because it resists satisfaction but because it is the effect of a difference which makes closure impossible. Desire is always an opening to the future; for Bataille 'Nothing seems more miserable and more dead than the stabilised thing, nothing is more desirable than what will soon disappear' (VE, 241). This reading has tried to read Bataille to the limit without turning him into a 'dead' stabilised thing. I have also tried to read Bataille as an opening to the future, to future readings that reopen the current theoretical delineation of objects, not least poststructuralism.

Reading cannot appropriate what it reads in advance, and even the most complete appropriation is haunted by a heterogeneity that it can never completely absorb. It is this remainder that makes reading possible, that reopens new possibilities of reading while remaining impossible to read. Theoretical appropriation succeeds but at the cost of reducing the object to a dead thing, to freezing the play of difference into a stable arrangement. Bataille prompts a different beginning of reading which begins at the promptings of an unsatisfied desire, a reading which reads the promptings of desire that underpin every reading, including the theoretical. The lesson of reading Bataille is that reading is a reading *of* desire, made by desire and which reads desire. It is also the desire that Bataille prompts in his readers; reading Bataille as the foreign body is an addictive experience, making us desire by never satisfying that desire. Bataille leaves us in a state of excitation which is the effect of difference, the difference that he traces in his singular style as a gift without return to us. What is left is a desire, the desire to begin reading Bataille.

Notes and References

Introduction

1. For two different examples of our contemporary fascination with excess see Charles Fleming, *High Concept: Don Simpson and the Hollywood Culture of Excess* (London: Bloomsbury, 1998) and Gordon Burn, *Happy Like Murderers: The True Story of Fred and Rosemary West* (London: Faber and Faber, 1998).
2. Harold Bloom, *The Western Canon: the Books and Schools of the Ages* (New York: Harcourt Brace, 1994) p. 551.
3. Alexander Nehamas, 'The Attraction of Repulsion: The Deep and Ugly Thought of Georges Bataille', *The New Republic*, 201: 17 (23 October 1989) p. 31.
4. See Pierre Klossowki's *Sade My Neighbour*, trans. Alphonso Lingis (London: Quartet Books, 1992) for Sade's opposition to the 'natural man' of the Enlightenment *philosophes*.
5. Geoffrey Bennington, 'Introduction to Economics: Because the World is Round' in C.B. Gill (ed.) *Bataille: Writing the Sacred* (London and New York: Routledge, 1995) p. 49.
6. Simone de Beauvoir, 'Must We Burn Sade?' in Marquis de Sade, *The One Hundred and Twenty Days of Sodom* (London: Arena, 1989) pp. 3–64.
7. Jean-Paul Sartre, 'Un nouveau mystique' in *Situations* I (Paris: Gallimard, 1947) p. 174.
8. See Jacques Lacan's *The Ethics of Psychoanalysis 1959–1960*, trans. Dennis Porter (London and New York: Routledge, 1992) for his discussion of the concept of *jouissance*.
9. Dylan Evans, 'From Kantian Ethics to Mystical Experience: An Exploration of Jouissance' in Dany Nobus (ed.) *Key Concepts of Lacanian Psychoanalysis* (London: Rebus Press, 1998) pp. 4–5.
10. For Bataille as a modernist see Julia Kristeva, 'Bataille, Experience and Practice' in Leslie Anne Boldt-Irons (ed.) *On Bataille: Critical Essays* (Albany: State University of New York Press, 1995) pp. 237–64; and for Bataille as a Catholic decadent see Susan Rubin Suleiman, 'Like Water in Water', in *London Review of Books* (12 July 1990) p. 23.

11. Paul Buck (ed.) *Violent Silence: Celebrating Georges Bataille* (London: The Georges Bataille Event, 1984) makes this mistake.
12. For more detailed chronologies of Bataille's life, which I have drawn on in the account that follows, see Michael Richardson (ed.) *Georges Bataille: Essential Writings* (London, Thousand Oaks, and New Delhi: Sage Books, 1998) pp. xi–xiv and Bataille's own chronology in his 'Autobiographical Note' (BR, 113–17).
13. See Georges Bataille *The Absence of Myth*, trans. and intro. Michael Richardson (London and New York: Verso, 1994) for Bataille's continuing engagement with the surrealists, although Michael Richardson's introduction (pp. 1–27) overstates the case for a rapprochement between Bataille and surrealism.
14. Breton quoted in Denis Hollier, *Against Architecture*, trans. Betsy Wing (Cambridge, Massachusetts and London, England: The MIT Press, 1992) p. 105.
15. Bataille quoted in Denis Hollier, *Absent Without Leave*, trans. Catherine Porter (Cambridge, Massachusetts and London: Harvard University Press, 1997) p. 133.
16. Bataille quoted in Elisabeth Roudinesco, *Jacques Lacan & Co.: A History of Psychoanalysis in France 1925–85*, trans. and intro. Jeffrey Mehlman (London: Free Association Books, 1990) p. 135.
17. Maurice Blanchot, *The Unavowable Community*, trans. Pierre Joris (New York: Station Hill Press, 1988) p. 13.
18. Hollier, *Absent*, p. 70.
19. Benedict de Spinoza, *Ethics*, trans. Edwin Curley (Harmondsworth: Penguin, 1996) p. 138 (part IV, proposition 39, scholium).
20. Gilles Deleuze and Claire Parnet, *Dialogues*, trans. Hugh Tomlinson and Barbara Habberjam (London: The Athlone Press, 1987) p. 47.
21. Julia Kristeva, *Tales of Love*, trans. Leon S. Roudiez (New York: Columbia University Press, 1987) p. 365.
22. Harry Cleaver, *Reading Capital Politically* (Austin: University of Texas Press, 1979), makes this argument.
23. Jacques Derrida, 'Structure, Sign, and Play in the Discourse of the Human Sciences' in *Writing and Difference*, trans. Alan Bass (Chicago: Chicago University Press, 1978) p. 278.
24. The exceptions to this rule are Lacan, whose case is discussed in Chapter 1 and Gilles Deleuze, who makes only a fleeting positive reference to Bataille in Gilles Deleuze and Félix Guattari, *Anti-Oedipus*, trans. Robert Hurley, Mark Seem,

and Helen R. Lane (Minneapolis: University of Minnesota Press, 1983), p. 4 note.

25. Two classic accounts of the thought of difference are Gilles Deleuze, *Difference and Repetition*, trans. Paul Patton (London: The Athlone Press, 1994) and Jacques Derrida, 'Différance' in *Margins of Philosophy*, trans. Alan Bass (Brighton: The Harvester Press, 1982). Deleuze does not mention Bataille at all and Derrida only briefly mentions him during a discussion of Hegel (p. 19).

1. The Subversive Image

1. Pierre d'Espezel quoted in Denis Hollier, *Absent Without Leave*, trans. Catherine Porter (Cambridge, Massachusetts, London, England: Harvard University Press, 1997) p. 126.

2. Sigmund Freud, *P.F.L. 12: Civilization, Society and Religion*, Albert Dickson (ed.) (Harmondsworth: Penguin, 1985) pp. 243–340.

3. Luis Buñuel, *The Exterminating Angel* (*El Angel, Exterminador*) (Mexico, 1962).

4. Luis Buñuel, *The Discreet Charm of the Bourgeoisie* (*Le Charme Discret de la Bourgeoisie*) (France, 1972).

5. See Michael Richardson, *Georges Bataille* (London and New York: Routledge, 1994) and Michael Richardson (ed.) *Georges Bataille: Essential Writings* (London: Thousand Oaks, and New Dehli: Sage, 1998) for a humanist and sociological interpretation of Bataille.

6. See William Pawlett, 'Utility and Excess: the radical sociology of Bataille and Baudrillard' in *Economy & Society*, vol. 26, no. 1 (February 1997) pp. 92–125 for the claim that Bataille is a 'radical' sociologist.

7. Theodor Adorno, *The Jargon of Authenticity*, trans. Knut Tarnowski and Frederic Will (London and Henley: Routledge, Kegan & Paul, 1973) p. 138.

8. Hollier, *Absent Without Leave*, p. 86.

9. André Breton, 'First Surrealist Manifesto' (1924) in Patrick Waldberg, *Surrealism* (New York and Toronto: Oxford University Press, 1978) p. 78.

10. Sigmund Freud, *P.F.L. 14: Art and Literature*, Albert Dickson (ed.) (Harmondsworth: Penguin, 1985) p. 352.

11. Jacques Lacan, *Écrits*, trans. Alan Sheridan (London: Routledge, 1977) pp. 1–7.

12. For an example of this Lacanian rediscovery of Lacan see Parveen Adams, *The Emptiness of the Image* (London and New York: Routledge, 1996).

13. Jacques Lacan, *The Four Fundamental Concepts of Psycho-Analysis*, trans. Alan Sheridan (Harmondsworth: Penguin, 1979) p. 89.
14. Lacan, *Fundamental*, p. 74.
15. Sigmund Freud, *P.F.L. 7: On Sexuality*, Angela Richards (ed.) (Harmondsworth: Penguin, 1977) pp. 99–106.
16. Lacan, *Fundamental*, p. 172.
17. Fred Botting, 'Relations of the Real in Lacan, Bataille and Blanchot' in *Sub-Stance*, vol. 73, no. 1 (1994) pp. 24–40. Botting assimilates both Bataille and Blanchot to Lacan's Real forcing them within a conceptuality that they both resist in different ways.
18. Lacan, *Fundamental*, p. 89.
19. For Lacan's institutional disputes see Elisabeth Roudinesco, *Jacques Lacan & Co.: A History of Psychoanalysis in France 1925–85*, trans. and intro. Jeffrey Mehlman (London: Free Association Books, 1990).
20. Yves-Alain Bois and Rosalind E. Krauss, *Formless: A User's Guide* (New York: Zone Books, 1997) p. 252.
21. Sarah Kent, *Shark Infested Waters: The Saatchi Collection of British Art in the 90s* (London: Zwemmer, 1994) pp. 36–7.
22. Damien Hirst in Kent, *Shark*, p. 37.
23. Julia Kristeva, *Powers of Horror: An Essay on Abjection*, trans. Leon S. Roudiez (New York: Columbia University Press, 1982).
24. Kristeva, *Powers*, p. 3.
25. Bois and Krauss, *Formless*, p. 40.
26. Guy Debord, *The Society of the Spectacle* (Detroit: Black & Red, 1983).
27. Jean-Paul Sartre, 'Un nouveau mystique' in *Situations* I (Paris: Gallimard, 1947) p .158.
28. Jacques Derrida, *Of Spirit: Heidegger and the Question*, trans. Geoffrey Bennington and Rachel Bowlby (Chicago and London: The University of Chicago Press, 1989) p. 68.

2. Inner Experience

1. Gilles Deleuze, 'Nomad Thought' in David B. Allison (ed.) *The New Nietzsche* (Cambridge, Massachusetts: The MIT Press, 1985) p. 147.
2. Friedrich Nietzsche, *Twilight of the Idols/The Anti-Christ*, trans. R.J. Hollingdale (Harmondsworth: Penguin, 1968) p. 21.
3. Deleuze, 'Nomad' p. 149 and also see Gilles Deleuze and Félix Guattari, *A Thousand Plateaus*, trans. Brian Massumi

(London: The Athlone Press, 1988) Plateaux 12 '1227: Treatise on Nomadology: The War Machine', pp. 351–423.

4. Michael Richardson, 'Introduction' in *Georges Bataille: Essential Writings*, Michael Richardson (ed. and trans.) (London: Thousand Oaks, and New Dehli: Sage, 1998) p. 2.

5. Friedrich Nietzsche, *Ecce Homo*, trans. R.J. Hollingdale (Harmondsworth: Penguin, 1979) p. 127.

6. Friedrich Nietzsche, *Beyond Good and Evil*, trans. R.J. Hollingdale (Harmondsworth: Penguin, 1973) p. 14.

7. Jean-Michel Besnier, 'Georges Bataille in the 1930s: A Politics of the Impossible', trans. Amy Reid, *Yale French Studies* 78: On Bataille (1990), ed. Allan Stoekl, pp. 176–7.

8. Friedrich Nietzsche, *Thus Spake Zarathustra*, trans. R.J. Hollingdale (Harmondsworth: Penguin, 1973) p. 237.

9. Klossowski quoted in Vincent Descombes, *Modern French Philosophy*, trans. L. Scott-Fox and J.M. Harding (Cambridge: Cambridge University Press, 1980), p. 183.

10. Pierre Klossowski, 'Nietzsche's Experience of the Eternal Return', trans. Allen Weiss, in David B. Allison (ed.) *The New Nietzsche* (Cambridge, Massachusetts: The MIT Press, 1985) p. 119.

11. Jean-Luc Nancy, *The Inoperative Community*, ed. Peter Connor, trans. Peter Connor et al. (Minneapolis and Oxford: University of Minnesota Press, 1991) p. 26.

12. Boris Souvarine quoted in Allan Stoekl, 'Truman's Apotheosis: Bataille, "*Planisme*," and Headlessness' in *Yale French Studies* 78: On Bataille (1990), ed. Allan Stoekl, p. 181.

13. Alexander Nehamas, 'The Attraction of Repulsion: The Deep and Ugly Thought of Georges Bataille' in *The New Republic*, 201: 17 (October 23, 1989) p. 35.

14. Richard Wolin, *The Terms of Cultural Criticism: The Frankfurt School, Existentialism, Post-Structuralism* (New York: Columbia University Press, 1992) p. 13, and Martin Jay 'The Reassertion of Sovereignty in a Time of Crisis: Carl Schmitt and Georges Bataille' in *Force Fields* (New York and London: Routledge, 1993) pp. 49–60.

15. Benjamin is indebted to Schmitt in *The Origin of German Tragic Drama*, trans. John Osborne (London: New Left Books, 1977), and also see Howard Caygill, Alex Coles and Andrzej Klimowski, *Walter Benjamin For Beginners* (Cambridge: Icon Books, 1998) pp. 98–9.

16. Nancy, *Community*, pp. 16–17.

17. Susan Rubin Suleiman, 'Bataille in the Street: The Search for Virility in the 1930s' in Carolyn Bailey Gill (ed.) *Bataille:*

Writing the Sacred (London and New York: Routledge, 1995) p. 36.

18. Besnier, 'Politics', p. 169.
19. Maurice Blanchot, *The Unavowable Community*, trans. Pierre Joris (New York: Station Hill Press, 1988) p. 17.
20. Suleiman, 'Street', p. 36.
21. Suleiman, 'Street', p. 40.
22. Roland Barthes, 'Inaugural Lecture, Collège de France', trans. Richard Howard in *A Barthes Reader*, (ed.) Susan Sontag (London: Fontana Press, 1983) p. 461.
23. Denis Hollier, *Against Architecture*, trans. Betsy Wing (Cambridge, Massachusetts and London: The MIT Press, 1989) pp. 25–6.
24. Nancy, *Community*.
25. Nancy, *Community*, p. 16.
26. For a critical review of contemporary 'communitarianism' and third way politics from a Foucauldian perspective see Nik Rose, 'Inventiveness in politics' in *Economy & Society*, vol. 28, no. 3 (August 1999) pp. 467–93.
27. Nancy, *Community*, p. 12.
28. Nancy, *Community*, p. 19.
29. Nancy, *Community*, p. 23.
30. Nancy, *Community*, p. 27.
31. Blanchot, *Inavowable*, p. 1.
32. Blanchot, *Inavowable*, p. 21.
33. Blanchot, *Inavowable*, p. 26.
34. Jacques Derrida, *The Politics of Friendship*, trans. George Collins (London and New York: Verso, 1997) p. 48, n. 15.
35. Jacques Derrida, 'The Politics of Friendship' in *The Journal of Philosophy*, 85 (1988) p. 642.
36. Suleiman, 'Street'.

3. Sovereignty

1. See Denis Hollier, *Absent Without Leave*, trans. Catherine Porter (Cambridge, Massachusetts, London, England: Harvard University Press, 1997) pp. 34–8.
2. Friedrich Nietzsche, *Beyond Good and Evil*, trans. R.J. Hollingdale (Harmondsworth: Penguin, 1973) p. 78.
3. Nick Land, *The Thirst For Annihilation* (London and New York: Routledge, 1992) p. 70.
4. André Breton in Jean-Michel Besnier, 'Georges Bataille in the 1930s: A Politics of the Impossible', trans. Amy Reid in *Yale French Studies* 78: On Bataille (1990), ed. Allan Stoekl, pp. 171–2.

5. Michel Foucault, *I Pierre Rivière, having slaughtered my mother, my sister, and my brother* ..., trans. Frank Jellinek (Lincoln and London: The University of Nebraska Press, 1975).

6. Étienne Balibar, 'Violence, Ideality, and Cruelty' in *New Formations*, 35 (Autumn 1998) p. 10.

7. Georges Sorel, *Reflections on Violence*, trans. T.E. Hulme (New York: Collier Books, 1961).

8. Friedrich Nietzsche, *The Nietzsche Reader*, trans. R.J. Hollingdale (Harmondsworth: Penguin, 1977) pp. 202–3.

9. Alexandre Kojève, *Introduction to the Reading of Hegel*, ed. Allan Bloom, trans. James H. Nichols Jr (New York and London: Basic Books, 1969) p. 21.

10. Michel Foucault, *The History of Sexuality*, trans. Robert Hurley (Harmondsworth: Penguin, 1981) p. 149.

11. Foucault, *History*, p. 148.

12. See Giorgio Agamben, *Homo Sacer: Sovereign Power and Bare Life*, trans. Daniel Heller-Roazen (Stanford, California: Stanford University Press, 1998).

13. Carolyn Bailey Gill, 'Bataille and the Question of Presence', *parallax* 4 (February 1997) p. 95.

14. Marc Augé, *Non-Places: Introduction to an Anthropology of Supermodernity*, trans. John Howe (London and New York: Verso, 1995) p. 60.

15. Kojève, *Introduction*, p. 6.

16. Alexandre Kojève, 'The Idea of Death in the Philosophy of Hegel', trans. Joseph J. Carpino in Robert Stern (ed.) *G.W.F. Hegel: Critical Assessments vol. 2* (London and New York: Routledge, 1993) p. 321. This essay was included in the French publication of Kojève's lecture notes.

17. Kojève, *Introduction*, p. 9.

18. Kojève, *Introduction*, p. 23.

19. Kojève, *Introduction*, pp. 29–30.

20. G.W.F. Hegel, *The Phenomenology of Mind*, trans. J.B. Baillie (London: George Allen & Unwin, 1955), p. 238.

21. Karl Marx, *The Marx Reader*, Christopher Pierson (ed.) (Cambridge: Polity Press, 1997) p. 88.

22. Nietzsche's attack on the formation of history by 'slave morality' is an obvious influence on Bataille, in particular *On the Genealogy of Morals*, trans. Walter Kaufmann and R.J. Hollingdale (New York: Vintage Books, 1969). However, Bataille also remarked that 'Nietzsche knew barely more of Hegel than a standard popularisation' (IE, 109) and that the *Genealogy* was a 'singular proof of ignorance in which the dialectic of master and slave has been held and remains to be held' (IE, 109).

23. Hegel, *Phenomenology*, p. 797.
24. Kojève, *Introduction*, p. 44.
25. Roger Callois quoted in CS, p. 86.
26. Jacques Derrida, *Spectres of Marx*, trans. Peggy Kamuf (London and New York: Routledge, 1994) p. 70.
27. Francis Fukuyama, *The End of History and the Last Man* (Harmondsworth: Penguin, 1992).
28. Mikkel Borch-Jacobsen, *Lacan: The Absolute Master*, trans. Douglas Brick (Stanford, California: Stanford University Press, 1991) p. 7.
29. Nietzsche, *Beyond*, p. 14.
30. Geoffrey Bennington, 'Introduction to Economics: Because the world is round' in C.B. Gill (ed.) *Bataille: Writing the Sacred* (London and New York: Routledge, 1995) p. 54.

4. The Tears of Eros

1. Geoffrey Bennington, 'Introduction to Economics: Because the World is Round' in C.B. Gill (ed.) *Bataille: Writing the Sacred* (London and New York: Routledge, 1995) p. 54.
2. Andrea Dworkin, *Pornography: Men Possessing Women* (London: Women's Press, 1981).
3. Leo Bersani, 'Is the Rectum a Grave?' in *October*, 43 (1987) p. 215.
4. Susan Rubin Suleiman, 'Bataille in the Street: The Search for Virility in the 1930s' in Carolyn Bailey Gill (ed.) *Bataille: Writing the Sacred* (London and New York: Routledge, 1995) p. 28.
5. Mitsou Ronat, 'The Glorious Body of Laure' in Paul Buck (ed.) *Violent Silence: Celebrating Georges Bataille* (The Georges Bataille event, 1984) pp. 33–6.
6. Marquis de Sade, *The Complete Justine, Philosophy in the Bedroom, and Other Writings*, trans. Richard Seaver and Austryn Wainhouse (New York: Grove Press, 1965) and *Juliette*, trans. Austryn Wainhouse (New York: Grove Press, 1976).
7. Denis Hollier, *Absent Without Leave*, trans. Catherine Porter (Cambridge, Massachusetts, London, England: Harvard University Press, 1997) p. 58.
8. Julia Kristeva, *Tales of Love*, trans. Leon S. Roudiez (New York: Columbia University Press, 1987) p. 370.
9. Pierre Klossowski, *Roberte Ce Soir* and *The Revocation of the Edict of Nantes*, trans. Austryn Wainhouse (New York and London: Marion Boyars, 1989).
10. Klossowski, *Roberte*, pp. 147–55.

11. Pierre Klossowski, 'Of the Simulacrum in Georges Bataille's Communication' in Leslie Anne Boldt-Irons (ed.) *On Bataille: Critical Essays* (Albany: State University of New York Press, 1995) pp. 118–25.
12. Nick Land, *The Thirst For Annihilation* (London and New York: Routledge, 1992) p. 63.
13. Immanuel Kant, *Critique of Pure Reason*, trans. Norman Kemp Smith (London and Basingstoke: Macmillan, 1929) p. 7.
14. Kant, *Critique*, p. 8.
15. Immanuel Kant, *Prolegomena to Any Future Metaphysics*, trans. Paul Carus and revised by James W. Ellington (Indianapolis and Cambridge: Hackett Publishing Company, 1977) p. 100.
16. Kant, *Prolegomena*, p. 57.
17. Kant, *Critique*, p. 383.
18. Georges Bataille, 'Letter to René Char on the Incompatibilities of the Writer' in *Yale French Studies: On Bataille* 78 (1990), Allan Stoekl (ed.) p. 35.
19. Michel Foucault, *The Order of Things*, trans. Alan Sheridan (London and New York: Tavistock/Routledge, 1970) p. 341.
20. G.W.F. Hegel, *Science of Logic*, trans. A.V. Miller (New Jersey: Humanities Press International, 1969) p. 134.
21. Hegel, *Science*, p. 431.
22. Hegel, *Science*, p. 435.
23. Jacques Derrida, *Margins of Philosophy*, trans. Alan Bass (Brighton: The Harvester Press, 1982) p. 8.
24. Michel Foucault, *The History of Sexuality*, trans. Robert Hurley (Harmondsworth: Penguin, 1981) p. 150.
25. Walter Benjamin, *Illuminations*, trans. Harry Zohn ed. and intro Hannah Arendt (New York: Shocken Books, 1968) p. 261.
26. Benjamin, *Illuminations*, p. 261.
27. Leslie Hill, *Blanchot: Extreme Contemporary* (London and New York: Routledge, 1997).

5. *The Accursed Share*

1. Jean-Paul Sartre, '*Un nouveau mystique*' in *Situations I* (Paris: Gallimard, 1947) pp. 133–74.
2. Loren Goldner, 'Amadeo Bordiga, The Agrarian Question and the International Revolutionary Movement' in *Critique*, 23 (1991) p. 79.
3. Wilkie Collins, *The Moonstone* (1868) (Harmondsworth: Penguin, 1998).

4. Marcel Mauss, *The Gift*, trans. Ian Cunnison (London: Routledge, 1988).

5. Theodor Adorno, *Minima Moralia*, trans. E.F.N. Jephcott (London: Verso, 1974) p. 42.

6. Adorno, *Minima*, p. 42.

7. Adorno, *Minima*, p. 43.

8. Greil Marcus, *Lipstick Traces* (London: Secker & Warburg, 1989) p. 396.

9. Probably the most accurate account of the role of the Situationists in the 'events' can be found in René Viénet, *Enragés and Situationists in the Occupation Movement, France, May '68* (New York: Autonomedia, 1992).

10. Ken Knabb (ed. and trans.) *Situationist International Anthology* (California: Bureau of Public Secrets, 1989) p. 155.

11. For a very sympathetic reading of Reich's later work see Adam Parfrey 'From Orgasm to UFOs: Wilhelm Reich's *Contact with Space*' in Adam Parfrey (ed.) *Apocalypse Culture* (New York: Amok Press, 1987) pp. 145–8.

12. Geoffrey Bennington, 'Introduction to Economics: Because the World is Round' in C.B. Gill (ed.) *Bataille: Writing the Sacred* (London and New York: Routledge, 1995) p. 49.

13. Bennington, 'Economics', p. 54.

14. Jacques Derrida, 'Politics and Friendship: An Interview with Jacques Derrida', trans. Robert Harvey in E. Ann Kaplan and Michael Sprinker (eds) *The Althusserian Legacy* (London and New York: Verso, 1993) p. 205.

15. See the exchange of letters between Bataille, Leiris and Callois on the status of sociology collected in CS, 353–9.

16. Jean Baudrillard, *Symbolic Exchange and Death*, trans. Iain Hamilton (London: Thousand Oaks, and New Dehli: Sage, 1993), also 'Death in Bataille' from this book is excerpted in CR, 139–45.

17. Jean Baudrillard, *The Transparency of Evil*, trans. James Benedict (London and New York: Verso, 1993) p. 81.

18. Baudrillard, *Transparency*, p. 106.

19. Bennington, 'Economics', p. 46.

20. Bennington, 'Economics', p. 48.

21. Bennington, 'Economics', p. 54.

22. See Marian Hobson, *Jacques Derrida* (London and New York: Routledge, 1998) p. 110.

Conclusion

1. Jorge Luis Borges, 'Pierre Ménard, Author of the *Quixote*' in *Labyrinths* (Harmondsworth: Penguin, 1970) pp. 62–71.

2. Jean-Jacques Lecercle, *Interpretation as Pragmatics* (Basingstoke and London: Macmillan, 1999) p. 180.

3. Neil Leach (ed.) *Rethinking Architecture: A reader in cultural theory* (London and New York: Routledge, 1997) p. 20.

4. Julian Pefanis, *Heterology and the Postmodern: Bataille, Baudrillard and Lyotard* (Durham and London: Duke University Press, 1991) p. 44.

5. Jacques Lacan, *The Four Fundamental Concepts of Psycho-Analysis*, trans. Alan Sheridan (Harmondsworth: Penguin, 1979) p. 49.

6. Robert Young, 'Poststructuralism – the improper name' in *Torn Halves* (Manchester and New York: Manchester University Press, 1996) pp. 70–5.

7. Michel Surya, *Georges Bataille La Mort à l'Œuvre* (Paris: Libraire Séguier, 1987).

8. Geoffrey Bennington, *Legislations* (London and New York: Verso, 1994) p. 261.

9. Alexandre Kojève, *Introduction to the Reading of Hegel*, ed. Allan Bloom, trans. James H. Nichols Jr (New York and London: Basic Books, 1969) p. 4.

10. Joseph Libertson, 'Bataille and Communication: *Savoir, Non-Savoir, Glissement, Rire*' in Leslie Anne Boldt-Irons (ed.) *On Bataille: Critical Essays* (Albany: State University of New York Press, 1995) p. 209.

Bibliography

In French, Bataille's writings are published in his *Œuvres complètes* (Paris: Gallimard, 1971–88) 12 volumes:

Volume I: *Early Writings, 1922–40: Histoire de l'oeil, L'Anus solaire, Sacrifices*, Articles.

Volume II: *Posthumously Published Writings, 1922–40.*

Volume III: *Literary Works: Madame Edwarda, Le Petit, L'Archangélique, L'Impossible, La Scissiparité, L'Abbé C., L'Être indifférencié n'est rien, Le Bleu du ciel.*

Volume IV: *Posthumously Published Literary Works*: Poems, *Le Mort, Julie, La Maison brûlée, La Tombe de Louis XXX, Divinus Deus, Ébauches.*

Volume V: *La Somme athéologique 1: L'Expérience intérieure, Méthode de méditation, Le Coupable, L'Alleluiah.*

Volume VI: *La Somme athéologique 2: Sur Nietzsche, Mémorandum.*

Volume VII: *L'Économie à la mesure de l'univers, La Part maudite, La Limite de l'utile, Théorie de la religion, Conférences 1947–48.*

Volume VIII: *L'Histoire de l'érotisme, Le Surréalisme au jour le jour, Conférences, 1951–53, La Souveraineté.*

Volume IX: *La Peinture préhistorique: Lascaux ou la naissance de l'art, Manet, La Littérature et le mal.*

Volume X: *L'Érotisme, Le Procès de Gilles de Rais, Les Larmes d'Éros.*

Volume XI: Articles, 1944–49.

Volume XII: Articles, 1950–61.

English Translations

Bataille, G. *Story of the Eye*, trans. J. Neugroschal (Harmondsworth: Penguin, 1982).

——, *Visions of Excess: Selected Writings 1927–1939*, ed. and intro. A. Stoekl, trans. Allan Stoekl, with C.R. Lovitt and D.M. Leslie Jr (Minneapolis: University of Minnesota Press, 1985).

——, *Literature and Evil*, trans. A. Hamilton (London and New York: Marion Boyars, 1985).

——, *Blue of Noon*, trans. H. Mathews (London and New York: Marion Boyars, 1986).

——, *Eroticism*, trans. M. Dalwood (London and New York: Marion Boyars, 1987).

——, *Inner Experience*, trans. and intro. L.A. Boldt (Albany: State University of New York Press, 1988).

——, *Guilty*, trans. B. Boone and intro. D. Hollier (California: The Lapis Press, 1988).

——, *L'Abbé C.*, trans. P.A. Facey (London and New York: Marion Boyars, 1988).

——, *Tears of Eros*, trans. P. Connor (San Francisco: City Lights Books, 1989).

——, *My Mother/Madame Edwarda/The Dead Man*, trans. A. Wainhouse (London and New York: Marion Boyars, 1989).

——, 'Letter to René Char on the Incompatabilities of the Writer', trans. C. Carsten, in A. Stoekl (ed.) *Yale French Studies 78: On Bataille* (1990) pp. 31–43.

——, *The Accursed Share Volume One*, trans. R. Hurley (New York: Zone Books, 1991).

——, *The Accursed Share Volumes Two and Three*, trans. R. Hurley (New York: Zone Books, 1991).

——, *The Trial of Gilles de Rais*, trans. R. Robinson (Los Angeles: Amok Books, 1991).

——, *The Impossible*, trans. R. Hurley (San Francisco: City Lights Books, 1991).

——, *The Theory of Religion*, trans. R. Hurley (New York: Zone Books, 1992).

——, *On Nietzsche*, trans. B. Boone and intro. S. Lotringer (London: The Athlone Press, 1992).

——, *The Absence of Myth: Writings on Surrealism*, ed., trans. and intro. M. Richardson (London and New York: Verso, 1994).

——, *The Bataille Reader*, F. Botting and S. Wilson (eds) (Oxford and Malden: Blackwell, 1997).

——, *Georges Bataille: Essential Writings*, M. Richardson (ed.) (London: Thousand Oaks, and New Dehli: Sage, 1998).

Other Works Consulted

Adams, P. *The Emptiness of the Image* (London and New York: Routledge, 1996).

Adorno, T. *The Jargon of Authenticity*, trans. K. Tarnowski and F. Will (London and Henley: Routledge, Kegan & Paul, 1973).

——, *Minima Moralia*, trans. E.F.N. Jephcott (London and New York: Verso, 1974).

Agamben, G. *Homo Sacer: Sovereign Power and Bare Life*, trans. D. Heller-Roazen (Stanford, California: Stanford University Press, 1998).

Augé, M. *Non-Places: Introduction to an Anthropology of Super-modernity*, trans. J. Howe (London and New York: Verso, 1995).

Balibar, É. 'Violence, Ideality, Cruelty', *New Formations*, 35 (Autumn 1998), pp. 7–18.

Barthes, R. *A Barthes Reader*, S. Sontag (ed.) (London: Fontana Press, 1983).

Baudrillard, J. *The Transparency of Evil*, trans. J. Benedict (London and New York: Verso, 1993).

——, *Symbolic Exchange and Death*, trans. I. Hamilton (London: Thousand Oaks, and New Dehli: Sage 1993).

Benjamin, W. *Illuminations*, trans. H. Zohn, H. Arendt (ed.) (New York: Schoken Books, 1968).

Benjamin, W. *The Origin of German Tragic Drama*, trans. J. Osborne (London: New Left Books, 1977).

Bennington, G. *Legislations* (London and New York: Verso, 1994).

——, 'Introduction to Economics I: Because the World is Round' in C.B. Gill (ed.). *Bataille: Writing the Sacred* (London and New York: Routledge, 1995), pp. 46–57.

Bersani, L. 'Is the Rectum a Grave?' in *October*, 43 (1987), pp. 197–227.

Besnier, J-M. 'Georges Bataille in the 1930s: a Politics of the Impossible', trans. A. Reid in A. Stoekl (ed.) *Yale French Studies, 78: On Bataille* (1990), pp. 169–80.

Blanchot, M. *The Unavowable Community*, trans. P. Joris (New York: Station Hill Press, 1988).

Bloom, H. *The Western Canon: the Books and Schools of the Ages* (New York: Harcourt Brace, 1994).

Bois, Y-A and R.E. Krauss, *Formless* (New York: Zone Books, 1997).

Boldt-Irons, L.A. (ed.) *On Bataille: Critical Essays* (Albany: State University of New York Press, 1995).

Borch-Jacobsen, M. *Lacan: the Absolute Master*, trans. Douglas Brick (Stanford, California: Stanford University Press, 1991).

Borges, J. L. *Labyrinths* (Harmondsworth: Penguin, 1970).

Botting, F. 'Relations of the Real in Lacan, Bataille and Blanchot' in *Sub-Stance*, vol. 43, no. 1 (1994), pp. 24–40.

Botting, F. and S. Wilson (eds). *Bataille: A Critical Reader* (Oxford and Malden: Blackwell, 1998).

Breton, A. 'First Surrealist Manifesto' (1924) in P. Waldberg, *Surrealism* (New York and Toronto: Oxford University Press, 1978), p. 78.

Brotchie, A. (ed.) *Encyclopædia Acephalica* (London: Atlas Press, 1995).

Buck, P. (ed.) *Violent Silence: Celebrating Georges Bataille* (London: The Georges Bataille Event, 1984).

Burn, G. *Happy Like Murderers: The True Story of Fred and Rosemary West* (London: Faber and Faber, 1998).

Caygill, H., A. Coles and A. Klimowski, *Walter Benjamin For Beginners* (Cambridge: Icon Books, 1998).

Cleaver, H. *Reading Capital Politically* (Austin: University of Texas Press, 1979).

Collins, W. *The Moonstone* (1868) (Harmondsworth: Penguin, 1998).

Debord, G. *The Society of the Spectacle* (Detroit: Black & Red, 1983).

Deleuze, G. and F. Guattari, *Anti-Oedipus*, trans. R. Hurley, M. Seem and H.R. Lane (Minneapolis: University of Minnesota Press, 1983).

——, 'Nomad Thought' in David B. Allison (ed.) *The New Nietzsche* (Cambridge, Massachusetts: The MIT Press, 1985), pp. 142–9.

——, and C. Parnet. *Dialogues*, trans. H. Tomlinson and B. Habberjam (London: The Athlone Press, 1987).

——, and F. Guattari, *A Thousand Plateaus*, trans. Brian Massumi (London: The Athlone Press, 1988).

——, *Difference and Repetition*, trans. P. Patton (London: The Athlone Press, 1994).

Derrida, J. *Writing and Difference*, trans. A. Bass (Chicago: Chicago University Press, 1978).

——, *Margins of Philosophy*, trans. A. Bass (Brighton: Harvester Press, 1982).

——, 'The Politics of Friendship', trans. G. Motzkin, in *The Journal of Philosophy*, 85 (1988), pp. 632–45.

——, *Of Spirit: Heidegger and the Question*, trans. G. Bennington and R. Bowlby (Chicago and London: The University of Chicago Press, 1989).

——, 'Politics and Friendship: an Interview with Jacques Derrida', trans. R. Harvey in E.A. Kaplan and M. Sprinker (eds) *The Althusserian Legacy* (London and New York, Verso, 1993), pp. 183–231.

——, *Spectres of Marx*, trans. P. Kamuf (London and New York: Routledge, 1994).

——, *Politics of Friendship*, trans. G. Collins (London and New York: Verso, 1997).

Descombes, V. *Modern French Philosophy*, trans. L. Scott-Fox and J.M. Harding (Cambridge: Cambridge University Press, 1980).

Dworkin, A. *Pornography: Men Possessing Women* (London: Women's Press, 1981).

Evans, D. 'From Kantian Ethics to Mystical Experience: An Exploration of Jouissance' in D. Nobus (ed.) *Key Concepts of Lacanian Psychoanalysis* (London: Rebus Press, 1998), pp. 1–28.

Fleming, C. *High Concept: Don Simpson and the Hollywood Culture of Excess* (London: Bloomsbury, 1998).

Foucault, M. *The Order of Things*, trans. A. Sheridan (London and New York: Tavistock/Routledge, 1970).

——, *I Pierre Rivière, Having Slaughtered my Mother, my Sister, and my Brother ...*, trans. F. Jellinek (Lincoln, Nebraska, and London, England: The University of Nebraska Press, 1975).

——, *The History of Sexuality vol. 1*, trans. R. Hurley (Harmondsworth: Penguin, 1981).

Freud, S. *P.F.L. 7: On Sexuality*, ed. A. Richards (Harmondsworth: Penguin, 1977).

——, *P.F.L. 12: Civilization, Society and Religion*, ed. A. Dickson (Harmondsworth: Penguin, 1985).

——, *P.F.L. 14: Art and Literature*, ed. A. Dickson (Harmondsworth: Penguin, 1985).

Fukuyama, F. *The End of History and the Last Man* (Harmondsworth: Penguin, 1992).

Gill, C.B. (ed.) *Bataille: Writing the Sacred* (London and New York: Routledge, 1995).

——, 'Bataille and the Question of Presence' in *Parallax*, 4 (February 1997), pp. 89–98.

Goldner, L. 'Amadeo Bordiga, The Agrarian Question and the International Revolutionary Movement' in *Critique*, 23 (1991), pp. 73–100.

Hegel, G.W.F. *The Phenomenology of Mind*, trans. J.B. Baille (London: George Allen and Unwin, 1955).

——, *Science of Logic*, trans. A.V. Miller (New Jersey: Humanities Press International, 1969).

Hill, L. *Blanchot: Extreme Contemporary* (London and New York: Routledge, 1997).

Hobson, M. *Jacques Derrida* (London and New York: Routledge, 1998).

Hollier, D. (ed.) *The College of Sociology 1937–39*, trans. B. Wing (Minneapolis: The University of Minnesota Press, 1988).

——, *Against Architecture: The Writings of Georges Bataille*, trans. B. Wing (Cambridge Massachusetts and London: The MIT Press, 1989).

——, *Absent Without Leave*, trans. C. Porter (Cambridge, Massachusetts, and London, England: Harvard University Press, 1997).

Jay, M. *Force Fields* (New York and London: Routledge, 1993).

Kant, I. *Critique of Pure Reason*, trans. N.K. Smith (London and Basingstoke: Macmillan, 1929).

——, *Prolegomena to Any Future Metaphysics*, trans. P. Carus and revised by J. W. Ellington (Indianapolis and Cambridge: Hackett, 1977).

Kent, S. *Shark Infested Waters: The Saatchi Collection of British Art in the 90s* (London: Zwemmer, 1994).

Klossowski, P. 'Nietzsche's Experience of the Eternal Return', trans. A. Weiss in D.B. Allison (ed.). *The New Nietzsche* (Cambridge, Massachusetts: The MIT Press, 1985), pp. 107–20.

——, *Roberte Ce Soir* and *The Revocation of the Edict of Nantes*, trans. A. Wainhouse (New York and London: Marion Boyars, 1989).

——, *Sade My Neighbour*, trans. A. Lingis (London: Quartet Books, 1992).

——, 'Of the Simulacrum in Georges Bataille's Communication' in L.A. Boldt-Irons (ed.) *On Bataille: Critical Essays* (Albany: State University of New York Press, 1995), pp. 118–25.

Knabb, K. (ed.) *Situationist International Anthology* (California: Bureau of Public Secrets, 1989).

Kojève, A. *Introduction to the Reading of Hegel*, ed. A. Bloom, trans. J.H. Nichols Jr (New York and London: Basic Books, 1969).

——, 'The Idea of Death in the Philosophy of Hegel, trans. J.J. Carpino in R. Stern (ed.) *G.W.F. Hegel: Critical Assessments vol. 2* (London and New York: Routledge, 1993), pp. 311–58.

Kristeva, J. *Powers of Horror: An Essay on Abjection*, trans. L.S. Roudiez (New York: Columbia University Press, 1982).

——, *Tales of Love*, trans. L.S. Roudiez (New York: Columbia University Press, 1987).

——, 'Bataille, Experience and Practice' in L.A. Boldt-Irons (ed.) *On Bataille: Critical Essays* (Albany: State University of New York, 1995), pp. 237–64.

Lacan, Jacques, *The Four Fundamental Concepts of Psycho-Analysis*, trans. A. Sheridan (Harmondsworth: Penguin, 1977).

——, *Écrits*, trans. A. Sheridan (London: Routledge, 1977).

——, *The Ethics of Psychoanalysis 1959–1960*, trans. D. Porter (London and New York: Routledge, 1992).

Land, N. *The Thirst for Annihilation: Georges Bataille and Virulent Nihilism (an essay on atheistic religion)* (London and New York: Routledge, 1992).

Leach, N. (ed.) *Rethinking Architecture: a Reader in Cultural Theory* (London and New York: Routledge, 1997).

Lecercle, J-J. *Interpretation as Pragmatics* (Basingstoke and London: Macmillan, 1999).

Libertson, J. 'Bataille and Communication: *Savoir, Non-Savoir, Glissement, Rire*' in L.A. Boldt-Irons (ed.) *On Bataille: Critical Essays* (Albany: State University of New York Press, 1995), pp. 209–30.

Marcus, G. *Lipstick Traces* (London: Secker & Warburg, 1989).

Marx, K. *The Karl Marx Reader*, ed. Christopher Peirson (Cambridge: Polity Press, 1997).

Mauss, M. *The Gift*, trans. I. Cunnison (London: Routledge, 1988).

Nancy, J-L. *The Inoperative Community*, ed. P. Connor, trans. P. Connor et al. (Minneapolis and Oxford: The University of Minnesota Press, 1991).

Nehamas, A. 'The Attraction of Repulsion: The Deep and Ugly Thought of Georges Bataille' in *The New Republic*, 201: 17 (23 October 1989), pp. 31–6.

Nietzsche, F. *Thus Spake Zarathustra*, trans. R.J. Hollingdale (Harmondsworth: Penguin, 1961).

——, *Twilight of the Idols/The Anti-Christ*, trans. R.J. Hollingdale (Harmondsworth: Penguin, 1968).

——, *On the Genealogy of Morals and Ecce Homo*, ed. W. Kaufmann (New York: Vintage Books, 1969).

——, *Beyond Good and Evil*, trans. R.J. Hollingdale (Harmondsworth: Penguin, 1973).

——, *The Nietzsche Reader*, trans R.J. Hollingdale (Harmondsworth: Penguin, 1977).

——, *Ecce Homo*, trans. R.J. Hollingdale (Harmondsworth: Penguin, 1979).

Parfrey, A. 'From Orgasm to UFOs: Wilhelm Reich's *Contact with Space*' in A. Parfrey (ed.) *Apocalypse Culture* (New York: Amok Press, 1987), pp. 145–8.

Pawlett, W. 'Utility and Excess: the Radical Sociology of Bataille and Baudrillard' in *Economy & Society*, vol. 26, no. 1 (February 1997), pp. 92–125.

Pefanis, J. *Heterology and the Postmodern: Bataille, Baudrillard and Lyotard* (Durham and London: Duke University Press, 1991).

Ronat, M. 'The Glorious Body of Laure' in P. Buck (ed.) *Violent Silence: Celebrating Georges Bataille* (London: The Georges Bataille Event, 1984), pp. 33–6.

Rose, N. 'Inventiveness in Politics' in *Economy & Society*, vol. 28, no. 3 (August 1999), pp. 467–93.

Roudinesco, E. *Jacques Lacan & Co.: A History of Psychoanalysis in France 1925–85*, trans. and intro. J. Mehlman (London: Free Association Books, 1990).

Sade, M. de. *The Complete Justine, Philosophy in the Bedroom, and Other Writings*, trans. Richard Seaver and Austryn Wainhouse (New York: Grove Press, 1965).

——, *Juliette*, trans. A. Wainhouse (New York: Grove Press, 1976).

——, *The One Hundred and Twenty Days of Sodom*, intro. S. de Beauvoir (London: Arena, 1989).

Sartre, J-P. *Situations I* (Paris: Gallimard, 1947).

Sorel, G. *Reflections on Violence*, trans. T.E. Hulme (New York: Collier Books, 1961).

Spinoza, B de. *Ethics*, trans. E. Curley (Harmondsworth: Penguin, 1996).

Stoekl, A. (ed.) *Yale French Studies 78: On Bataille* (1990).

——, 'Truman's Apotheosis: Bataille, "*Planisme*," and Headless-ness', in A. Stoekl (ed.) *Yale French Studies 78: On Bataille* (1990), pp. 181–205.

Suleiman, S. R. 'Like Water in Water' in *London Review of Books*, 12:13 (12 July 1990), pp. 22–3.

——, 'Bataille in the Street: The Search for Virility in the 1930s' in C.B. Gill. (ed.) *Bataille: Writing the Sacred* (London and New York: Routledge, 1995), pp. 26–45.

Surya, M. *Georges Bataille La Mort à l'Œuvre* (Paris: Libraire Séguier, 1987).

Viénet, R. *Enragés and Situationists in the Occupation Movement, France May '68* (New York: Autonomedia, 1992).

Wolin, R. *The Terms of Cultural Criticism: The Frankfurt School, Existentialism, Post-Structuralism* (New York: Columbia University Press, 1992).

Young, R. *Torn Halves* (Manchester and New York: Manchester University Press, 1996).

Index

abject, 33, 34, 109
   art, 4, 33–4
accursed share, the, 13, 103, 104,
   105, 106, 111, 112, 113,
   114, 115, 117, 119, 120,
   121, 122, 123, 124, 129
Acéphale, 9, 45, 46, 47, 48, 62,
   65, 73
Adams, Parveen, 144n
Adorno, Theodor, 25, 109, 144n,
   151n
Agamben, Giorgio, 148n
Aquinas, 48
Aristotle, 46
Aron, Raymond, 7
Augé, Marc, 72, 148n

Balibar, Étienne, 148n
Barthes, Roland, 29, 49, 147n
Bataille, Georges,
   Blanchot, friendship with, 1, 9,
      56, 127
   Catholicism, relation to, 11,
      12, 93–4
   contemporary, as, 1, 33, 102,
      117–24
   death of, 3, 13, 14
   fascism, resistance to, 8, 39–47
   feminism, and, 57, 88
   fictional writings, 87–94
   Hegel, displacement of, 7–8,
      23, 26–7, 30–1, 72–3,
      75–81, 85, 98–102
   isolation of, 1
   Lacan, appropriation by 3, 31–3
   laughter of, 36, 37, 38
   Life events, 3, 5–14, 131–2,
      143n
   Marx, and, 13, 56, 106, 110
   Nietzsche, identification with,
      6, 38, 51–3

philosophy, resistance to, 6, 39,
   58–9
   psychoanalysis of, 6, 12
   Sade, relation to, 2–5
Bataille, Sylvia, 31
Baudrillard, Jean, 13, 118, 120,
   121, 122, 151n
   The Transparency of Evil, 121,
      151n
Bäumler, Alfred, 40, 42
Beauvoir, Simone de, 2, 142n
Benjamin, Walter, 43, 44, 101,
   102, 146n, 150n
Bennington, Geoffrey, 81, 114,
   122, 123, 132, 142n, 149n,
   151n, 152n
Bersani, Leo, 88, 149n
Besnier, J-M, 41, 47, 146n, 147n
bio-power, 71
Blanchot, Maurice, 1, 9, 43, 47,
   50, 53, 56, 57, 102, 127,
   143n, 145n, 147n
Bloom, H., 142n
Bois, Y-A, 33, 34, 35, 145n
Borch-Jacobsen, Mikkel, 37, 80,
   149n
Bordiga, Amadeo, 106, 150n
Borel, Adrian, 12, 25
Borges, J. L., 126, 151n
Botting, Fred, 32, 118, 122, 145n
Breton, André, 6, 27, 28, 62,
   143n, 144n, 147n
Buck, Paul, 143n, 149n
Buñuel, Luis, 21, 29, 144n
Burn, Gordon, 142n

Callois, Roger, 45, 46, 60, 149n,
   151n
Caygill, Howard, 146n

chance, 11, 12, 19, 52, 53, 101,
119, 128, 130
Châteaubriant, Alphonse de, 45
'Che' Guevara, Ernesto, 22
Christianity, 26, 40
Cleaver, Harry, 143n
Coles, Alex, 146n
College of Sociology, the, 9, 44,
45, 46, 57
Collins, Wilkie, 107, 150n
communication, 25, 26, 27, 35,
43, 50, 51, 52, 53, 55, 57,
65, 74, 84, 89, 136
communism, 43, 54, 56, 106,
110, 111
community, 8, 9, 13, 28, 42, 43,
45, 46, 47, 48, 50, 51, 52,
53, 54, 55, 56, 57, 58, 59,
130, 134, 139
Counter-Attack, 8, 44, 89
counterculture, 1, 25, 33
Crawford, Joan, 28, 29

Dali, Salvador, 28, 29
de Man, Paul, 8
death, 1, 3, 7, 8, 10, 11, 13, 14,
18, 24, 25, 26, 27, 31, 34,
36, 37, 39, 41, 48, 51, 53,
60, 62, 69, 70, 71, 72, 73,
76, 77, 78, 82, 83, 84, 86,
88, 92, 93, 94, 101, 118,
120, 121, 126
Debord, Guy, 36, 145n
Deleuze, Gilles, 12, 38, 132,
143n, 144n, 145n
democracy, 46, 47, 54, 61, 80
Democratic Communist Circle, 8
Derrida, Jacques, 16, 37, 56, 57,
59, 66, 75, 76, 78, 79, 84,
85, 100, 104, 113, 116, 124,
133, 135, 143n, 144n, 145n,
149n, 150n, 151n
différance, 100, 144n,
general economy, and, 116
Spectres of Marx, 149n
The Politics of Friendship, 56–7,
147n
Descombes, Vincent, 146n
d'Espezel, Pierre, 144n

difference, 16, 17, 27, 28, 33, 39,
60, 65, 71, 82, 83, 84, 85,
86, 87, 88, 93, 94, 97, 99,
100, 101, 102, 103, 104,
105, 106, 108, 111, 113,
115, 116, 117, 122, 123,
124, 125, 126, 127, 129,
130, 131, 132, 133, 134,
135, 136, 137, 138, 139,
140, 141
Documents, 6, 7, 18, 19, 25, 36,
58
Durkheim, Emile, 45
Dworkin, Andrea, 88, 149n

eroticism, 2, 11, 25, 82, 83, 84,
88, 90
eternal recurrence, 42, 43, 48
Evans, D., 142n
excess, 1, 13, 17, 36, 45, 49, 59,
61, 65, 67, 70, 85, 91, 94,
103, 111, 112, 113, 114,
116, 117, 119, 120, 121,
122, 123, 124, 127, 129, 134
existentialism, 3, 103
expenditure, 64, 65, 71, 73, 78,
104, 105, 106, 107, 108,
109, 110, 111, 113, 115,
116, 118, 123

fascism, 8, 33, 38, 40, 41, 42, 43,
44, 45, 46, 47, 49, 50, 54,
55, 130
Fleming, Charles, 142n
foreign body, 4, 12, 16, 44, 57,
125, 130, 132, 133, 141
formless, 33, 34, 35, 36, 37
Förster-Nietzsche, Elisabeth, 40
Foucault, Michel, 62, 71, 95, 96,
97, 98, 100, 101, 122, 133,
148n, 150n
*I, Pierre Rivière, having
slaughtered my mother, my
sister, and my brother ...*,
62–3, 148n
The History of Sexuality, 71,
101, 148n, 150n
The Order of Things, 98, 150n
Frankfurt school, the, 43, 44